Sophisticated Entertaining

Spirited Food for Grown-Up Parties

J EANNE B ENEDICT

HPBOOKS

HPBooks
Published by The Berkley Publishing Group
A division of Penguin Putnam Inc.
375 Hudson Street
New York, New York 10014

First edition: October 2000

Published simultaneously in Canada.

The Penguin Putnam Inc. World Wide Web site address is
http://www.penguinputnam.com

LIBRARY OF CONGRESS CATALOGING-IN-PUBLICATION DATA

Benedict, Jeanne.
　　Sophisticated entertaining/Jeanne Benedict.—1st ed.
　　　p. cm.
　　Includes index.
　　ISBN 1-55788-345-9
　　1. Entertaining. I. Title.

TX731 .B413 2000
642'.4—dc21
　　　　　　　　　　　　　　　　　　00-033507

Printed in the United States of America

10 9 8 7 6 5 4 3 2 1

For Dylan:
My creative little spirit.

Contents

Acknowledgments

May all who have dined at my table enjoy the laughter and love that we shared in an evening over the course of a lifetime.

As always, my fabulous sister Laura, my genius brother Bob.com, my connoisseur father, my smart mother, and the wonderful Sparanos who are an inspiration and source of constant support. Thank you.

My adorable brother Daniel the Naniel, for being the most generous and loving brother and uncle a family could have. There are not enough thank-yous.

Tom Bartlett and Darby Rowe, whose hearts and minds are always present in my life. Thanks, guys.

Thank you to the ultimate sophisticate, John Duff, whose voice is pure "Park Avenue" class, and to Jeanette Egan, who always has an innovative suggestion and great ideas to make it better. To Steve Wrubel, photographer extraordinaire; to the gifted Sharon Bonney; and to everyone who helped make the cover of *Sophisticated Entertaining* spectacular, thank you so very much.

John and Dylan, my life and loves. Thank you to my beautiful little son for laughing and clapping at the sound of the mixer, for finally learning what "hot" meant the day I finished the book, and for his radiant smile. Thank you to my exquisite husband, John, with a talent for everything and a fathomless love that he shares with me, and Mr. D.

Sophisticated Entertaining

Introduction:
The Height of Sophistication

Sophistication has long been associated with a highbrow culture. In the past, only those with ample means had access to the finer things in life or the best chef in town. An event executed by an expensive caterer is lovely for guests. Creating a party from your own inventive resources is like a gift from the heart. *Sophisticated Entertaining* gives you all the tools necessary to whip up fabulous parties with a professional flair in your own home. With the catering trade secrets revealed in this book, your event, be it a dinner for two or an elegant buffet for fifty, will be a guaranteed success.

Sophisticated Entertaining holds the host's hand through the entire party process. I've organized over 150 gourmet food recipes flavored with spirits and wine into multicourse menus. A Food and Drink Planner listing a meal preparation schedule follows each bill of fare along with specific cocktail and wine suggestions. And you can learn how to select the perfect wine for your dinner in the chapter titled, "Under the Cork" (page 17). Finally, timesaving substitutions give you, the busy host, alternatives so you can make a few dishes and complete your menu with commercially prepared food.

The truly professional party focuses on presentation. Innovative Table Setting and Decorating Ideas, offering an imaginative theme, accompany each menu. Designs range from elegant and fun concepts for sit-down dinners to constructing lavish buffets. Many suggestions refer to the chapters "The Art of the Table" and "Formula for a Feast" (pages 3 and 9), which offer helpful hints and guidelines on everything from color combinations for table linen to the mechanics of a multiple food station event. A Proportion Chart for Food and Beverages solves problems such as "How much ice do I buy for my number of invited guests?" And, as in my last book, *The Sophisticated Cookie*, a beverage glossary describing the flavor characteristics of different spirits will provide you with the option of substituting liquor on hand for a similar one in the recipe.

A social event should feel like a vacation from the demands of daily life for both the guests and the host. For some a relaxing day might be spent cooking in the kitchen. Others prepare a couple of food items and indulge themselves by crafting an intricate centerpiece. And there are those of us who go all out for an occasion and make no apologies for extravagance. Whether you enjoy one or all aspects of entertaining, I hope *Sophisticated Entertaining* will be your one-stop food, beverage, and table decor guide for throwing an inspired and memorable event.

For more entertaining tips and delicious recipes, visit my website at www.iceentertainment.com.

The Art of the Table

hink of your dinner table as the landscape for your food. The perfect table should reflect the cuisine, enhance the atmosphere, and spark conversation. As a guest, I love taking my seat at an artistic table. If the host has put that much thought into the dinner table or buffet, I imagine the food will taste wonderful. Also, a beautiful table shows guests that you care about your time spent together. What better way is there to start off the evening than with a visual compliment to your guests?

Fortunately, we live in a more relaxed era where a formal or acceptable table setting doesn't involve a day of polishing the silver and praying that the wedding china survives. The do-it-yourself mentality bred by all those crafting and food shows on television has given us permission to shop at tag sales, serve food on secondhand plates, and design unique tabletops. An eclectic assortment of teapots purchased at a swap meet becomes a group of quaint flower vases at a luncheon. I've even used old LP records as base plates at a martini dinner party. These inexpensive and creative accents are the essence of a great table.

$\mathcal{T}$ABLE DESIGNS FOR SIT-DOWN AFFAIRS

Table-setting and decorating ideas appropriate to the cuisine follow each menu in this book. Consider plating meals in the kitchen or setting serving bowls on a side table if your table display is elaborate. The three basic table designs that I've found work beautifully for sit-down affairs are the following:

Garland Design

A garland base of greenery or pooled fabric is spread along the center of the table. Depending on your table size, the base should be about 6 to 12 inches wide; the ends of the garland should not touch the plates at the head and foot of the table. Embellish the garland as you would a wreath, by adding flowers, leaves, nuts, and appropriate trinkets.

Floating Flowers and Candles

Miniature bud vases and votive candles, the small candles in little glass holders, are placed around the table. The traditional bud vase may be replaced with teacups, wine glasses, antique inkwells, rustic cruets, small watering cans, or anything that holds water. This design works well with ornamental or fragrant flowers such as orchids, gardenias, and roses.

Traditional Candlesticks with Accents

Two candlesticks are placed at an equal distance from the ends of the table and from each other in the table's center. A floral accent such as a low, tasteful flower arrange-ment is placed between them, or a wreath of greenery and flowers encircles the candlestick bases. Ivy and flowers may be gracefully draped down the stems of taller candlesticks. Candelabra can stand alone without additional accents.

The traditional design also works well with two tall topiary flower arrangements replacing the candlesticks. The topiary looks like a mini flowering tree: a stem or entwined branches extend a few feet above a potted base and a ball of greenery rests on top. Flowers are placed in the ball and around the branch at the base. The topiary's flower ball should be higher than the guests' line of vision across the table. Topiaries are absolutely exquisite and romantic, especially when satin ribbons are strewn from one flower ball to the other.

In keeping with the designs listed above, some good rules are the following:

- No monstrous centerpieces on the dinner table. Though lovely to look at in a hallway, a giant flower arrangement can be a nuisance as guests crane their necks to see one another across the table. You can achieve the same majesty and grandeur with a little innovation. The exception to this rule is the buffet table, where a large flower arrangement would be perfect.

- Keep it organic. Most hosts choose fresh flowers and candles to adorn their table, with the occasional kitsch items at a 60s party or confetti tossed on a New Year's spread. Whatever the theme may be, employ similar materials in your decorating. Some florists use fruit, rocks, and branches as filler, creating amazing flower arrangements. I've seen tiny champagne grapes spilling over the lip of a vase and halved pomegranates peering through a glass bowl containing yellow roses.

- Less is more. It's easy to go overboard in a decorating frenzy. Visualize the table with bowls of food, glasses, and plates. Does the table look cluttered? When in doubt, draw a rough sketch of your intended design or ask an honest friend's opinion. Simple is best.

- Always use candles. Everyone looks and feels good in candlelight. If nothing else, light a few candles, and you have instant atmosphere. Votive candles are most popular on the caterer's table. A set of six or more votives is a great investment. And while you may love the pungent mulberry-scented candle from your favorite boutique, it may send one of your guests into an asthmatic fit. Shelve the aromatic candles; they compete with the scents of the food. Candles, full of ritual and romance, breathe life into every occasion.

- Choose colors within the same palette. Generally, party colors are based on holidays, seasons, or are specific to the party's theme. It may be difficult for you to determine which shades of color are compatible with another. You can purchase a palette/color wheel at your local art supply or craft store, or page through an interior design book. I usually choose a main color and then accent it with ivory, white, black, gold, or silver. If you want to introduce a third color, perhaps for napkins or flowers, stay within the same color family, but chose a shade from a different primary color. For example, within the winter hues, put cranberry red with hunter green, not cranberry red with burgundy.

  The experienced eye can implement a more sophisticated design, such as pairing two tones of the same color, like steel blue with smoky blue. To achieve a blended look, the tones should be close to each other on the color spectrum. Tones that are too diverse stand out like a corporate logo because the contrast is too bold. You want those viewing your display to think of the food first and then discover its surroundings.

COLOR FAMILIES AND COMPLEMENTARY SHADES

Below is a list of some basic color families and complementary shades that should help when you are choosing your party colors.

Spring Pastels: white, ivory, mint green, aqua, peach, lavender, sky blue, pale yellow, light pink

Autumn Tones: ivory, tan, rust, burnt umber, pumpkin, pine green, marigold, cranberry red, indigo, royal purple

Winter Hues: ivory, cranberry red, burgundy, hunter green, deep purple, metallic gold and silver, black

Summer Brights: white, bubble-gum pink, candy apple red, royal blue, kelly green, lemon yellow, sunset orange

- Choose suitable fabrics for your design. Fabric texture and weight affect your design choice. I use the two-tone approach with silky fabrics, which will fuse together gracefully. The standard polyester-based catering linen is too thick for this method and would look like someone draped a cheerleading uniform over the table. I usually use catering linen as a base tablecloth and swirl a silk or light cotton fabric throughout the arrangements and food platters to compose a glorious table.

The Formula for a Feast

How many times have you seen party guests race to the buffet table in fear of standing in line for an hour? Although the caterer rarely runs out of food, somehow the first pick seems more appealing than the bottom of the pan. It's time to chop up the mile-long buffet line into anxiety-free stops for fabulous food.

In the world of catering a buffet, be it large or small, each serving area is often referred to as a station. For larger parties the stations are strategically positioned throughout the event space to avoid human traffic jams. If your big bash is in a small space, some crowding is unavoidable. I catered an omelet party for 150 people that the client wanted to take place on his 20-foot-square patio. The star attraction at this breakfast party was the omelet bar, and guests had no choice but to cluster and form a line; there was nowhere else to go. The client was not happy that his party began to feel like a military drill, but he didn't want to expand the event space into the house, which would have solved the problem.

Hotels are notorious for talking clients into one grand buffet station, because they can double up on service personnel. They promise that their system of calling each individual table up to the buffet is seamless. I always feel like I'm on a field trip waiting to board the bus when dinner is executed in this manner. As an event coordinator, I have negotiated with hotels on behalf of many clients for a several station setup, because the hotels' catering departments do not like to stray from their normal procedure.

Why are several stations better than one buffet? Guests feel as though they are on their own schedule and therefore are more relaxed. They can enjoy the food at their leisure without following an agenda that is convenient for the caterer. They can visit the antipasto table, dance a little, and then hit the tenderloin station. I've also found that stations are more successful when differentiated by theme as opposed to meal courses for larger events. If you put all the entrees on one table, you're back to one stagnant buffet. Give your guests the freedom to enjoy themselves by creating a movable feast.

$\mathcal{P}$RACTICAL TIPS AND IDEAS FOR FOOD STATIONS

Along with the design ideas mentioned in "The Art of the Table" (page 3), here are some professional tips and industry secrets specific to a food station setup.

Create Varying Levels on the Buffet

Platters of food set on different levels make a more interesting presentation. Create levels with risers of varying heights. Use books, bowls, upside-down pots, or even a stack of plates. Place risers underneath the tablecloth or accent cloth and set the serving platters on top. Make sure the riser is sturdy and the platter is stable, so guests don't tip the platter over when serving themselves. I usually set any item that guests will be cutting into, such as a cheese torte or butter, directly on the table. I place items easily served with a spoon or finger food on risers. Don't elevate something that seems too heavy, like an ice sculpture.

Use a small riser under one side of the bottom of bread and cracker baskets to create a tilted effect. I have a horn-shaped basket that I fill with bread or crudités, and I elevate the back so the food overflows like a cornucopia. Decorative risers can also be made from items in your home. A large metal stand designed to hold a glass vase or candle may be used to hold a bowl. Even a rustic jewelry box or a kitchen tin may work perfectly as a riser or to hold silverware.

Create a Thematic Display on the Buffet

I have friends who only do display. In lieu of a floral centerpiece, these artists take thematic items and arrange them into table exhibits. Chile pepper plants, a sombrero, and a Mexican blanket can transform a tabletop with a mere bowl of chips and salsa into a stunning Southwest station. A wok, fans, greenery, and even a butterfly kite are fantastic items for a Chinese New Year's table.

The display doesn't always have to be in the center of the table, unless the food is accessible from all sides. If this is the case, I almost always use a floral centerpiece elevated on a plastic milk crate beneath the cloth and then swag accent fabric from the centerpiece down onto the table. If the table is against a wall, I'll put the display on one side of the table and build it into the catering equipment. For example, a beach-themed crab cake station will have a wooden crate or a lobster trap strewn with a knotty fisherman's net on one end of the table. The setup may be on a bed of sand with starfish, shells, and fern plants for color. The sand will extend beneath the chafing dishes on to the serving side of the table. The shells and greenery will adorn the table in between and in front of the food dishes. Obviously, the sand must not touch the food, and any item with a strong scent, such as seaweed, is not a good idea. Always consider the scents of display items.

Invest in Essential Elements

If you entertain often, purchase a set of votive candles, banquet cloths, and perhaps a chafing dish or two. Party rental fees can really add up. If you live in certain parts of California or Arizona, GBS Linens (714-778-6448) sells and rents very inexpensively. GBS's rental price on most cloths is $10.00 a week, including extremely reasonable (or sometimes free) delivery if you live in the area. You can purchase a table drape, which is a cloth designed to reach to the floor all the way around a 6- or 8-foot table, for about $30.00. Or, if you've been trying to find the perfect color cloth and matching napkins for your round patio table with a center umbrella, these are the people to call. There are shipping costs involved if you live out of area, but it may still be worth it. For catering equipment, call your local party or restaurant supply store, or check the Internet.

Keep Food Fresh

Often a dip for crudités, which usually has a sour cream base, will sit unrefrigerated on a buffet table for hours. Few would leave sour cream on their kitchen counter for more than 15 minutes. A bowl of ice under creams and perishable foods is a good idea and is a must on a hot day. Keep foods fresh by setting out small but ample amounts at a time. Don't leave the same platter of turkey out all day at your 10 A.M. to 5 P.M. holiday open house. If the party is outdoors, consider the elements. Rent an outdoor umbrella to shade the food if the event is on a sunny day. Use common sense and take reasonable precautions.

Ensure That Your Table Is Safe

I'll never forget the time I catapulted over a famed baseball pitcher at the Bob Hope Classic golf tournament to stomp out a flaming ball of Spanish moss. Keep flammable décor, plastic plates, and paper napkins away from candle flames and lighted Sterno fuel under the chafing dish. On windy days, wrap foil or place tiles around the base of the chafing dish to keep the flame lit and to avoid the flame blowing into another item on the buffet.

The Cocktail Hour

When will someone 'break the ice'?" the panicked host wonders while passing yet another round of mini quiches. The stress of a party's first hour can be brutal. Arm yourself with the right tools, which are amazing hors d'oeuvres and terrific cocktails, and your worries will be over. Guests just need something to talk about, and good food and drink is an easy subject. Along with incredible edibles, here are a few points to remember during the cocktail hour.

Establish a relaxed pace.

People will ease into their own comfort level, but they often take their cue from the host. Don't rush the food out in droves or ply guests with too many cocktails before dinner. Guests will pick up on your angst, and it will affect the whole mood of the party. Setting a relaxed pace is important. Offer a cocktail and an appetizer tray as soon as guests arrive, and then chat with them. You may have to pop in and out of the kitchen for the final food preparations, but you're not breaking any records for speed.

Choose cocktails and hors d'oeuvres that will blend with the flavors of the evening.

Although cocktails and hors d'oeuvres are suggested in most of the menus, you may have some tidbits that you always serve. The attitude of the cocktail hour is whimsical, and you can offer food and drink with extreme tastes, but the palate has its limits. You may love chips and salsa, but they won't mesh with filet mignon in a béarnaise sauce. And a sweet drink such as Kahlua and cream may not be a great partner for salmon on brioche. You can't control guests' taste buds when serving a full bar, but when one cocktail is featured, make sure its flavor is compatible with that of the food.

Enjoy the cocktail hour, but serve your meal on schedule.

The beauty of the cocktail hour is that it allows for flexibility so the presentation of your main meal is right on target. Take the time to enjoy yourself and your guests' company, but don't forget that people are relying on you to feed them at a reasonable hour. There are those occasions when people haven't seen each other for years and a catch-up conversation can last the entire evening. That's fine, but usher guests to their seats at your scheduled dining time. If they've been talking, chances are they haven't been nibbling on hors d'oeuvres and will come to the table famished.

*L*ET YOUR GUESTS KNOW WHAT TO EXPECT.

Let guests know what to expect by written invitation or a telephone conversation. Generally, cocktails last for an hour and then dinner is served. If you plan on showing your vacation video between hors d'oeuvres and the main entrée, guests need to know. They may resent having to sit through a boring video, but at least they won't despise you for starving them. Or if you are hosting an hors d'oeuvres-only event that starts as early as 7 P.M., inform your guests that dinner will not be served.

Just as it isn't fair to spring any surprises on your guests, so it is within your right to deal with potential upsets. For important or formal events, I tell the notorious latecomers, some of my dearest friends, to be on time. It's better to calmly confront the problem beforehand than to answer the door an hour into dinner. Specifying an "end time" will usually ensure guests' prompt arrival and departure.

*B*E A RESPONSIBLE HOST.

While this may not seem a part of the cocktail hour, it is important, because the host sets the evening's tone from the outset. If necessary, you can control the amount people drink prior to the meal by keeping the wine and liquor behind the bar or in a cabinet. Offer the guests a drink when they arrive and then disappear into the kitchen to fill their request. Replenish the cocktail when it is getting low and use a light hand when pouring. By the third round, dinner will be ready or the guests will probably ask you instead of helping themselves. Be prepared to offer a woozy guest a bed for the night or cab fare should he or she need assistance in getting home.

Under the Cork

Wine tasting as an art form has few masters and many happy pretenders. Diners enjoy putting on their amateur sommelier caps to perform the tasting ritual, but most are faking it. Who can blame them? The pomp surrounding the ordering a bottle of wine is regal. It's a nice perk for the price you pay in most restaurants. Every time you participate in the wine ceremony, you further your knowledge of the grape. This education is invaluable for the home entertainer when it comes to choosing a complementary wine for your menu.

We are the experts on our taste buds and our wallets, which determine most people's choice of wine. But what do the connoisseurs look for under the cork? An excellent wine balances the flavor of the grape with the aromatic tones of the cask and the vintner's special crafting secrets. Experts also have their technical checklist of tannins, acidity, weight, and so on, which they mentally compute with every sip. Perhaps the best indication of a wine's quality is the aftertaste or finish. A wine that pleasantly lingers on your palate for 20 to 30 seconds is usually considered to be outstanding. Let's put the professional standards aside and focus on the key elements for matching food with drink, which I believe to be the aroma, taste, and texture.

If winemakers used "scratch and sniff" labels, we'd all save hours of time in the store searching for that Chardonnay with a scant trace of vanilla and a hint of butter. Our four basic tastes (sweet, sour, bitter, and salty) don't really tell us about the nuances of a wine. It's our sense of smell that identifies flavor characteristics. Wine is consumed through our mouth, so we use the term "taste." But it is the marriage of our nose and our tongue that sends a signal to the brain that says, "Oh, yeah, vanilla." The complex bouquet of an individual wine is primarily achieved by a combination of where the grape is grown and how the wine is aged. A spicy crop of Cabernet grapes may have come to fruition near a grove of pepper trees. A Chardonnay with the overpowering aroma of oak may have spent a generous amount of time aging in an oak cask. The talented winemaker parents the grape from the vine to the bottle, blending nature with nurture to create the perfect glass of wine.

Until grocery stores host daily wine tastings, we have to rely on what we've read, heard, or enjoyed in restaurants when selecting wine for a meal. Some hosts offer a new bottle of wine with every course. Most people base their wine selection on the main entrée. An archaic rule of thumb suggests that red wine should be served with red meat and white wine should be served with fish and poultry. One school of thought behind this rule is that the heavier textured reds with their smoky, fruity, or spicy aromas are more compatible with red meat. The whites, generally lighter in texture, tickle the senses with nuts, butter, citrus, and flavors more suitable to poultry and fish. This theory makes sense, but what do you do if you are serving a red-friendly smoked ham with an apple glaze that cries out for a white? You use your best judgment and start with the predominant flavors within your menu. And typically those who turn their nose up when you serve or order red wine with chicken are naked emperors with bad manners.

I choose wine according to how I am preparing the main entrée. With the apple-glazed smoked ham, I would serve a hearty white wine that would highlight the apple. Obviously, a wine choice centered on the main course may not compliment the taste of appetizers and opening courses. However, it is perfectly acceptable and budget-wise to select only one wine for the entire menu.

$\mathcal{G}$UIDELINES TO CHOOSING WINE FOR YOUR MENU

Wine with a meal should provide a backdrop for the food rather than overpower it. Here are some tricks and creative guidelines that I use when choosing wine for a menu.

How am I preparing the main entrée?

My goal is to accent the entrée with wine. First, I consider the sauce being served with the entrée. Is it a tart lemon caper sauce? Is it a nouveau pesto with pistachio nuts and basil? The descriptions we use for many wines can easily apply to sauces. If your sauce has a strong presence—whether tart, herbal, or fruity—look for a subtle wine such as a Chianti or Chardonnay blend. Many Pinot Grigios, for example, are too bright or tart, and would compete with a lemony sauce. On the other hand, a simple butter and parsley sauce could use a little Pinot Grigio pick me up.

If your sauce is delicate or you are not using a sauce, consider other factors in your entrée preparation. Grilled food will pick up the smoky aromas of mesquite and would be great with a woody red or white. Fruit-tomato salsa, a popular summer condiment for fish and chicken, would taste terrific with the berry tones of a Pinot Noir. Think about the texture of both the wine and the entrée. A lush Cabernet Sauvignon with beef is lovely, unless the wine's body is so heavy that you are full in two sips and a bite. Merlot is a lighter-bodied red, which I prefer with heartier meat dishes.

I know which flavors I want to highlight in my menu. How do I find the right wine?

The artistry of winemaking has made its way to the labels. Check the wine label for a description. An impressionistic illustration of nuts and autumn leaves can be very telling. Or the label may read "a rich, full-bodied wine with a fruity aroma." Tell the clerk at your liquor or grocery store you want to speak with the person who buys the wine. Say, "I am serving a seafood lasagna with artichokes, and I don't want anything too bright. What do you recommend?" Often the response will be "White or red? Dry or sweet?" In the wine world, "dry" means less sweet. I've read that many Americans prefer their wine on the sweeter side. This may be true, unless you have a guest list of wine-savvy gourmands.

Browse through wine magazines at a newsstand or research wine on the Internet. There is a fascinating industry web site at smartwine.com. You'll find insider information on vintners and a great consumer section as well. *Food & Wine* magazine has a web site at foodwinemag.com that I've also found to be very thorough. The best wine lesson I've ever had was from a romantic wine tasting trip through the Napa Valley. The wealth of knowledge gained from the winemaker's tales while overlooking a flourishing vineyard is priceless.

I have a certain price range in mind.

Don't be shy about buying a less expensive wine. Wine can be pricey, especially if you are paying for a dinner party. Usually, more money will ensure a better quality wine. At a grocery store in Los Angeles, where prices are inflated, I seldom spend less than $7.00 on a 750-ml bottle for a dinner party. Anything over $15.00 per bottle is usually excellent. As the guest count rises, the wine price drops. For a party of 20 or more, I spend around $5.00 per bottle. If you are shopping in a mega-discount store, you may find something palatable for $3.99. Rarely will you find a respectable bottle of wine under $3.99. Your guests may not be able to tell the difference at the party, but the next day their cloudy heads will betray your thrift. Finally, never serve wine from a box.

How much wine should I buy?

There are about 5 (6-ounce) glasses of wine per bottle. The wine flows as abundantly as the conversation at small dinner parties. You can figure about 3 glasses per person when wine is the main beverage. Some drink more, some less, so it all averages out. See the Proportion Chart for Beverages (page 361) for drink proportions at larger parties.

Is there anything else I should look for when selecting wine?

Alcohol content is something you may want to consider. If you have gone to the trouble of preparing a fabulous meal, you want your guests to have the presence of mind to enjoy it. Some people drink wine like water, and it quickly goes to their head. I threw my brother a gourmet 30th birthday party, and his friend Jasmine was in charge of the wine. Jasmine, who owns a wine business, chose a wine with a low alcohol content of 11 percent (the average alcohol content is a modest 13.5 percent). She knew the crowd to be heavy drinkers and wanted the party to remain civilized throughout dinner. It was a smart idea for which I was grateful.

During dinner, I like to keep the wine on the table for guests to enjoy at their leisure. I pour the initial glass and thank my friends for joining me with a toast. As the evening progresses, I take pleasure when guests feel comfortable enough to fill each other's glass.

The Wine List

This wine guide lists the nuances and flavor characteristics of the wines suggested in the *Sophisticated Entertaining* menus. Most of these wineries have long-standing reputations of excellence and their wines are widely available in most areas. The vintages suggested below are mostly 1997 and 1998. Because these wineries produce good quality wines, you should always be able to find a great bottle of wine from them at similar prices. The NV or nonvintage designation means that the wine contains a blend of grapes harvested in different years.

This wine list is designed to provide you with information for finding a decent dinner party wine at a reasonable price. Should you wish to impress the wine connoisseur at your table with a superior vintage, I suggest that you start with the wineries listed below. Inquire at your local wine shop about exceptional vintages.

Along with a description of the wine, you'll find the general price range for an average size bottle, approximately 750 milliliters. The ranges are shown below.

$ BELOW $10	$$ BETWEEN $10-$20	$$$ ABOVE $20

$\mathcal{W}$HITE WINES

1997 Ashley Nicole Chardonnay, California ($)

This trendy white wine from California's central coast is well balanced and has less oak than the average Chardonnay.

1997 Beaulieu Vineyard Coastal Chardonnay, California ($$)

BV is a giant winery producing both less expensive wines, such as this crisp Chardonnay with citrus tones, and award-winning bottles of liquid gold.

1998 Bollini Pinot Grigio, Italy ($$)

A well-crafted wine, this has more body and subtle citrus nuances than many Pinot Grigios, which are released too bright and young.

1997 Cakebread Cellars Chardonnay, California ($$$)

This absolutely excellent wine never disappoints with its nuances of citrus, green apples, and ripe pears within an oaky milieu. In my opinion, Cakebread is one of the finest wineries in the Napa Valley.

1998 Cape Indaba Sauvignon Blanc, South Africa ($$)

A nose of lemon and lime with a hint of pineapple makes for a terrific and easy to drink white wine.

1997 Clos du Bois Late Harvest Semillon, California ($$)

This superior dessert wine is sweetened by flavors of ripe pears and berries.

1997 De Loach Vineyards Early Harvest Gewurztraminer, California ($$)

An aromatic, sweet wine with tones of grapefruit, it is a good choice for an exotic and diversely flavored menu.

1998 B. R. Cohn Carneros Chardonnay, California ($$$)

Delightful fruity blend with hints of vanilla and toasted oak with a rich finish.

1998 Duckhorn Sauvignon Blanc, California ($$)

This dry, crisp white wine with citrus notes will provide a light and pleasant backdrop for spicy foods.

1997 Estancia Chardonnay, California ($)

I love the simple and elegant label of this affordable white that has more fruit and less oak than most Chardonnays. It's a good buy and a popular selection for large parties.

1997 Geyser Peak Sauvignon Blanc, California ($)

A white wine with lemon and herb notes that is a great pairing with a menu full of spicy dishes.

1998 Glen Ellen Proprietor's Reserve Chardonnay, California ($)

Probably the highest-selling label, Glen Ellen mass-produces a respectable Chardonnay with traces of oak at a fabulous price. This is great for large parties when cost is a concern.

1997 Grgich Hills Cellars Chardonnay, California ($$$)

A king crafter of Chardonnay, this Napa Valley winery has created a lovely rich, buttery wine. It's an excellent choice for an elegant dinner party.

1998 Husch Mendocino Sauvignon Blanc, California ($)

An inventive blend of orange and nectarine makes this lively white a natural for salads.

1997 Kendall-Jackson Vintner's Reserve Chardonnay, California ($$)

A rich, buttery Chardonnay with a strong presence of oak, this wine is so popular on the restaurant scene that its fans have nicknamed it "KJ."

1997 Kendall-Jackson Vintner's Reserve Sauvignon Blanc, California ($$)

This medium-bodied, bright wine is a little sweet, making it a good compliment for spicy foods.

Ozeki Karatamba Sake, Japan ($$)

> *This fruity rice wine is a bit sweet and blends harmoniously with the salty, spicy flavors of Japanese cuisine.*

1998 Robert Mondavi Fumé Blanc, California ($)

> *Mr. Mondavi is credited with inventing the term "fumé blanc." This dry white wine with its overtones of pear and melon is a nice complement to a menu whose flavors are on the sweeter side.*

1997 Rosemount Estate Diamond Semillon-Chardonnay, Australia ($)

> *An excellent value from Down Under, this white wine blend of crisp Semillon with hearty Chardonnay is a real crowd pleaser at cocktail parties.*

1997 Tiefenbrunner Pinot Grigio, Italy ($)

> *Bright, light, and aromatic, as are most Pinot Grigios, it has citrus and nut overtones.*

1998 Trefethen Vineyards Dry Riesling, California ($$)

> *A lemony, zesty white, this pairs beautifully with exotic cuisine such as Indian and Malaysian.*

1997 Teruzzi & Puthod Terre di Tufi, Italy ($$)

> *I enjoyed this amazing white Tuscan wine about a year ago at a restaurant and found that not a wine store in Los Angeles carried it. Since then it has popped up all over the gourmet scene. This wine is practically perfect, an exquisite blend of fruit making it balanced and ultra smooth.*

RED AND ROSÉ WINES

1997 Acacia Pinot Noir, California ($$$)

> *A complex blend of silky, smooth berries makes this Pinot Noir an excellent choice for a dinner party.*

1998 Beringer "LVS" White Zinfandel/Chardonnay, California ($)

> *An inexpensive wine from a highly regarded winery, this medium-body and fruity blend is perfect for large parties.*

1997 Blackstone Winery Merlot, California ($)

Growing in popularity is this top-selling Merlot with hints of berry and a little sweet-ness. It can still be found for a very reasonable price at large wine stores.

1997 Cakebread Cellars Rubaiyat, California ($$$)

Inspired by the quote from Omar Khayyam's poem The Rubaiyat, *"a jug of wine, a loaf of bread and thou," this romantic blend of Syrah and Pinot Noir has notes of plum and fresh berries.*

1998 Cakebread Cellars Vin de Porche, California ($$)

Described by the owner of this stellar winery as "a pizza and hot dog" wine, this exper-imental rosé with a blend of Syrah and Pinot Noir grapes is a fun, casual wine with a more serious price.

1998 Fetzer Eagle Peak Merlot, California ($)

A decent Merlot with a candied, fruity nose at a great price, it is a first choice for large parties.

1997 Firestone Cabernet Sauvignon, California ($$)

A superb wine with a blend of cherries and plums, it is perfect with grilled steak and smoky flavors.

1997 Francis Ford Coppola California Rosso, California ($)

An amazing four-grape blend of Zinfandel, Sangiovese, Syrah, and Cabernet, this refreshing red table wine is a real winner and one of the most affordable in the Niebaum-Coppola portfolio.

1998 Glen Ellen Proprietor's Reserve Cabernet Sauvignon, California ($)

An American favorite that can be found in almost every grocery store at a great price, this full-bodied, hearty red will not disappoint at larger parties.

1998 Glen Ellen Proprietor's Reserve Gamay Beaujolais, California ($)

A top seller in its category, this fruity blush wine is pleasantly smooth and blends well with many styles of food. It's a great budget buy for large parties.

1995 Jordan Vineyard and Winery Cabernet Sauvignon, California ($$$)

A subtle Cabernet, it has notes of blackberry, cherry, and plum. Jordan is a master crafter of Cabernet Sauvignon.

1998 Louis Jadot Beaujolais Villages, France ($$)

Louis Jadot is a premiere producer of blush wine with a smooth, slightly sweet blend of berries.

1998 Niebaum-Coppola Talia Rosé, California ($$)

A lovely blush wine with a refreshing fruity blend, it lends a supreme accent to roast pork or pasta in a light cream sauce.

1999 Rosemount Estate Grenache-Shiraz, Australia ($)

A wonderful, subtle red with the flavors of ripe, red berries and a touch of licorice, it's a very affordable wine that will appeal to the tastes of many.

1997 Santa Rita Merlot, Chile ($)

A well-blended, fruity red wine designed to highlight the spicy fare of South America.

CHAMPAGNE, SPARKLING WINES, AND OTHER SUGGESTIONS

1991 Domaine Carneros Blanc de Blanc, California ($$$)

A tangy, sparkling wine perfect for an afternoon tea or brunch, it's from a winery that is co-owned by master Champagne producer Taittinger.

NV Domaine Chandon Cuvée Brut, California ($$)

This lively, crisp bubbly is a top seller because it is a great sparkling wine for a great price. Both balanced and elegant, a glass of Chandon Brut can stand on its own or blend beautifully in a cocktail.

NV Freixenet Brut Cordon Negro, Spain ($)

Known as a great value, this popular, imported sparkling wine is attractively packaged in a frosted black bottle. Its dry, smooth character makes it a great mixer with sweet liqueurs and fresh fruit juice, as in a Mimosa.

NV Leustau Amontillado Bodegas Vieja, Portugal ($$$)

> *This nonvintage sherry has a touch of sweetness with a good deal of age and is lovely with dessert. Dry sherry is an acquired taste, so a little sugar may please more palates.*

NV Piper Sonoma Cellars, Blanc de Noirs, California ($$)

> *A cheerful pink sparkler with hints of red berry and citrus, it's fun and festive for a birthday toast or a Sunday afternoon refresher.*

1988 Veuve Clicquot Champagne Brut Reserve, France ($$$)

> *A dry, crisp, lively Champagne from first-class producers, this bubbly has nuances of apple.*

Wine Tasting 101

Here's a very elementary lesson in wine tasting. If you want more information, don't be embarrassed to ask the server or sommelier for assistance when selecting and tasting a bottle of wine in a restaurant.

1. BOTTLE PRESENTATION: The bottle is presented to you so you can check the label and make sure it is the wine you ordered.

2. CORK OPENING: The bottle is uncorked and you are given the cork for examination. The cork should be marked with the vintner's imprint, which assures you that the label is indeed accurate. You smell the cork in hopes of a pleasant aroma. You make sure that the cork's end is moist, which means the bottle has been properly stored on its side. Apparently the true expert needs but one whiff of the cork to determine if the wine is acceptable.

3. SWIRL AND SMELL: You cue the server to proceed and the wine is poured. You swirl the glass and the wine within to release the aroma. You smell the wine. (Once again, the expert can distinguish good wine from bad.) If the aroma is extremely unpleasant, chances are that the wine is not good, but this is rarely the case. By holding the glass up to the light, you check the wine's color. White wine should be bright and various shades of gold. If white wine is especially dark, it may indicate that it is beginning to oxidize. Red wine should have a rich, saturated color. Red wine that appears brown at the rim may have aged prematurely.

4. TASTE: Take a nice big sip of the wine and swirl it around in your mouth. Note the length of time that the wine lingers on your palate. If you are blissfully savoring the wine's aftertaste for more than 20 seconds after it leaves your mouth, you've probably selected a terrific bottle of wine. If the wine is perfectly acceptable, but you do not care for its taste, express your opinion to the server. Very rarely will he or she accommodate you with another selection unless the bottle is technically bad. If it's a matter of taste, enjoy the characteristic of the wine you've chosen and ask a few more questions of the server when you order the next bottle.

Sit-Down Dinners for Holidays & Special Occasions

A TOASTY THANKSGIVING FOR 6

Grand Marnier Roasted Turkey

Rum and Cherry Cornbread Stuffing

Anise Pecan Sweet Potatoes

Cranberry-Orange Relish

Irish Cream Pumpkin Pie

DERBY DAY DINNER FOR 8

Broiled Apple Brandy Herbed Lamb Chops

Mint Julep Chunky Applesauce

Bourbon-Glazed Carrots

Creamy Corn and Bourbon Custard

Kentucky Derby Pie

THE CHRISTMAS SPIRIT FOR 10

*Pink and Green Peppercorn-Crusted Roast Beef
Tenderloin in a Cabernet Sauce*

Roasted Garlic Wine Mashed Potatoes

Christmas Spinach and Brandied Red Pepper Timbales

Chocolate Frozen Eggnog Mousse Bûche de Noël

A TOASTY THANKSGIVING FOR 6

*I*n keeping with the spirit of this holiday, my annual thanks given to our dinner guests is as follows: "Thank you to all the confirmed vegetarians here who are secretly eating turkey." Living in Los Angeles, we have a lot of die-hard veggie friends and family . . . 364 days of the year. As considerate hosts, we offer a variety of foods from the garden, but I am always complimented when they indulge in the bird.

For many, certain dishes epitomize Thanksgiving. My mother has to have pearl onions and peas, a dish from her Irish background, and my friend Ira always rounds out his turkey dinner with macaroni and cheese. Be sensitive to guests' need for tradition. Should a guest show up at your dinner with a platter of squid, graciously offer it on a side table. Give thanks that your friend thought enough of you to share his or her heritage on this day.

———

Grand Marnier Roasted Turkey

Rum and Cherry Cornbread Stuffing

Anise Pecan Sweet Potatoes

Cranberry-Orange Relish

Irish Cream Pumpkin Pie

———

FOOD AND DRINK PLANNER

ONE DAY BEFORE: Make Cranberry-Orange Relish. Make Irish Cream Pumpkin Pie. Make Rum and Cherry Cornbread Stuffing. Thaw turkey in refrigerator.

PARTY DAY: Stuff and cook turkey. Make Anise Pecan Yams.

COCKTAIL SUGGESTION: Cape Cod: Pour 1 ounce vodka over ice in a short glass; fill glass with cranberry juice.

WINE SUGGESTION: 1997 Kendall-Jackson Vintner's Reserve Chardonnay (see "The Wine List," page 23, for more information).

MENU EXTRAS: Traditional dishes or your family favorites.

TIMESAVERS: Substitute canned sweet potatoes for Anise Pecan Sweet Potatoes. Substitute canned cranberry sauce for Cranberry-Orange Relish. Purchase a prepared pumpkin pie.

TABLE SETTING AND DECORATING IDEAS: A Harvest Feast (see "Traditional Candlesticks with Accents," page 4)

TABLE LINEN: Use autumn tones suggested in "Color Families and Complementary Shades" (see page 6).

Elegant Mini Pumpkins and Flower Display

Place 6 mini pumpkins in the bottom of a glass bubble bowl that is the size of a basketball. Fill the bowl with water. Trim stems on autumn-colored flowers to 2-inch lengths. Arrange flowers in the bowl so top has a neat rounded shape. Another display idea: cut a hole in the top of a large pumpkin and remove seeds and pulp. Place a low glass container in pumpkin. Fill container with water and arrange autumn-colored flowers.

Corn Husk Napkin Bows

Soak dried corn husks in hot water for 5 minutes to soften them. Drain, separate into individual pieces, and pat dry. Tightly knot 2 pieces together at the narrow ends. Roll napkins lengthwise, place them on husks, and, with the knot in back of napkin roll, bring each husk around napkin roll and tie into a large knot. Fan out wide ends of husk, forming a bow shape. If desired, insert a rust-colored flower into the large knot.

Mini Pumpkin Place Cards

Write each person's name on a mini pumpkin in gold or silver ink.

Mini Pumpkin Votives

Hollow mini pumpkins and/or gourds and use them as holders for votive candles.

Grand Marnier Roasted Turkey

MAKES 6 SERVINGS

*C*an you remember the first time you cooked the bird? What an awesome task that seemed! A marinade is a must for poultry, especially when the anticipated cooking time is over 2 hours. This Grand Marnier glaze will ensure a moist, exquisitely flavored turkey.

---

1 (15-POUND) TURKEY

SALT AND BLACK PEPPER

RUM AND CHERRY CORNBREAD STUFFING (PAGE 35)

½ CUP GRAND MARNIER

½ CUP OLIVE OIL

2 TABLESPOONS FINELY CHOPPED CHIVES

2 TABLESPOONS FRESH LEMON JUICE

If turkey is frozen, thaw for 1 to 2 days in the refrigerator or in cold water, changing the water often.

Preheat oven to 325F (165C). Remove the plastic wrapping from turkey. Remove the neck and bag of giblets from body cavities. Rinse the turkey, including cavities, thoroughly with cold water. Pat dry with paper towels. Rub salt and pepper inside cavities and on skin.

Loosely fill the neck and body cavities with stuffing. Fold the neck flap skin under turkey. Pull the wings back and place the tips under the turkey. Tie the legs together and place turkey, breast side up, in a large roasting pan.

Whisk together the Grand Marnier, oil, chives, lemon juice, and 2 teaspoons salt. Brush mixture over entire surface of turkey. Insert a meat thermometer into thickest part of thigh without touching the bone.

Roast the turkey, basting occasionally with Grand Marnier mixture, for about 4 hours or until the thermometer registers 180F (80C). During the last half hour, loosely tent turkey with foil to prevent skin from becoming too brown. Let the turkey stand for 15 minutes and then remove the stuffing before carving.

Carve each breast half on the bias, pull off the thighs and legs, cut off the wings, and arrange the meat on a large platter. Pour the Grand Marnier drippings into a gravy boat and serve on the side.

Rum and Cherry Cornbread Stuffing

MAKES 8 CUPS

*N*ot being a huge fan of celery, I am forever trying stuffing recipes that omit this staple ingredient. I also find that turkey sausage (rather than pork sausage) blends nicely with the sweeter flavors of cherry and creamed corn. This recipe is my younger brother Danny's favorite new dish year-round.

¾ CUP DRIED CHERRIES

¾ CUP RUM

¾ CUP BUTTER

1 LARGE BROWN ONION, COARSELY CHOPPED

3 MEDIUM CARROTS, COARSELY CHOPPED

1 (12-OUNCE) PACKAGE CORNBREAD STUFFING

1 POUND TURKEY SAUSAGE

1 (15-OUNCE) CAN CREAM-STYLE CORN

1 TABLESPOON ANISE SEEDS

1 CUP CHICKEN BROTH

1 TEASPOON SALT

½ TEASPOON BLACK PEPPER

Soak the cherries in the rum overnight. Drain cherries and reserve rum.

Melt ½ cup of the butter in a large skillet over medium-high heat. Add the onion and carrots and cook until just tender, about 8 minutes. Add the reserved rum and cherries and cook over medium-high heat until liquid reduces completely. Remove from heat and transfer to a large bowl. Stir in the cornbread stuffing until combined.

Remove the sausage from casings and crumble it into a large skillet. Cook over medium-high heat until browned, stirring to break up sausage. Add the sausage, corn, and anise seeds to the stuffing mixture and stir well.

Melt the remaining ¼ cup butter and add to the chicken broth. Stir into stuffing mixture until it is thoroughly moistened. Season with the salt and pepper. (Stuffing may be made a day in advance and stored in an airtight container in the refrigerator. Stuff the bird just before cooking.)

Stuff the mixture into body and neck cavities of turkey. Place leftover stuffing in a baking dish and bake at 350F (175C) for 15 minutes or until top is crusty. When the turkey is done, remove stuffing from bird and place it in a serving dish.

Anise Pecan Sweet Potatoes

MAKES 6 SERVINGS

These sweet potatoes pack quite a punch. Sambuca gives this dish a sweet herbal edge with the essence of licorice.

5 POUNDS SWEET POTATOES, PEELED AND CUT INTO 1-INCH CHUNKS

⅓ CUP ROMANA SAMBUCA LIQUORE CLASSICO

½ CUP CHOPPED PECANS

Place the sweet potatoes in a large stockpot and cover with water. Bring to a boil over medium-high heat and cook until tender, about 15 minutes. Drain sweet potatoes and transfer to a large bowl.

Preheat oven to 350F (175C). Spray a 1-quart casserole with nonstick cooking spray. Mash sweet potatoes until smooth. Stir in Sambuca and pecans until blended. (You can store the mixture, covered, in the refrigerator for up to 2 days. Increase baking time to 30 minutes.)

Spoon potato mixture into prepared casserole. Cover and bake for 10 minutes or until heated through. Spoon into a serving dish and serve hot.

Cranberry-Orange Relish

MAKES ABOUT 5 CUPS

*A*s an alternative to canned cranberry sauce, serve this tart, delicious relish laced with spirit.

1½ POUNDS FRESH CRANBERRIES, RINSED

1 CUP CHOPPED FENNEL OR ANISE BULB

1 CUP CHOPPED BARTLETT PEAR

½ CUP MINCED DRIED PEACHES

½ CUP GRAND MARNIER

½ CUP FRESH ORANGE JUICE

½ CUP SUGAR

2 TABLESPOONS FRESH LEMON JUICE

Place all the ingredients in a large saucepan. Cook over medium heat, stirring occasionally, until cranberries are just tender and mixture thickens, about 20 minutes. Remove from heat and cool to room temperature.

Spoon relish into a bowl and serve. Or store it in an airtight container in the refrigerator for up to 2 days. Bring to room temperature before serving.

Irish Cream Pumpkin Pie

*B*aileys Original Irish Cream is the number one liqueur in the world for good reason. Its superior flavor is an excellent enhancement for this popular Thanksgiving dessert.

FILLING	RICH CRUST
1½ CUPS CANNED PUMPKIN	1¾ CUPS ALL-PURPOSE FLOUR
2 EGGS	2 TABLESPOONS POWDERED SUGAR
¾ CUP PACKED LIGHT BROWN SUGAR	6 TABLESPOONS UNSALTED BUTTER, CHILLED, CUT INTO PIECES
½ TEASPOON GROUND CINNAMON	1 EGG
½ CUP HEAVY CREAM	2 TABLESPOONS COLD WATER
¼ CUP BAILEYS ORIGINAL IRISH CREAM	

To make the crust: Place the flour, powdered sugar, and butter in a food processor and pulse until mixture resembles coarse meal. Beat together 1 egg and water. Add to the flour mixture and process until it forms a ball. Form a flat disk from the dough. Cover with plastic wrap and chill for 1 hour.

Preheat the oven to 425F (220C). Roll out dough into a 12-inch circle on a heavily floured surface. Transfer dough circle to a 10-inch pie pan. Trim and crimp the edges of the dough. Prick bottom of dough 5 times with a fork.

To make the filling: Reduce oven to 350F (175C). Beat the pumpkin and 2 eggs in a medium bowl until creamy. Beat in the brown sugar and cinnamon until smooth. Add the cream and Baileys, and beat until thoroughly combined. Pour pumpkin mixture into chilled crust.

Bake for 45 to 55 minutes or until a knife inserted off-center in pie comes out clean. Remove the pie from the oven and cool to room temperature. (Store it for up to 3 days, covered, in the refrigerator.)

Cut into wedges and serve.

TIP: If crust edges become too brown during baking, cover them with foil.

Turkey Tricks

Talk show stints as a chef/crafting guest have kept me occupied for countless hours thinking about a spin on the traditional. These quirky ideas were a big hit!

ICE CREAM TURKEY—A latex glove is the perfect mold for a turkey. Fill a clean latex glove with softened ice cream. Knot the open end as you would a balloon. Place glove, knot side down, on a flat surface in your freezer. When frozen, remove the glove, coat ice cream with chocolate, and decorate with mini M&M candies. Serve in a bowl with the finger feathers upright, resembling a turkey.

MINI TURKEY ICE SCULPTURE—Fill a clean latex glove with fruit juice or, colored water and whole cranberries or slivered citrus peels. Follow preparation and freezing directions above. Put this mini turkey ice sculpture in punch or surround it with crudités or fresh fruit.

COOKIE TURKEY—Trace the outline of your hand on thin cardboard. Cut out the tracing and use as a pattern for cookies. Place the pattern on rolled out cookie dough and cut around the edges. Decorate with gourmet jellybeans or M&M candies before baking, or with icing and candy after baking.

DERBY DAY DINNER FOR 8

Although I've never attended the Kentucky Derby, its celebrated day is filled with special memories and cherished traditions. My husband, John, and I were wed on Derby Day, and were reminded of that fact every year by our friend Jim Eastwood, now deceased. Jim, whose father was a horse trainer, was happy to attend our wedding, but frequently had to excuse himself from the church and reception to hear the race highlights on a transistor radio.

The Kentucky Derby is the only event I can think of that has an official cocktail. Mint Juleps (see below) are served throughout the day to women in fancy hats and to patrons clutching their betting slips. We always make an event of the day, be it a private anniversary dinner or a sit-down gala for once-in-a-lifetime friends like Eastwood.

Broiled Apple Brandy Herbed Lamb Chops

Mint Julep Chunky Applesauce

Bourbon-Glazed Carrots

Creamy Corn and Bourbon Custard

Kentucky Derby Pie

FOOD AND DRINK PLANNER

ONE DAY BEFORE: Make Mint Julep Chunky Applesauce. Make Kentucky Derby Pie.

PARTY DAY: Make Creamy Corn and Bourbon Custard.

JUST BEFORE SERVING: Make Bourbon Glazed Carrots. Make Apple Brandy Herbed Lamb Chops.

COCKTAIL SUGGESTION: Mint Julep: Crush 3 mint sprigs in a silver mint julep mug or tall glass. Add 1 teaspoon powdered sugar and 1 ounce water, and stir. Add ice and 1 ounce bourbon, and stir. Garnish with fresh mint sprigs.

WINE SUGGESTION: 1997 Acacia Pinot Noir (see "The Wine List," page 23, for more information).

TIMESAVERS: Substitute canned cream-style corn for Creamy Corn and Bourbon Custard. Substitute prepared applesauce for Mint Julep Chunky Applesauce.

TABLE SETTING AND DECORATING IDEAS: Kentucky Derby Tribute

TABLE LINEN: Use white, cream, or hunter green table linen.

Horseshoe and Red Rose Place Card Displays

Thoroughly clean one horseshoe for each person. Spray-paint horseshoes gold, silver, or black, or leave as is for a rustic look. Paint each person's name across the top of horseshoe with acrylic paint or red nail polish. Or write names on cloth ribbons and drape them diagonally across horseshoes. Set horseshoes at the top (or 12 o'clock position) of the plates.

To make horseshoes stand upright, fill 2 baby food or small jars halfway with gravel to weight down the jars. Insert each end of horseshoe into a jar, working the end into the rocks until the horseshoe is upright and steady. Mask the jar by gluing green moss or leaves to the outside. Fill remainder of jar with water and insert red roses and greenery into jar. You can also tie a ribbon around jars or horseshoes and decorate with baby ivy. Set bud vases of red roses around the table.

Straw Place Mats

Make a sparse bed of straw for a place mat. Use a base plate or charger on top of the straw and under the dinner plate. Or make a display of straw, horseshoes, and red roses in the center of the table. Candles are not recommended; the flames may ignite the straw.

Mini Saddle Napkin Holders

Purchase a miniature horse saddle at a toy store for each person. Roll a napkin lengthwise and fasten the saddle straps around the middle of the napkin. Or use a piece of leather tied in a bow or knot as a napkin ring.

Broiled Apple Brandy Herbed Lamb Chops

MAKES 8 SERVINGS

These lamb chops are also wonderful when cooked on an outdoor grill. Place chops on a clean grill about 6 inches above medium coals. Cook for 5 minutes on one side, flip the chops over and cook for another 5 minutes or until desired doneness.

Serve with Mint Julep Chunky Applesauce (page 43).

1 CUP (2 STICKS) BUTTER, MELTED	½ CUP MINCED FRESH THYME
1 CUP OLIVE OIL	3 CLOVES GARLIC, MINCED
¼ CUP LAIRD'S APPLEJACK OR APPLE BRANDY	1½ TEASPOONS SALT
½ CUP FRESH LEMON JUICE	½ TEASPOON BLACK PEPPER
½ CUP MINCED FRESH ROSEMARY	16 (4-OUNCE) LOIN LAMB CHOPS, ABOUT 1¼ INCHES THICK
½ CUP MINCED FRESH SAGE	8 CLOVES GARLIC, QUARTERED

Whisk together the butter, oil, Applejack, lemon juice, rosemary, sage, thyme, minced garlic, salt, and pepper in a medium bowl. Place the lamb chops in a large baking pan. Pour mixture over chops. Marinade, covered, in the refrigerator for 1 hour, turning over after 30 minutes.

Preheat oven to 350F (175C). Remove the lamb chops from the marinade and set them aside. Place the pan with hardened marinade in the oven for 3 to 5 minutes or until marinade melts. Remove the herbs with a slotted spoon and place on a plate. Dip the lamb chops in the marinade and coat the flat sides with the herbs. Cut 2 slits into top of each lamb chop and insert garlic quarters into each slit.

Preheat the broiler to high. Place the lamb chops on a rack in broiler pan. Broil the chops 6 inches from heat. For medium-rare chops, broil 5 minutes on each side. For medium chops, broil 7 minutes on each side. Remove from broiler and serve hot.

Mint Julep Chunky Applesauce

MAKES ABOUT 4 CUPS

A mint julep is the traditional Kentucky Derby drink. The aroma of fresh mint in this hearty applesauce replaces the mint jelly with a fresh fruit alternative.

3 POUNDS RED DELICIOUS APPLES, PEELED, CORED, AND DICED

¾ CUP BOURBON

1½ CUPS APPLE JUICE

2 TABLESPOONS FRESH LEMON JUICE

¾ CUP FRESH MINT LEAVES, COARSELY CHOPPED

Place the apples, bourbon, juices, and mint in a medium saucepan. Cook over medium heat, stirring occasionally, until apples are very tender, about 45 minutes. Remove from heat.

Drain the apples and reserve ¼ cup of the liquid. Remove 1 cup of the drained apples and set aside. Place the remaining apples in a food processor and process until smooth. Transfer to a bowl and stir in reserved liquid and apples until combined. Cool to room temperature. (Can be stored in an airtight container in the refrigerator for up to 2 days.)

Bourbon-Glazed Baby Carrots

MAKES 8 SERVINGS

*B*aby carrots are usually washed, peeled, and prepackaged, which makes preparation a breeze. You can also find them unpackaged in the produce section with their decorative green tops attached.

¼ CUP BUTTER

2 POUNDS BABY CARROTS

3 TABLESPOONS MINCED FRESH PARSLEY

3 TABLESPOONS LIGHT BROWN SUGAR

3 TABLESPOONS BOURBON

Melt the butter in a large skillet over medium-high heat. Add the carrots and parsley and cook, stirring occasionally, for 10 minutes. Stir in the brown sugar and bourbon. Cook, stirring occasionally, until sugar dissolves and glazes carrots, about 3 minutes. Remove from heat.

Transfer to a bowl and serve hot.

Creamy Corn and Bourbon Custard

MAKES ABOUT 15 CUSTARDS

*A*s with most custard dishes, the baking pan is placed in a bain-marie or a warm water bath. The pan containing the food is placed in the larger pan of water and then both pans are placed in the oven. The water remains at a constant temperature, helping the food cook more evenly.

2 (15-OUNCE) CANS CREAM-STYLE CORN	2 TABLESPOONS BOURBON
4 EGGS	2 TABLESPOONS MINCED FRESH PARSLEY

Preheat oven to 325F (165C). Line 15 cups of muffin pans with foil baking cups. Spray cups with nonstick cooking spray. Beat the corn, eggs, and bourbon in a large bowl until combined. Fill prepared foil cups with batter.

Fill 2 large baking pans halfway with water. Set each muffin pan inside a pan of water and place pans in the oven. Bake 1 hour or until knife inserted off-center in custard comes out clean. Remove from heat and cool 10 minutes.

Gently remove foil from each custard and place custards, upside down, on a serving platter. Garnish each custard with minced parsley.

Kentucky Derby Pie

MAKES 12 SERVINGS

*M*y friend Ruth Shure brought this gooey pie to a Kentucky Derby party thrown by my high school buddy Justine and her Southern hubby, David. After devouring three pieces, I cornered her and got the secret recipe! More like a giant, chewy cookie in a piecrust, this dessert is best served warm. Thanks, Ruth!

½ CUP GRANULATED SUGAR

½ CUP PACKED LIGHT BROWN SUGAR

¾ CUP ALL-PURPOSE FLOUR

2 EGGS, BEATEN

2 TABLESPOONS MAKER'S MARK BOURBON

½ CUP UNSALTED BUTTER, MELTED AND COOLED

¾ CUP WALNUTS

¾ CUP CHOCOLATE CHIPS

1 (9-INCH) UNBAKED PIE SHELL

Preheat oven to 350F (175C). Sift together the sugars and flour into a medium bowl. Beat in the eggs and bourbon. Add the butter and mix until combined. Stir in the walnuts and chocolate chips. Pour batter into pie shell.

Bake 30 minutes or until a knife inserted in center comes out clean. Cool completely. (Store in an airtight container at room temperature for up to 2 days.)

Cut into wedges and serve.

THE CHRISTMAS SPIRIT FOR 10

*C*hristmas dinner is a grand occasion full of spirit and rituals. Each family has its own way of celebrating with food, gifts, and ceremony. At age nine, my sister rallied my brothers and me into filling Christmas stockings for my parents. I can still remember the look on their faces when they happened upon the stuffed socks.

Christmas starts earlier every year with merchants selling reindeer candle-holders and an array of angel-themed items. The marketplace has become so creative with festive trinkets that it's easy to spend a fortune on dinnerware alone. Adorn your holiday table with a blend of Yuletide heirlooms and the magical decorating and food ideas listed here.

Pink and Green Peppercorn-Crusted Beef Tenderloin in a Cabernet Sauce

Roasted Garlic and Wine Mashed Potatoes

Christmas Spinach and Brandied Red Pepper Timbales

Chocolate Frozen Eggnog Mousse Bûche de Noël

FOOD AND DRINK PLANNER

ONE DAY BEFORE: Make Chocolate Hazelnut Genoise cake for Bûche de Noël. Make frozen eggnog Mousse for Bûche de Noël.

PARTY DAY: Make Christmas Spinach and Brandied Red Pepper Timbales.

JUST BEFORE SERVING: Make Pink and Green Peppercorn-Crusted Beef Tenderloin in a Cabernet Sauce. Make Roasted Garlic and Wine Mashed Potatoes. Assemble Chocolate Frozen Eggnog Mousse Bûche de Noël.

COCKTAIL SUGGESTION: Champagne with a framboise float.

WINE SUGGESTION: 1995 Jordan Vineyard and Winery Cabernet Sauvignon (see "The Wine List," page 23, for more information).

TIMESAVERS: Substitute a prepared pie for the Chocolate Frozen Eggnog Mousse Bûche de Noël. Substitute a steamed green vegetable for Christmas Spinach and Brandied Red Pepper Timbales.

TABLE SETTING AND DECORATING IDEAS: A Golden Yuletide Garland (see "Garland Design," page 4).

TABLE LINEN: Use Winter Hues suggested in "Color Families and Complementary Shades" (see page 6).

Shimmering Pine Cone Garland

Place the cloth on the table. Lay gold lamé fabric in a flowing pooled fashion along the center of the table. Arrange pine boughs close together in a wavy strip along the center of the fabric or use an assembled pine garland purchased from a Christmas tree lot or store. Spray-paint pine cones and unopened nut shells with various metallic colors like copper, chrome, and gold. Scatter cones and nuts throughout pine boughs. Gold and silver ball ornaments also look beautiful in this design. Or decorate the pine boughs as you would a Christmas tree with tiny ornaments and balls. If desired, spray gold glitter on pine cones.

Pearled String and Ornament Napkin Ties

Purchase a pearled string at the notions department of your local fabric store. Cut into 1-foot lengths (1 for each person). Fold napkins accordion style. Wrap pearled string twice around middle of napkin. Feed one end of string through hanging loop of a miniature Christmas ball. Tie ends into a loose bow and place napkin on dinner plate. Gold cord is a good substitute if pearled string is not available.

Silver or Crystal Candlesticks or Candelabra

Place your finest candleholders in the center of table, worked into the garland design.

Miniature Wrapped Gift Place Cards

Place a small gold gift box of chocolates or trinkets on each plate. Tie a bow around the gift box and affix a name tag to the bow or box.

Pink and Green Peppercorn-Crusted Beef Tenderloin in a Cabernet Sauvignon Sauce

MAKES 10 SERVINGS

With its confetti crust of pink and green peppercorns this melt-in-your-mouth tenderloin is a festive main entrée for a holiday dinner. This dish with its ruby-colored shallots is so delectable that you may want to prepare a few extra portions, if you have a hungry crowd and can handle the cost.

½ CUP WHOLE PINK PEPPERCORNS	2 CUPS BEEF BROTH
½ CUP WHOLE GREEN PEPPERCORNS	1½ CUPS CABERNET SAUVIGNON
¼ CUP SALT	5 MEDIUM SHALLOTS, CUT INTO SLIVERS
2 (2½-POUND) OR 1 (5-POUND) WHOLE BEEF TENDERLOIN OR FILET MIGNON	6 TABLESPOONS BUTTER

Preheat oven to 375F (190C). Lay a sheet of waxed paper on a flat surface. Toss the peppercorns together and scatter on the waxed paper. Lay another sheet of waxed paper on top of peppercorns. Place a heavy frying pan on top of waxed paper and press down, cracking peppercorns into coarse bits.

Rub the salt over the surface of the beef. Roll the beef in the cracked peppercorns until the outer surface is coated. Place beef in a large roasting pan and insert a meat thermometer into the thickest part. Roast for about 20 minutes per pound or until desired doneness. The thermometer will register 140F (60C) for rare meat and 170F (75C) for well-done meat. Remove the beef from oven and transfer to a plate. Tent with foil to keep warm.

Meanwhile, place broth, wine, and shallots in a large skillet and cook over high heat until mixture boils and reduces by half, 15 to 20 minutes. Remove from heat and swirl in butter, 1 tablespoon at a time. Pour drippings from roasting pan into mixture and stir until combined.

Cut beef into thick slices and arrange on a serving platter or individual plates. Spoon sauce over beef and serve hot.

NOTES: Though most sauces start with the drippings from the pan, in this recipe you add the drippings at the end of the cooking process. The Cabernet Sauvignon sauce takes about 20 minutes to prepare, and you don't want perfectly cooked tenderloin to cool just because you needed the drippings.

A whole beef tenderloin weighing 5 pounds may be hard to find. Ones weighing 2½ pounds should be more readily available. Special cuts of beef can be ordered from a butcher or the meat department of your local market.

Roasted Garlic and Wine Mashed Potatoes

MAKES 10 TO 12 SERVINGS

My Irish mother is a mashed potato fiend. Her potatoes are always fluffy and light because she never uses an electric beater to do the mashing for her. She shared her potato expertise with me in perfecting this recipe. Love ya, B. J.!

---

8 CLOVES GARLIC, PEELED

2 TABLESPOONS OLIVE OIL

2 TABLESPOONS WHITE WINE

8 LARGE RUSSET POTATOES (ABOUT 4 POUNDS TOTAL), PEELED AND CUT INTO 1-INCH CUBES

1 TABLESPOON PLUS 1½ TEASPOONS SALT

6 TABLESPOONS BUTTER

¼ TEASPOON WHITE PEPPER

¾ CUP HEAVY CREAM

Preheat oven to 400F (205C). Cut the garlic lengthwise into quarters. Place the garlic, oil, and wine in a small baking dish and bake about 15 minutes or until garlic is deep golden brown.

Place potatoes in a stockpot and add 1 tablespoon salt and enough water to cover. Bring to a boil over medium-high heat and cook until potatoes are tender, about 15 minutes. Drain potatoes in a colander.

Transfer potatoes to a large bowl and use a potato masher to mash them until smooth. Add the butter, 1½ teaspoons salt, and pepper to potatoes and mash until butter is melted. Add the garlic and any wine left in the baking dish and mash until incorporated. Stir in cream until blended. (You can make ahead, then store in an airtight container in the refrigerator for up to 2 days.)

Serve warm in a large bowl or on individual plates.

Christmas Spinach and Brandied Red Pepper Timbales

MAKES ABOUT 18 TIMBALES

Traditional dessert timbales are brioche pastry cups filled with a fruity mixture. This version of the timbale, a cup-shaped custard with minced vegetables, is a lovely side dish for elegant meals. This recipe allows for extra timbales because guests rarely eat just one.

---

2 (10-OUNCE) PACKAGES CHOPPED FROZEN SPINACH, THAWED	1/2 TEASPOON BLACK PEPPER
1/4 CUP BUTTER	1 CUP HEAVY CREAM
2 LARGE BROWN ONIONS, MINCED	8 EGGS
1 1/2 CUPS FRESHLY GRATED PARMESAN CHEESE	3 TABLESPOONS OLIVE OIL
	2 RED BELL PEPPERS, MINCED
1 1/2 TEASPOONS SALT	1/2 CUP SPICED BRANDY

Squeeze all excess water from the spinach and place spinach in a large bowl.

Melt the butter in a large skillet over medium-high heat. Add the onions and cook, stirring occasionally, until translucent, 3 to 5 minutes. Add onions to spinach and stir until combined. Stir in the cheese, 1 teaspoon of salt, and black pepper.

Preheat oven to 325F (165C). Line 18 cups of muffin pans with foil cups. Spray cups with nonstick cooking spray. Beat the cream and eggs in a large bowl until just blended. Pour egg mixture into spinach and stir until combined.

Pour mixture into prepared foil cups. Fill 2 large baking pans halfway with hot water. Set the each muffin pan in a pan of water and place pans on lower rack of oven. Bake 35 to 40 minutes or until knife inserted off-center of a timbale comes out clean. Remove from heat and cool for 10 minutes. (To make ahead, cool the timbales in the pan. Remove them from the pan, keeping timbales in their foil cups. Place the timbales on a plate, cover with plastic wrap and refrigerate up to 2 days. When ready to serve, gently peel foil cups away from the timbales and place them, upside down, on a baking sheet. Warm timbales in a 350F [175C] oven for 10 minutes. Or place timbales, upside down, on a plate and microwave until warm.)

Meanwhile, heat the oil in a large skillet over medium-high heat. Add bell peppers and cook, stirring occasionally, for 5 minutes. Add the brandy and remaining ½ teaspoon salt and cook, stirring occasionally, until peppers are softened, about 5 minutes. Reserve ⅓ cup of the peppers and place remaining peppers and liquid in a blender. Puree until smooth.

Remove timbales from muffin pans and gently peel away foil cups. Place, upside down, on a serving platter or individual plates. Spoon 2 teaspoons bell pepper puree over top of each timbale and garnish with a pinch of reserved bell peppers.

Chocolate Frozen Eggnog Mousse Bûche de Noël

MAKES 10 SERVINGS

Few have been exposed to the bûche de Noël, a classic French Christmas dessert shaped like a Yule log. I attribute its rare appearances to the lengthy preparation it requires during the time-challenging holidays. The good news is that you can make the cake 3 days in advance, the mousse filling a day in advance, and then assemble all the elements on Christmas Day. An applause-inspiring dessert, this dinner finale is well worth the effort.

CHOCOLATE HAZELNUT GENOISE CAKE	FROZEN EGGNOG MOUSSE
3 EGGS	4 OUNCES GOOD-QUALITY WHITE CHOCOLATE, CHOPPED
1 EGG YOLK	2 EGG YOLKS, PREFERABLY PASTEURIZED (SEE NOTE, BELOW)
1 CUP GRANULATED SUGAR	2 TABLESPOONS SUGAR
¾ CUP CAKE FLOUR	2 TABLESPOONS DARK RUM
⅓ CUP UNSWEETENED COCOA POWDER	1 CUP HEAVY WHIPPING CREAM, CHILLED
1 TEASPOON BAKING POWDER	3 EGG WHITES, PREFERABLY PASTEURIZED (SEE NOTE, BELOW)
⅛ TEASPOON SALT	1 TEASPOON FRESHLY GRATED NUTMEG
2 TABLESPOONS BUTTER, MELTED AND COOLED	
½ CUP GROUND HAZELNUTS	FOR ASSEMBLY
½ CUP POWDERED SUGAR	2 TABLESPOONS FRANGELICO
	½ CUP POWDERED SUGAR

To make the cake: Center a rack in the oven and preheat oven to 350F (175C). Butter a 15 × 10-inch jelly roll pan and line it with waxed paper. Butter and flour waxed paper, shaking off excess flour.

Beat the eggs and egg yolk in a medium bowl until pale yellow. Gradually beat in granulated sugar until eggs thicken and ribbons form when beaters are lifted. Sift together the flour, cocoa powder, baking powder, and salt, and gently fold, ¼ cup at a time, into egg mixture. Fold in the butter, 1 tablespoon at a time.

Pour mixture into prepared jelly roll pan. Smooth top with a rubber spatula, and sprinkle hazelnuts over top. Bake for 12 minutes or until center springs back to the touch. Cool in pan 5 minutes on a wire rack.

Lay a clean kitchen towel on a flat surface and dust with the powdered sugar. Trim ¼ inch off all sides of the cake, using a sharp knife. Lift waxed paper under cake away from pan and invert cake on the towel. Peel waxed paper away from cake. Starting at a 10-inch end, roll up cake, jelly roll style, in towel. Place roll on a wire rack and cool completely. Wrap cake roll and towel in plastic wrap and refrigerate until ready to use or for up to 3 days.

To make the mousse: Melt the white chocolate in top of a double boiler until smooth, stirring occasionally. Cool 5 minutes. Beat the egg yolks and sugar in a large bowl until thick and pale yellow. Add the melted chocolate and rum, and beat until blended. Using clean beaters, whip the cream in a small metal bowl until thick and fold it into egg mixture. Using clean beaters, beat egg whites in another small bowl until stiff peaks form. Fold egg whites and nutmeg into yolk mixture. Cover and freeze until firm and ready to use.

To assemble: Bring the cake to room temperature or warm slightly in a microwave before unrolling, or it may crack. Carefully roll out cake on a flat surface. Brush cake surface with Frangelico. Spread frozen mousse in an even layer on cake. Re-roll cake and place, seam side down, on a serving platter. Dust with powdered sugar and serve immediately. Cut into rounds at the dinner table and serve.

NOTE: Pasteurized eggs, both in liquid form and in the shell, are becoming more available. Use them as you would unpasteurized eggs. They have one main advantage—the pasteurization destroys salmonella, often the culprit in food poisoning. Raw eggs should not be consumed by children, pregnant women, the elderly, or any one with serious health issues.

Let's Get This Party Started!

EXCELLENT TRAY PASSED HORS D'OEUVRES FOR 50

Cinnamon Liqueur Pumpkin Ravioli

Bacon-Wrapped Sea Scallops in a Port Wine Glaze

Coconut Rum Shrimp Appetizers

Port Wine Cheese Beignets with Blackberry Brandy Dipping Sauce

Tempura California Sushi Roll with Ponzu Sauce

Japanese Eggplant and Goat Cheese Rolls

THE NEW ITALIAN BUFFET FOR 50

Tuscan Bean Spread

Zesty Bread

Seafood and Artichoke White Lasagna

Pinot Grigio Chicken Piccata

Caesar Salad with Toasted Capers

B-52 Tiramisu

SPIKED SHOWSTOPPERS FOR AN HORS D'OEUVRES
STATION FOR 100

Calvados Caramelized Apples Brie en Croûte

Caviar Torte with Champagne Onions

Orange Liqueur Shrimp Wrapped in Snow Peas on Shredded Red Cabbage

Smoked Salmon with Pumpernickel and Lively Mustard Dill Sauce

EXCELLENT TRAY PASSED HORS D'OEUVRES FOR 50

*T*he perfect hors d'oeuvre is an edible architectural feat and the serving tray is its city block. I find the creation of these little masterpieces to be the most challenging and rewarding aspect of the food business. I am constantly thinking of new ways to twist smoked salmon on brioche or form tempura into tiny sculptures.

Don't limit yourself to the old doily on silver tray presentation, as anything goes these days in the catering world. Hors d'oeuvres kick off the party and the recipes in this section are both impressive to the eye and on the palate. Once you discover the artistry of the appetizer, you may never make a full meal again. (See "Proportion Chart for Foods," pages 359–360).

———

Cinnamon Liqueur Pumpkin Ravioli

Bacon-Wrapped Sea Scallops in a Port Wine Glaze

Coconut Rum Shrimp Appetizers

Port Wine Cheese Beignets with Blackberry Brandy Dipping Sauce

Tempura California Sushi Roll with Ponzu Sauce

Japanese Eggplant and Goat Cheese Rolls

———

FOOD AND DRINK PLANNER

ONE DAY BEFORE: Make Port Wine Cheese Beignet dough and Blackberry Brandy Dipping Sauce. Make Japanese Eggplant and Goat Cheese Rolls.

PARTY DAY: Make Cinnamon Liqueur Pumpkin Ravioli. Marinade shrimp in Malibu rum. Make California Sushi Roll and Ponzu Sauce.

DURING PARTY: Assemble and fry Coconut Rum Shrimp.
Fry Cinnamon Liqueur Pumpkin Ravioli.
Make Bacon-Wrapped Scallops in a Port Wine Glaze.
Fry Port Wine Cheese Beignets.
Fry Tempura California Sushi Roll.

COCKTAIL SUGGESTION: Offer full bar (see "Proportion Chart for Beverages," page 361.)

WINE SUGGESTIONS: 1997 Blackstone Winery Merlot and 1997 Rosemount Estate Diamond Semillon-Chardonnay (see "The Wine List," page 23 for more information).

TIMESAVERS: Substitute restaurant or store-bought sushi for Tempura Sushi Roll.

MENU EXTRAS: Make vegetable cups and fillings from Easy Hors d'Oeuvre Cups with Gourmet Fillings (see page 109).

TABLE SETTING AND DECORATING IDEAS: Ten Interesting Trays

Ten Interesting Trays

Garnish a food tray with flowers, shells, rocks, or greenery around the dipping bowl or in the tray's center. If the surface is slick, tape the bowl to the tray. To avoid spilling when it's passed, don't overfill the dipping bowl. Clean all nontraditional serving trays thoroughly before placing food on them. Always when passing hors d'oeuvres, have the tray in one hand and a stack of cocktail napkins in the other.

LP Record: Fun conversation starter; no garnish is necessary.

Chessboard: Use wood boards only, not fold-up cardboard. They're perfect for round hors d'oeuvres like cucumber cups, tarts, or mini quiches.

Mirror: Very elegant look for fussy canapés. Make sure edges are safe.

Basket Lined with Kale: Great for fried food because kale soaks up the excess oil.

Thin Marble Slab: Modern look makes a nice backdrop for intricately shaped food.

Picture Frame: Nostalgic look for family parties; photo or fabric is protected under the glass.

Hatbox Lid Upside Down: Lovely Victorian look: rest the food on greenery.

Large Palm Frond or Tropical Leaf: Exotic presentation; use clean, sturdy leaves.

Washboard: Rustic feel; use for Italian appetizers or country themes.

Large Floor Tile: Contemporary look with many colors available. Make sure edges are safe.

Cinnamon Liqueur Pumpkin Ravioli

MAKES 50 RAVIOLIS

*W*ithout fail, the comment always made by guests offered these amazing hors d'oeuvres is *"Pumpkin in ravioli? Interesting . . . great!"* Using Chinese wonton skins instead of pasta is a cuisine trend that popped up in Los Angeles a few years ago. Many of the cooks around town boil the stuffed wonton skins, which is also an excellent way to prepare this recipe. For an appetizer, I like to fry them into crisp, delectable finger food that is easy for guests to pick up and dip into the Amaretto Orange Sauce.

1 (15-OUNCE) CAN PUMPKIN PULP	1 CUP CORNMEAL
½ CUP GOLDSCHLAGER CINNAMON LIQUEUR	1 (50-COUNT) PACKAGE ROUND WONTON WRAPPERS
1 TABLESPOONS FRESH SAGE, FINELY CHOPPED	OLIVE OIL
3 TABLESPOONS LIGHT BROWN SUGAR	AMARETTO ORANGE SAUCE (SEE BELOW)

Cook the pumpkin, liqueur, sage, and brown sugar in a large skillet over medium heat, stirring occasionally, for 15 minutes.

Line baking sheets with waxed paper and scatter a thick layer of cornmeal over the paper.

Moisten edge on one side of wonton wrapper with water. Place 1 teaspoon pumpkin mixture in center of wonton. Fold wonton in half and pinch together edges to seal. Place on prepared baking sheet. Repeat with remaining wrappers and filling. Be sure there is space between wontons. Refrigerate, covered, until ready to cook (up to 3 hours).

Heat 1 tablespoon olive oil in a large skillet over medium-high heat. Cook about 6 raviolis at a time until golden brown on one side, 3 to 5 minutes. Flip raviolis and cook until golden on other side. Remove with a slotted spatula to paper towels to drain excess oil. Repeat process, using 1 tablespoon of oil for each batch. Serve immediately.

Cinnamon Liqueur Pumpkin Ravioli as an Entree

MAKES 6 SERVINGS

Bring water and 1 tablespoon olive oil to boil in large pot. Cook the ravioli for 3 minutes. Remove with a slotted spoon and drain in a colander. Serve warm with a light, white wine cream sauce. The Amaretto Orange Sauce suggested for the appetizer version of this recipe is good in small dipping doses, but it is too sweet as an entree sauce.

TIP: When moistened, wonton skins are extremely sticky. A sticky dough problem is usually solved with flour, but cornmeal is much more effective for this recipe. Use plenty of cornmeal on the baking sheet to prevent the ravioli from sticking to each other.

Amaretto Orange Sauce

MAKES ABOUT 2 CUPS

This pungent sauce is very sweet. I recommend its use only as a dipping sauce for hors d'oeuvres or on desserts.

½ CUP AMARETTO	2 TABLESPOONS FRESHLY GRATED ORANGE ZEST
½ CUP FRESH ORANGE JUICE	2 CUPS SOUR CREAM

Boil the amaretto, orange juice, and zest in a small saucepan over medium-high heat until liquid reduces to one-third, about 5 minutes. Remove from heat and cool to room temperature.

Stir the orange mixture into sour cream until blended. Cover with plastic wrap and chill until ready to use.

Bacon-Wrapped Sea Scallops in a Port Wine Glaze

MAKES 50 SCALLOPS

*C*aramelized bacon is appearing on more and more restaurant menus. At first thought, this sweetened pork sounded odd, but it tastes terrific. Rumaki, an hors d'oeuvre of chicken liver wrapped in bacon, has never appealed to me. However, sea scallops in a sugar-crusted smoky wrap are exquisite.

WARNING: Adding liquor or wine to bacon fat in a hot skillet may cause the liquid to flame up. Should this occur, quickly cover skillet with a lid.

25 BACON SLICES, CUT IN HALF CROSSWISE	2 CUPS PORT
50 LARGE SEA SCALLOPS (ABOUT 3 POUNDS)	4 TABLESPOONS BUTTER

Wrap half a bacon slice around each scallop so bacon ends overlap. Insert a wooden pick through scallops to secure bacon.

Heat a large skillet over medium-high heat. Add one-third of the wrapped scallops, bacon side down, and cook 5 minutes. Using tongs, carefully turn the scallops and cook until bacon is crisp on all sides, about 5 minutes. Remove scallops to paper towels to absorb excess bacon fat. Pour off bacon fat from pan and repeat cooking process two times with remaining scallops. After cooking final batch, pour off all but 1 tablespoon of the bacon fat.

Reduce heat to medium. Add the Port to the pan and scrape up the browned bits and drippings with a spatula. Cook until liquid reduces to half, 5 to 7 minutes. Remove from heat and swirl in the butter, 1 tablespoon at a time.

Drizzle the sauce over the scallops and arrange on a tray. Serve immediately.

Coconut Rum Shrimp Appetizers

Toasted coconut on a rum-soaked shrimp is sheer heaven. Serve these appetizers piping hot from the skillet. As is the case with most fried foods, after an hour the shrimp will lose its crispness.

1 POUND (50-COUNT) MEDIUM RAW SHRIMP, PEELED AND DEVEINED	1 (16-OUNCE) PACKAGE TEMPURA BATTER MIX
1 CUP MALIBU RUM	ICE WATER
1 CUP ALL-PURPOSE FLOUR	VEGETABLE OR CANOLA OIL
1 TABLESPOON CHILI POWDER	1½ CUPS PURCHASED FRUIT CHUTNEY
1 TEASPOON SALT	
1 (8-OUNCE) PACKAGE SWEETENED, FLAKED COCONUT	

Marinate the shrimp in Malibu rum for 1 hour, covered, in the refrigerator.

Toss together the flour, chili powder, and salt in a medium bowl until combined. Place coconut on a dinner plate and set aside. Drain shrimp, discarding rum. Toss shrimp in flour mixture until coated. Prepare tempura batter according to instructions on box, using ice water. It should be the consistency of pancake batter, and ice cold.

Pour 3 inches of oil in a medium saucepan and heat over medium-low heat. Coat shrimp with tempura batter and roll in coconut. Drop 3 to 5 shrimp at a time in hot oil and cook until golden brown, 1 to 2 minutes. Remove with a slotted spoon and drain on paper towels.

Place fruit chutney in a small dipping bowl and set on a serving tray or in kale-lined basket. Arrange shrimp on tray or in basket and serve hot.

NOTES: Always test how hot the oil is before cooking. For me, the test is always the product. The shrimp in this recipe should not take more than 2 minutes to fry. Drop a prepared shrimp into the oil. If the coconut browns too quickly, the oil is too hot and the inside may not cook thoroughly, so turn down the heat. If it does not brown quickly, the oil is not hot enough; the product will soak up the oil and be soggy. Also, the oil is not ready if the product stays on the bottom of the pot instead immediately floating to the surface of the oil.

Oil can be used for frying for a total of 1 to 2 hours. After that, the oil breaks down. Most people keep oil hot for no more than 15 minutes, in which case it can be reheated and used again, up to 1 to 2 hours of total frying time.

To reuse, allow the oil to cool, strain it, and pour it through a funnel back into the bottle.

Port Wine Cheese Beignets with Blackberry Brandy Dipping Sauce

MAKES ABOUT 50 BEIGNETS

*C*ream puff dough, also known as pâte à choux, is the basis for these beignets. Many know this New Orleans specialty as a light pastry with powdered sugar sprinkled on top.

The addition of cheese to this recipe brings these airy appetizers closer to the classic cheese puff or a fritter. (See page 63 for information on cooking with hot oil.)

---

1 CUP WATER	3 EGGS
½ CUP (1 STICK) BUTTER	1 CUP PORT CHEESE SPREAD
1 TEASPOON SALT	VEGETABLE OIL
¼ TEASPOON WHITE PEPPER	BLACKBERRY BRANDY DIPPING
¾ CUP ALL-PURPOSE FLOUR	SAUCE (SEE BELOW)

Place the water, butter, salt, and white pepper in a medium saucepan and bring to a boil over medium heat. When butter has melted, remove from heat and immediately stir in the flour. Return pan to high heat and stir mixture vigorously until a film forms on the bottom of the pan, 1 to 2 minutes. Remove pan from heat and cool for 5 minutes.

Add the eggs, one at a time, to mixture, stirring well to incorporate after each addition. Stir in cheese until well blended. Cover with plastic wrap and refrigerate for at least 1 hour.

Line a baking sheet with wax paper. Form 1 teaspoon chilled mixture into a ball, using a melon baller. Insert a wooden pick into each ball and set aside on baking sheet.

Pour about 2 inches of oil into a medium saucepan and heat over medium-high heat. Gently drop balls into hot oil and cook 6 at a time for 30 seconds or until golden brown. Remove balls with a slotted spoon and place on paper towels to absorb excess oil. Arrange in a basket of kale or on a doily-lined tray and serve hot with Blackberry Brandy Dipping Sauce.

Blackberry Brandy Dipping Sauce

MAKES 1 CUP

1 CUP SEEDLESS BLACKBERRY JAM

1 TABLESPOON BLACKBERRY
BRANDY OR CRÈME DE CASIS

Place jam and brandy in a small saucepan. Cook over low heat until jam melts. Stir mixture until blended. Bring to room temperature and pour into a small bowl.

Tempura California Sushi Roll with Ponzu Sauce

MAKES 48 PIECES

*S*ushi is always a big production requiring special utensils like a bamboo rolling mat. Once you master the sushi-rolling challenge, preparing this creative and healthy cuisine may become a weekly habit.

Sushi with a tempura coating has an interesting crunch, and less adventurous guests will try it because it looks cooked—"Oh, it's cooked, so it's safe." (See Notes below.)

1 CUCUMBER, PEELED AND SEEDED	WASABI PASTE (OPTIONAL, SEE NOTE BELOW)
1 RIPE AVOCADO	1 (16-OUNCE) BOX TEMPURA BATTER MIX
2 (6-OUNCE) CANS CRABMEAT	
6 SEAWEED SHEETS (NORI), TOASTED	ICE WATER
SUSHI RICE (PAGE 69)	VEGETABLE OR CANOLA OIL
SESAME SEEDS	DAIKON SPROUTS
	PONZU SAUCE (PAGE 70)

Cut the cucumber into long, thin strips. Cut the avocado in half lengthwise and remove the pit. Gently peel away the skin and cut the flesh into thin strips. Drain any excess liquid from the crabmeat.

Toast the seaweed by carefully holding each sheet, shiny side down, over an open flame for 5 seconds, or place in your toaster oven on a light setting. Place seaweed sheet, shiny side down, with the long side lying left to right on a bamboo rolling mat. With moistened hands, gently press ⅔ cup rice over seaweed, leaving a ½-inch margin at the long side that is farther from you. Moisten the margin with water. Make a groove from left to right along the center of rice. Spread a tiny amount of wasabi along the groove, if desired. Lay 1 cucumber strip, 1 avocado strip, and one-sixth of the crabmeat along the length of the groove. Sprinkle sesame seeds over rice and other ingredients.

You may need a few trial runs when first using the bamboo mat. Roll the sushi, starting at the long end closer to you. Place your thumbs under the mat and your fingers over the roll with your fingertips on the ingredients, holding them in the groove. As you begin to roll, the mat will come over the sushi roll and support the seaweed. Tuck the long end that you started rolling with into the sushi roll when the end meets the rice. Continue rolling tightly until complete; secure the sushi roll by pressing the moistened margin along the roll. Repeat process with remaining ingredients to make 6 sushi rolls. Wrap sushi rolls in plastic wrap and refrigerate until ready to use. Sushi is best when prepared and served on the same day.

Prepare the tempura batter according to instructions on the box, adding enough ice water so that it is the consistency of cake batter. Fill a medium pot or wok halfway with oil and heat over medium-high heat for 10 minutes.

Dip sushi roll in tempura batter and fry until golden brown and puffy, 30 to 60 seconds. Remove from oil with a wok basket or slotted spoon and place on paper towels to absorb excess oil. Cool for 5 minutes.

Place the tempura sushi roll on a cutting board and, using a sharp knife, cut crosswise into 8 pieces. Cut off the stems of the daikon sprouts about 1 inch down from the leafy tops. Place sushi slices, rice side up, on a serving tray and insert a daikon sprout in the center of each piece. Serve with Ponzu Sauce.

VARIATION

For traditional sushi, omit frying the sushi roll in tempura batter. After rolling the sushi, cut the roll crosswise into 8 pieces and serve.

NOTES: Bamboo rolling mats resemble 9-inch-square island rafts made from sticks and string. They provide a rigid backing against the seaweed, allowing you to roll the sushi tightly. You can find a bamboo rolling mat in your grocery store, at an Asian market, or at a gourmet cooking store like Williams-Sonoma.

Wasabi is a very hot, green horseradish. You can buy it as a powder and add water to form a thick paste. Prepared wasabi is usually available in the Asian section of your grocery store. Although the California Sushi Roll typically has a tiny bit of wasabi smeared along the inside of the rice, I don't recommend its addition for a large party; it is too strong for most people.

Daikon sprouts are from the radish family and resemble clover. They are usually sold in plastic containers in the produce section of your grocery store. If daikon sprouts are not available, alfalfa sprouts will do, but are not nearly as charming.

Sushi Rice

MAKES 4 CUPS

When short-grain rice is cooked, it becomes sticky, which means that it holds together well for sushi or rice balls.

2 CUPS SHORT-GRAIN RICE	½ CUP SEASONED RICE WINE VINEGAR
2 CUPS COLD WATER	

Soak the rice for 5 minutes in a bowl of cold water. With clean hands, gently stir rice until water becomes cloudy. Drain rice in a sieve and set aside, in sieve, for 30 minutes.

Place the rice in a medium pot and add the 2 cups of cold water. Cover and cook over medium-high heat until rice steams, 5 to 8 minutes. Turn heat to high and cook for 2 minutes more. Reduce heat to medium and cook for 5 minutes more, until you hear a crackling sound. Do not lift lid during cooking process. Turn off heat and allow rice to stand, covered, for 15 minutes.

Remove the lid and fluff the rice with a bamboo paddle or a wide wooden spoon. Cover and let stand another 15 minutes.

Spread the rice along the bottom and up the sides of a large nonmetallic bowl or platter. Sprinkle the vinegar over the rice, tossing rice with a wooden paddle to incorporate vinegar. Fan rice with a paper fan or piece of cardboard for about 2 minutes. Cover the bowl with a clean, damp towel until rice cools to room temperature.

Prepare sushi as soon as rice cools for the best results. Do not store rice in the refrigerator; chilled rice loses its stickiness.

Ponzu Sauce

MAKES ABOUT 2 CUPS

*H*ere's a very elementary lesson in Japanese. I humbly request the pardon of my neighborhood sushi chef for this adaptation of his beautiful language. "Pon" loosely means citrus and "zu" means vinegar. The "z" changes to an "s" when the consonant starts a word, hence "sushi" means "vinegar-rice." You may never dip into soy sauce again after tasting this zesty alternative.

---

1 CUP SOY SAUCE	3 TABLESPOONS FRESH LEMON JUICE
⅔ CUP RICE VINEGAR	2 TABLESPOONS FINELY MINCED
½ CUP SAKE	CHIVES

Whisk together the soy sauce, vinegar, sake, and lemon juice in a small bowl. Pour some of the sauce into a dipping bowl and float a teaspoon of minced chives on top. Replenish dipping bowl with sauce and fresh chives as necessary.

NOTE: Some grocery stores sell bottled ponzu sauce. You'll find it near the soy sauce in the Asian section.

Japanese Eggplant and Goat Cheese Rolls

MAKES ABOUT 50 ROLLS

Japanese eggplant may be labeled as baby eggplant in your grocery store. You can go overboard on the food-to-guest ratio with these because they are tiny and scrumptious.

10 JAPANESE EGGPLANT

OLIVE OIL

SALT AND BLACK PEPPER

1 (8-OUNCE) PACKAGE CREAM
CHEESE, ROOM TEMPERATURE

1 (4-OUNCE) PACKAGE GOAT
CHEESE, ROOM TEMPERATURE

1 CUP SUN-DRIED TOMATOES (DRY
PACK)

1 TABLESPOON PLUS 1 TEASPOON
SAKE

Cut the stem off the eggplant. Slice the eggplant lengthwise into wafer-thin strips.

Heat 1 tablespoon oil in a large skillet over medium-high heat. Place eggplant strips flat in pan and sear each side until eggplant is translucent, 2 to 4 minutes. Season with a dash of salt and pepper. Remove eggplant to paper towels and drain excess oil. Repeat process, adding 1 tablespoon oil to skillet with every batch. Cool the eggplant completely. Cover with plastic wrap and store in the refrigerator until ready to use (up to 1 day).

Place sun-dried tomatoes in a small pot of boiling water for 5 minutes to rehydrate. Drain, cool for 5 minutes, and mince. Whip the cream cheese and goat cheese together until creamy. Stir in the sun-dried tomatoes and sake until distributed evenly throughout mixture.

Place ½ teaspoon of goat cheese mixture on wide end of each eggplant strip. Roll up eggplant, enclosing the cheese inside. Secure roll by spreading a dab of goat cheese on loose end of eggplant and adhering end to roll. Stand eggplant rolls, cheese side up, on a serving platter. (To make ahead, store up to 2 days, wrapped in plastic wrap, in the refrigerator.)

THE NEW ITALIAN BUFFET FOR 50

rattorias featuring cuisine more commonly found in northern Italy are all over Los Angeles. This menu with a white lasagna and Tuscan Bean Spread features foods from Italy's upper regions.

North Italian cuisine always reminds me of the floating city of Venice, where I enjoyed a fabulous meal in a restaurant overlooking the Grand Canal. I ordered seafood pasta full of cuttlefish and offended the waiter by requesting Parmesan cheese to top this dish. Apparently America's favorite Italian condiment is a big no-no on seafood in Venice. I'm sure the tourist faux pas happens nightly. I found the incident quite humorous, especially after a bottle of wine and a gondola ride in the rain.

———

Tuscan Bean Spread

Zesty Bread

Seafood and Artichoke White Lasagna

Pinot Grigio Chicken Piccata

Caesar Salad with Toasted Capers

B-52 Tiramisu

———

FOOD AND DRINK PLANNER

ONE DAY BEFORE: Make Zesty Bread Croutons for salad. Make Tuscan Bean Spread. Make Seafood and Artichoke White Lasagna. Make Caesar Salad Dressing. Make B-52 Tiramisu.

PARTY DAY: Prepare and brown Pinot Grigio Chicken Piccata. Toast capers for Caesar Salad.

JUST BEFORE SERVING: Finish cooking Pinot Grigio Chicken Piccata. Reheat Seafood and Artichoke Lasagna. Make Zesty Bread. Make and toss Caesar Salad.

COCKTAIL SUGGESTION: Harvey Wallbanger: Pour 1 ounce vodka over ice in a tall glass. Fill glass with orange juice and float Galliano liqueur on top.

WINE SUGGESTIONS: 1997 Tiefenbrunner Pinot Grigio and 1997 Francis Ford Coppola California Rosso (see "The Wine List," page 23, for more information).

TIMESAVERS: Purchase prepared garlic bread or a loaf of Italian bread with butter. Purchase a dessert such as a sheet cake or cheesecake. Serve salad of romaine lettuce and prepared Caesar salad dressing. Purchase prepared Caesar-flavored salad croutons.

TABLE SETTING AND DECORATING IDEAS: Italian Marketplace with Multiple Stations (see "Practical Tips and Ideas for Food Stations," page 10.)

TABLE LINEN: Use Autumn Tones suggested in "Color Families and Complementary Shades" (see page 6).

Self-Serve Wine Bar

Place a dark cloth on the table—spilled red wine is inevitable. Purchase a flowering plant and set in a plastic-lined basket with a handle. Cover plant soil with moss or greenery. Place basket on one side of the table. Hang ivy and Champagne grapes over side of basket and up around handle, and allow ivy and grapes to spill onto table. Arrange wineglasses, upside down, on other side of table. Set wine bottles, ice bucket, wine opener, and other accessories in center of table.

Garden Station for Bread and Lasagna

Place a cloth on the table. Set a plastic milk crate or sturdy riser on one side of table and cover with accent cloth. Place baskets of green plants on and around covered crate. Arrange fresh vegetables like eggplant, zucchini, tomatoes, yellow squash, and garlic in a chain around crate and on table. Fill in any bare spots with kale or salad savoy. Place Zesty Bread and lasagna in containers on cloth-covered risers or directly on table. Allow additional vegetables and greenery to spill onto table in front of food.

Old World Charm Station for Salad and Chicken

Place a cloth on the table. Set a couple of baskets of tall green plants in middle of table. Place a variety of baskets and an interesting Italian container or two in front and on sides of center display. Fill containers with various shapes and sizes of bread. Baguettes can be vertical in baskets, round loaves can be directly on table, and bread-sticks can be in a large, empty olive oil can with a beautiful label. Finish off display with large, sealed jars of marinated vegetables. Place salad and chicken in front, on either side of display.

Fruit Orchard Dessert Station

Place a cloth on the table. Purchase a flowering plant and set in a plastic-lined basket with a handle. Cover plant soil with moss or greenery. Place a basket on one side of table. Hang ivy and Champagne grapes over side of basket and around handle, and allow ivy and grapes to spill onto table. Cut some oranges in half and place them and a few whole oranges around basket on table. Set coffee urn, cream, sugar, and cups on other side of table. Set B-52 Tiramisu in center of the table.

Tuscan Bean Spread

MAKES ABOUT 2 CUPS

This Tuscan spread is reminiscent of a Greek hummus. You can vary the consistency of the spread by the length of time you process the olive oil. The longer the mixture whips in the processor, the thicker its texture will be.

Make 3 batches of dip for a party of 50 guests.

2 CLOVES GARLIC, PEELED

2 (15-OUNCE) CANS WHITE BEANS (GREAT NORTHERN OR CANNELLINI), DRAINED AND RINSED

1 TABLESPOON WHITE WINE

1 TABLESPOON FRESH LEMON JUICE

1/2 TEASPOON SALT

1/2 CUP OLIVE OIL

Place the garlic in a food processor and process until minced. Add the beans, wine, juice, and salt, and process into a puree. With processor running, slowly add the olive oil in a steady stream through the feed tube. Process until mixture thickens, 1 to 2 minutes.

Spoon into a dish and serve as a spread for bread or crackers. Store in an airtight container in the refrigerator up to 1 day. Bring to room temperature before serving.

Zesty Bread

Too easy! You can use just about any dry soup mix, salad dressing mix, or seasoning blend you wish with this recipe. Choose a blend that has bits of vegetable in the mix. The veggies will soften when heated with the melted butter and your bread will have a colorful, festive appearance.

1 CUP (2 STICKS) BUTTER	1 (1-OUNCE) PACKAGE DRY VEGETABLE OR ONION SOUP MIX
1 TABLESPOON WHITE WINE	2 LOAVES ITALIAN BREAD

Preheat oven to 350F (175C). Heat the butter and wine in a microwave-safe bowl or in a small saucepan over low heat, until butter is melted. Stir in the soup mix until combined.

Cut the loaves in half lengthwise. Brush cut side of bread halves with butter mixture. Place bread halves, cut side up, on baking sheets. Bake for 10 to 12 minutes or until toasted. Remove from oven and cut bread crosswise into 1-inch slices. Arrange in a napkin-lined basket and set on buffet table.

VARIATIONS

Zesty Cheese Bread

Scatter ⅓ cup grated Parmesan or Cheddar cheese on top of bread halves just before baking.

Zesty Bread Croutons

For great homemade croutons, cut 1 loaf of Italian bread into cubes and place in a large bowl. Combine melted butter, wine, and soup mix as in the recipe and pour over croutons until moistened. Place croutons on a baking sheet and bake at 350F (175C) for 10 minutes or until toasted.

Seafood and Artichoke White Lasagna

*E*veryone has an Italian pal who has procured Grandma's heirloom lasagna recipe. Making this traditional and time-consuming dish is a great way to introduce children to the kitchen. After you cook and prepare the ingredients, let the little fingers build the lasagna as you supervise. Once assembled, lasagna can be frozen and then reheated for an easy supper.

Make three lasagnas for a party for 50.

1 TEASPOON SALT

2 TABLESPOONS OLIVE OIL

1 (1-POUND) BOX LASAGNA NOODLES

½ CUP FRESH BASIL LEAVES, SHREDDED, FOR GARNISH

SEAFOOD LAYER

2 TABLESPOONS OLIVE OIL

½ POUND BAY SCALLOPS

½ POUND COOKED BAY SHRIMP

1 (8½-OUNCE) CAN ARTICHOKE HEARTS, CHOPPED

CHEESE LAYER

1 CUP (4 OUNCES) SHREDDED SWISS CHEESE

1 CUP (4 OUNCES) SHREDDED GRUYÈRE CHEESE

RICOTTA CHEESE LAYER

2 TABLESPOONS BUTTER

2 TABLESPOONS OLIVE OIL

2 CLOVES GARLIC, FINELY MINCED

2 LARGE LEEKS, CHOPPED

½ CUP DRY WHITE WINE

1 (2-POUND) CONTAINER RICOTTA CHEESE

3 TABLESPOONS FINELY CHOPPED FRESH BASIL

2 EGGS

1 TEASPOON SALT

½ TEASPOON BLACK PEPPER

WHITE SAUCE

½ CUP (1 STICK) BUTTER

6 TABLESPOONS ALL-PURPOSE FLOUR

1¾ CUPS CHICKEN STOCK

2 CUPS HALF-AND-HALF

1 CUP FRESHLY GRATED PARMESAN CHEESE

3 EGGS, LIGHTLY BEATEN

1 TEASPOON SALT

½ TEASPOON WHITE PEPPER

To cook the noodles: Add the salt and olive oil to a large pot of water and bring to a boil over medium-high heat. Add the lasagna noodles and cook until tender, about 15 minutes. Gently remove the noodles with tongs and drape over the sides of several pots or large bowls. Do not overlap noodles; they will stick to each other and tear.

To make the seafood layer: Heat the olive oil in a large skillet over medium heat. Add the scallops and cook until scallops are white, 5 minutes. Stir in the shrimp and remove from heat. Toss together the scallops, shrimp, and artichoke in a large bowl. Cover bowl and set aside.

To make the cheese layer: Toss together the cheeses in another bowl; cover and set aside.

To make the ricotta cheese layer: Heat the butter, oil, and garlic in a large skillet over medium-high heat. Add the leeks and wine, and cook over medium-high heat until leeks are tender and liquid reduces completely, 8 to 10 minutes.

Spoon ricotta cheese into a large bowl. Add the leek mixture, basil, eggs, salt, and pepper; mix until blended. Cover bowl and set aside.

To make the white sauce: Melt the butter in a large saucepan over medium heat. Whisk in the flour until smooth and cook, stirring constantly, for 1 minute. Add the chicken stock, ½ cup at a time, stirring constantly, to incorporate liquid. Add the half-and-half and stir as sauce thickens. Stir in the Parmesan cheese until blended. Add ½ cup of the hot sauce to bowl with beaten eggs and stir to temper eggs. Add eggs to sauce and stir constantly for 2 minutes more, then remove from heat. Season with salt and pepper. Preheat oven to 350F (175C).

To assemble the lasagna: Spread white sauce on the bottom of a 13 × 9-inch baking pan. Lay 3 noodles, side by side, over bottom of pan. Cut broken noodles to fill in any gaps or to extend noodles the length of the pan. Dollop ½ cup of the ricotta cheese mixture over the noodles. Scatter ⅓ cup of the seafood mixture over the cheese layer. Spoon ⅓ cup of the white sauce over the seafood layer and top with ½ cup of the cheese mixture. Repeat layers three more times. Top the final layer with noodles and spoon sauce over top. Sprinkle the cheese over the sauce.

Bake for 45 minutes or until top is bubbling. Remove from oven and cool for 10 minutes. (To make ahead, lasagna may be prepared and cooked up to 2 days before serving. Cover cooked lasagna and refrigerate. When ready to serve, reheat lasagna at 350F [175C] for 20 to 30 minutes or until hot. Or freeze for up to 2 weeks, thaw overnight in the refrigerator, and reheat.)

Cut lasagna into 3-inch squares and place pan on a trivet or hot plate on the buffet table. Garnish with shredded basil leaves.

𝒱egetable Lasagna

Whenever I serve lasagna, inevitably there is a guest who wants a vegetarian version. This is an easy request to fill; there are often enough ingredients left over to build a small lasagna. Simply sauté á medley of 2 cups chopped vegetables and substitute the vegetables for the shrimp and scallops. A mixture of fresh or sun-dried tomatoes, chopped olives, and pine nuts is also a wonderful alternative.

Pinot Grigio Chicken Piccata

MAKES 50 SERVINGS

Veal piccata is more commonly seen on restaurant menus. However, when trying to please a crowd, especially on the West Coast, choose chicken. This delicious dish is prepared a little differently than the usual piccata recipes, to prevent the chicken from drying out (see Notes, below).

50 BONELESS, SKINLESS CHICKEN BREASTS HALVES	PICCATA SAUCE
	1 CUP (2 STICKS) BUTTER
4 CUPS ALL-PURPOSE FLOUR	3 TABLESPOONS OLIVE OIL
4 TABLESPOONS SALT	6 SHALLOTS, CUT INTO SLIVERS
2 TABLESPOONS BLACK PEPPER	1 (6-OUNCE) JAR CAPERS, DRAINED
OLIVE OIL	2 CUPS PINOT GRIGIO
	½ CUP FRESH LEMON JUICE

Pound the chicken breasts with a kitchen mallet to ¼-inch thickness. Toss together the flour, salt, and pepper, and place on a dinner plate. Coat chicken in flour mixture.

Heat 1 tablespoon olive oil in a large skillet over high heat. Add 4 or 5 chicken breasts and cook until flour coating is lightly browned, 3 to 5 minutes on each side. Repeat process with remaining chicken breasts, adding 1 tablespoon of oil for every batch. Place chicken in overlapping rows in 13 × 9-inch baking pans (see Notes, below). Cover with plastic wrap and refrigerate.

To make the piccata sauce: In same skillet, immediately after chicken is browned, add ¼ cup of the butter, oil, and shallots; cook over medium-high heat for 2 minutes. Add capers and wine and cook until reduced by half, 3 to 5 minutes. Add the lemon juice and cook for 2 minutes. Remove from heat and swirl in the remaining ¾ cup butter, 2 tablespoons at a time. Drizzle sauce over chicken in baking pans. Cover and return to refrigerator until ready to use. (Chicken may be prepared up to this point on the morning of the event, then fully cooked and served in the evening.)

Preheat over to 325F (165C). Uncover pans of chicken and place in oven. Cook for about 15 minutes or until chicken is no longer pink in the center. Arrange in a chafing dish or on a large platter and spoon the sauce from pan over the top. Serve hot.

NOTES: You will need at least 3 (13 × 9-inch) baking pans to make all 50 chicken breasts. I've found about 15 breasts fit nicely into one pan. You can use 8-inch square baking dishes or whatever you have in the kitchen. Or purchase disposable aluminum pans at the grocery store.

In many chicken piccata recipes, the chicken is cooked in the skillet. For larger parties, over 20 guests, I recommend cooking the chicken, drizzled with piccata sauce, in the oven. The chicken will be more moist and all the chicken breasts will be hot and ready to serve at the same time. Plus, you won't have to slave over a hot stove while your guests are chatting in the other room.

Caesar Salad with Toasted Capers

It is my understanding that the Caesar salad originated at a restaurant in Mexico and is named for its creator. However, a restaurateur friend of mine debates that fact, stating that the salad was first offered at the famed Beverly Hills eatery Chasen's. I had the pleasure of attending a private informal birthday party at this legendary place a few months after its doors had officially closed. Best of all, I got to cook in the kitchen and happily took over the hors d'oeuvres preparation. This may not seem like fun for most, but it was the party of a lifetime for me. Chasen's has reopened in a new location and is fabulous.

You will need two batches of the dressing for 50. It is easier to make one batch at a time because the larger amount may not fit into your food processor.

1 TABLESPOON OLIVE OIL

1 CLOVE GARLIC, MINCED

2 (4-OUNCE) JARS CAPERS, DRAINED

2 TABLESPOONS WHITE WINE

12 LARGE HEADS ROMAINE LETTUCE, CUT INTO BITE-SIZE PIECES

CAESAR ZESTY BREAD CROUTONS (SEE PAGE 76)

2 (6-OUNCE) WEDGES PARMESAN CHEESE

CAESAR DRESSING

7 CLOVES GARLIC, PEELED

1 (2-OUNCE) CAN ANCHOVY FILLETS, DRAINED

1½ CUPS MAYONNAISE

3 EGGS, PREFERABLY PASTEURIZED (SEE NOTE, PAGE 55)

¼ CUP OLIVE OIL

¼ CUP FRESH LEMON JUICE

2 TABLESPOONS CAPERS

1½ TABLESPOONS WORCESTERSHIRE SAUCE

1 TABLESPOON GRAINY BROWN MUSTARD

½ CUP FRESHLY GRATED PARMESAN CHEESE

1 TEASPOON FRESHLY GROUND PEPPER

Heat the oil and garlic in a large skillet over high heat. Add the capers and wine; cook, stirring occasionally, until the capers are crisp and toasted, about 10 minutes. Remove from heat and set aside. Cool to room temperature.

Meanwhile, to make the Caesar Dressing: Place the garlic and anchovies in a food processor and process until minced. Add remaining ingredients and process until mixture is smooth and blended. Pour into a large plastic container with an airtight lid.

Make a second recipe of dressing and add it to the plastic container. Store in the refrigerator until ready to serve (for up to 1 day). One recipe makes 3 to 3½ cups dressing.

To assemble: For each head of lettuce, add ⅓ cup dressing, 1 heaping tablespoon toasted capers, and ½ cup croutons to a large bowl. Toss salad until thoroughly coated and transfer to a serving bowl or large platter. Repeat process, in these proportions, as necessary to replenish the buffet table.

Using a vegetable peeler, shave wide strips from Parmesan wedge over top of salad. Most like their Caesar salad to be overflowing with cheese, especially when it is in wafer-thin shavings. Serve immediately.

Caesar Zesty Bread Croutons

Follow the recipe for Zesty Bread Croutons (page 76) substituting a dry Caesar salad dressing mix for the dry soup mix. Prepare 2 batches of croutons for a salad that serves 50 guests.

TIPS: Keep each chopped head of lettuce in a separate large plastic bag and store in the refrigerator. The lettuce will remain fresh and you will be able to maintain the dressing-to-lettuce ratio. Do not dress the salad until just before serving, or it will become soggy.

B-52 Tiramisu

MAKES 70 SERVINGS

*T*iramisu is a scrumptious cheese-custard type of dessert traditionally made with mascarpone cheese. Mascarpone, a sweet Italian cream cheese, is not widely available, so this recipe combines common ingredients to replicate it. Often this creamy dessert is prepared and served in a regular baking pan, but an unmolded tiramisu is a much more impressive presentation (see Note below on making a tiramisu mold).

ORANGE COCOA SPONGE CAKE

4 EGGS, SEPARATED

1 CUP SUGAR

2 TABLESPOONS BUTTER, MELTED AND COOLED

2 TABLESPOONS GRAND MARNIER

¾ CUP CAKE FLOUR

¼ CUP UNSWEETENED COCOA POWDER

1 TEASPOON BAKING POWDER

⅛ TEASPOON SALT

TIRAMISU CREAM

4 (8-OUNCE) PACKAGES CREAM CHEESE, SOFTENED

¾ CUP SOUR CREAM

1 CUP HEAVY CREAM

1 CUP BAILEYS ORIGINAL IRISH CREAM

7 EGGS

1 CUP GRANULATED SUGAR

3 TABLESPOONS KAHLUA

¼ CUP UNSWEETENED COCOA POWDER

¼ CUP POWDERED SUGAR

¼ CUP CHOCOLATE-COVERED COFFEE BEANS

To make the cake: Center a rack in the oven and preheat oven to 350F (175C). Butter a 15 × 10-inch jelly roll pan and line pan with waxed paper. Butter and flour waxed paper, shake off excess flour.

Beat the egg yolks and ½ cup of the sugar in a medium bowl until pale yellow. Add the butter and Grand Marnier, and beat until blended. In another large bowl, using clean beaters, beat the egg whites on high speed until soft peaks form. Gradually add the remaining ½ cup sugar and beat until stiff peaks form. Fold the yolk mixture into egg whites. Sift together dry ingredients and gently fold into mixture.

Pour the cake batter into prepared jelly roll pan and smooth surface with a rubber spatula. Bake for 15 minutes or until center springs back to the touch. Remove from oven and cool in the pan for 5 minutes on a wire rack.

Prepare tiramisu mold according to instructions under Note below. Lay a sheet of waxed paper on a flat surface. Trim ¼ inch off all sides of cake, using a sharp knife. Invert cake on new waxed paper and remove waxed paper from cake bottom. Lift new waxed paper with cake and invert cake, right side up, onto bottom of prepared mold.

To make the tiramisu cream: Beat the cream cheese, sour cream, heavy cream, and Baileys in a large bowl until smooth. Set aside until ready to use.

Fill a large pot halfway with water and place over medium-high heat until water simmers. Beat the eggs and granulated sugar in a medium stainless-steel bowl until smooth. Place bowl over simmering water (do not allow bowl bottom to touch water) and beat until eggs have tripled in volume, about 5 minutes. Remove from heat and continue beating mixture until cool, 5 minutes. Add the egg mixture to the cream cheese mixture and beat until blended.

Sprinkle the Kahlua over the cake in the mold. Pour the tiramisu cream in an even layer over the cake and smooth top with a rubber spatula. Refrigerate uncovered, keeping the tiramisu flat, for 2 hours or until mixture is firm.

To serve, combine the cocoa and powdered sugar and sift over top of the tiramisu. Gently cut away cardboard sides from box mold. Cut away extra plastic wrap for a neat presentation. The tiramisu will be supported and served on the sturdy cardboard under it. Arrange the chocolate-covered coffee beans in a decorative pattern over the top. Place the tiramisu on buffet and cut into 2 × 1-inch squares. Serve cold.

VARIATION

Happy Birthday Tiramisu

You can spell "Happy Birthday" or any words you wish on top of the tiramisu, using sweetened cocoa powder and letter stencils. Purchase stencils at a stationery store and arrange them on top of the tiramisu. Sift a combination of cocoa powder and powdered sugar over the stencils. Remove stencils to reveal words. Also, a checkered harlequin design made with square stencils and sweetened cocoa powder looks amazing on top of this dessert.

NOTE: Because oversize rectangular baking pans with removable sides do not exist, you have to fashion your own 15 × 10-inch mold. Purchase a half sheet cake board, which is approximately 20 × 14 inches, from your local cake decorating supply store or craft store. Find a large, sturdy cardboard box. Cut 2 (10 × 3-inch) strips and 2 (15 × 3-inch strips from the cardboard. Form a 15 × 10-inch frame from cardboard strips. Secure corners with wide tape. Wrap foil around frame to further secure. Place the 15 × 10-inch frame on cake board. Line inside bottom and sides of box mold with plastic wrap. (If cake board is not available, wrap a sturdy, 20 × 14-inch piece of cardboard with regular or decorative foil purchased from a cake supply or crafting store.)

SPIKED SHOWSTOPPERS FOR AN
HORS D'OEUVRES STATION FOR 100

*Y*ears in the catering business have taught me to stick with what works. People will sing your praises as a chef when you serve the Calvados Caramelized Apples Brie en Croûte and Caviar Torte with Champagne Onions. But the presentation of the Orange Liqueur Shrimp Wrapped in Snow Peas on Shredded Red Cabbage is the real showstopper. This dish offers an outstanding hors d'oeuvres display technique that you can use for just about any skewered appetizer.

Best of all, you can make some of these amazing dishes the day before, reheat on the party day, set them on the table, and walk away. I highly recommend this buffet menu if you wish to feel like a guest (who receives compliments and is toasted all evening) at your own party.

———

Calvados Caramelized Apples Brie en Croûte

Caviar Torte with Champagne Onions

Orange Liqueur Shrimp Wrapped in Snow Peas on Shredded Red Cabbage

Smoked Salmon with Pumpernickel and Lively Mustard Dill Sauce

———

FOOD AND DRINK PLANNER

ONE DAY BEFORE: Make Calvados Caramelized Apples Brie en Croûte. Make Caviar Torte with Champagne Onions. Make Lively Mustard Dill Sauce.

PARTY DAY: Marinate Orange Liqueur Shrimp.

JUST BEFORE SERVING: Reheat Calvados Caramelized Apples Brie en Croûte. Assemble Shrimp Wrapped in Snow Peas on Shredded Red Cabbage. Assemble Salmon Platter.

COCKTAIL SUGGESTION: Offer full bar (see Proportion Chart for Beverages, page 361).

WINE SUGGESTIONS: 1997 Beaulieu Vineyard Coastal Chardonnay, 1999 Rosemount Estate Grenache-Shiraz, Beringer "LVS" White Zinfandel/Chardonnay (see "The Wine List," page 23 for more information on these wines).

TIMESAVERS: Substitute cheese platter for Caviar Torte. Substitute prepared honey mustard for Lively Mustard Dill Sauce.

TABLE SETTING AND DECORATING IDEAS: Grand Floral Display (see "Practical Tips and Ideas for Food Stations," page 10).

TABLE LINEN: Use Winter Hues or Spring Pastels suggested in "Color Families and Complementary Shades" (see page 6).

Grand Floral Centerpiece with Strewn Flowers

Place a cloth on the table. Set a sturdy milk crate in the center of the table and arrange food risers around table. Cover crate and risers with shimmering or silky white fabric. Allow fabric to flow onto table and between the dishes. Purchase a large but simple centerpiece from a florist or create one by placing a dozen large long-stemmed white roses or Casablanca stems (large, white lillies) in an elegant footed urn. Fill in the centerpiece with greenery and hang amaranthus over the side of the urn. Place the flower urn on the crate in the center of the table. Work a few elegant flowers into table design around bottom of the risers.

Votive Candles

Place votive candles around table. Be careful to set them so guests don't have to reach across them.

Calvados Caramelized Apples Brie en Croûte

MAKES ABOUT 50 APPETIZER SERVINGS

There have been many versions of pastry-wrapped Brie, but none quite as delicious as this one with caramelized apples. I make one Brie per 30 to 40 guests for an hors d'oeuvres-only party, and one Brie per 50 to 60 guests for a dinner buffet. When your menu calls for a second Brie, choose a different filling (as suggested in the Variation).

For this menu you will need two wheels of Brie.

2 TABLESPOONS UNSALTED BUTTER	1 (2.2-POUND) WHEEL OF BRIE
2 GRANNY SMITH APPLES, PEELED AND DICED	1 (17.3-OUNCE) PACKAGE PUFF PASTRY DOUGH, ROOM TEMPERATURE
3 TABLESPOONS CALVADOS	1 EGG, BEATEN
3 TABLESPOONS LIGHT BROWN SUGAR	FRENCH BAGUETTE SLICES OR CRACKERS
2 (8-OUNCE) PACKAGES CREAM CHEESE, SOFTENED	

Preheat oven to 350F (175C). Line a baking sheet with foil.

Melt the butter in a large skillet over medium-high heat. Add the apples and Calvados, then sauté, stirring occasionally, until apples are tender, about 10 minutes. Add the brown sugar and cook until sugar caramelizes, 5 minutes. Remove from heat and cool for 5 minutes.

Place the cream cheese in a large bowl. Add the apple mixture and stir until thoroughly combined. Remove the plastic wrapping and labels from the Brie. Spread the apple-cream cheese mixture on top of the Brie, directly onto the thick white skin, forming a flattened dome.

Lay a sheet of puff pastry on a prepared baking sheet. Place Brie in center of pastry. Wrap pastry up along sides of Brie. Center another sheet of puff pastry over cream cheese dome. Fold pastry down along the sides and under the Brie. Brie must be completely enveloped in pastry or cheese may leak out. Seal any open edges. Brush entire surface of pastry with beaten egg to give a golden brown color when baked. Bake for 20 to 30 minutes or until pastry is golden brown. Remove Brie from oven and place baking sheet on a flat surface. (If you are preparing Brie a day in advance of party, cool the baked Brie to room temperature. Keep the Brie on the baking sheet, cover with plastic wrap, and refrigerate until ready to serve. Reheat on baking sheet in 350F [175C] oven for 10 minutes.)

Cut a 5-inch-diameter circle in center of top crust. Remove the circle and gently mix the apple-cream cheese mixture with the Brie. Be sure to run spoon deep down and into sides to combine completely, but be careful not to break the crust. If the cheese is not thoroughly melted, place the Brie back in oven for 5 minutes or until cheese is melted.

Carefully remove the Brie to a serving tray, using two spatulas. Or support Brie with the foil and lift it off baking sheet and onto your serving tray. Tear foil from side of Brie for a cleaner presentation.

Place a metal tray on top of a round chafing dish to keep warm. Place a spoon in Brie opening and serve immediately with thin slices of bread or crackers.

VARIATIONS

Instead of caramelized apples, substitute ½ cup chopped sun-dried tomatoes and ½ cup pine nuts; ¾ cup sautéed sliced mushrooms and 1 to 2 tablespoons chopped fresh tarragon; or ½ cup chopped proscuitto and 1 to 2 tablespoons chopped fresh basil.

NOTES: If Brie breaks, take a piece of bread and place it over leak as if you were plugging a leaky dam. It should stop or at least slow the leak.

If a round chafing dish is not available, fill a fondue pot with water, light Sterno canned heating fuel, and place a silver or metal tray on top of the fondue pot. Be sure the tray is sturdy, or it may tip as people dip into the Brie.

Caviar Torte with Champagne Onions

MAKES 100 SERVINGS ON AN HORS D'OEUVRE BUFFET

*B*eluga caviar would be a once-in-a-lifetime treat on this dish, unless you're a Trump family. Lumpfish roe is perfectly fine, because this triple layer torte has many dynamic flavor combinations.

---

1 CUP FINELY CHOPPED RED ONION

1 CUP CHAMPAGNE

2 (8-OUNCE) PACKAGES CREAM CHEESE, WHIPPED

16 EGGS, HARD-COOKED, COARSELY CHOPPED

½ CUP MAYONNAISE

1 TEASPOON SALT

½ TEASPOON WHITE PEPPER

4 LARGE, RIPE AVOCADOS, MASHED

½ CLOVE GARLIC, MINCED

2 TEASPOONS FRESH LEMON JUICE

12 OUNCES BLACK CAVIAR OR LUMPFISH ROE

WATER CRACKERS

Place the onions and Champagne in a large skillet over medium-high heat. Cook until the Champagne reduces completely, 10 minutes. Remove from heat and stir into the cream cheese. Cover and set aside.

In another bowl, mix together the eggs and mayonnaise. Season with ½ teaspoon of the salt and ¼ teaspoon of the pepper, and mix until thoroughly combined. Cover and set aside.

In another bowl, mix together the avocados, garlic, and lemon juice. Season with the remaining ½ teaspoon salt and ¼ teaspoon pepper, and mix until thoroughly combined.

Layer ingredients in a 10-inch springform pan. Spread the egg mixture on the bottom and smooth the top until even. Spread the avocado mixture on top of the egg mixture and smooth the top until even. Spread the cream cheese mixture on top of the avocado mixture and smooth the top until even. Cover with plastic wrap and chill at least 3 hours or until firm. (Torte can be made up to 2 days in advance.)

Just before serving, spread an even layer of caviar on top of torte. Place the torte on a silver tray or serving platter. Undo the springform pan latch. Carefully run a knife around the edge of the torte to loosen from the pan. Gently lift away the pan's side. Wipe the side of the serving tray if necessary. Place flowers or a thin lemon or lime slice in the center of the torte. Set crackers around the base of the torte and place on the buffet table with a serving knife.

Red Caviar Star in Torte Center:

Cut a 5-point star, approximately 5 inches in diameter, from thin cardboard. Remove torte from refrigerator and unmold. Place star on top center of torte. Spread black caviar on top of torte around outline of star. Remove cardboard star and fill in star shape with 4 ounces red caviar or lumpfish roe.

Orange Liqueur Shrimp Wrapped in Snow Peas on Shredded Red Cabbage

*H*ors d'oeuvres presented on a magenta bed of shredded red cabbage are stunning. This technique will work well with almost any appetizer that is speared with a pick.

Save yourself a little time and effort by asking the deli counter clerk at your grocery store to shred the bottom third of the cabbage head, using the meat slicer. The cabbage is "shredded" by being sliced crosswise and pulled into long shreds.

---

¹/₃ CUP GRAND MARNIER

¹/₄ CUP FRESH LIME JUICE

³/₄ CUP OLIVE OIL

3 TABLESPOONS SOY SAUCE

1 TABLESPOON FINELY MINCED FRESH GINGER

¹/₄ CUP SESAME OIL

2 TEASPOONS SALT

¹/₂ TEASPOON BLACK PEPPER

50 MEDIUM COOKED SHRIMP (ABOUT 1¹/₂ POUNDS), PEELED AND DEVEINED

50 LARGE SNOW PEAS

3 CUPS WATER

1 TEASPOON SALT

1 LARGE HEAD RED CABBAGE

Whisk together the Grand Marnier, lime juice, olive oil, soy sauce, ginger, sesame oil, 1 teaspoon of the salt, and pepper in a large bowl. Place the shrimp in the marinade and refrigerate, covered, for 1 hour.

Place the snow peas, remaining 1 teaspoon salt, and enough water to cover in a large pot. Bring to a boil over medium-high heat and boil peas for 5 minutes. Drain and then plunge the peas into a bowl of ice water. This will stop the cooking process and intensify the color. Drain and refrigerate, covered, until ready to use.

Cut off the bottom one-third of the cabbage head. Set remaining intact cabbage head aside. Cut bottom one-third into ¹/₈-inch-thick slices. Pull apart the slices and make a bed of cabbage shreds on a serving platter. Place the intact cabbage head, flat side down, in the center of the platter, surrounded by the shredded cabbage.

An hour before serving, assemble the dish. Imagine that a shrimp is the letter "C." Form a snow-pea flat along the outer curve of the shrimp, also taking the form of the

LET'S GET THIS PARTY STARTED! / 93

letter "C." Stick a pick through the bottom of the "C," spearing the snow pea and shrimp, and then up through the top of the "C," again spearing and securing the snow pea to the shrimp. The shrimp/snow pea and pick should now resemble the cent symbol.

Insert the shrimp pick into the cabbage head. Repeat the process, arranging the shrimp and snow peas in the cabbage head. Spear extra shrimp and snow peas with picks and refrigerate, covered. Replenish cabbage head with shrimp as necessary throughout party.

Top Ten Catering No-Nos

Some of these taboos may seem painfully obvious, but years in the catering business have taught me that they are not.

1. If possible, remove a buffet dish from the table and go into the kitchen to replenish it. Or bring the food out in a tasteful serving bowl to fill the dish on the table. Never refill food from the manufacturer's carton or kitchenware such as pots and pans. An exception is made when transferring a full catering pan into a hot chafing dish.

2. A server should never set a bottle of wine on the table after filling glasses at a dinner party if the wine is not purposely set on the table during the meal—not even to clear dirty plates.

3. A bartender should never use his or her hands to put ice into a glass. A glass should never be used in place of an ice scoop; as it could break into the ice used for drinks. A bartender should never place his or her fingers inside the glass, whether the intent is to stir the liquid or refill the drink.

4. A server should always ask a guest, "May I remove your plate?" before clearing a partially empty plate, no matter how neatly the silverware is laid upon it.

5. Neither a server manning a buffet or sit-down affair nor a bartender should ever be seen consuming food or drink.

6. Never put a dirty plate or refuse on a tray that has a fresh plate of food to be served.

7. Never pick up a dropped napkin, silverware, or the like from the floor and give it to a guest.

8. Never light the Sterno with a flaming paper napkin or other paper product. Use a long match or electric lighter. Although tongs or a metal spoon dipped into flaming Sterno can be used to transfer the fire to a fresh Sterno, never use a utensil that is being used for food. Use caution with Sterno because its hot blue flame is barely visible.

9. When in doubt, ask someone who knows before giving out information! For example, caffeinated coffee can cause a sleepless night to someone not accustomed to it, and those with severe allergies need to know what's in the food. Guests aren't just being nosy. Some mistakes can cost the server his or her job or the caterer a future event.

10. Never insult a guest with a phrase like "These appetizers are really fattening . . . are you sure you need another?" If the guest insults the server, I feel that a clever retort is fine. A person who is serving food isn't less of a human, and guests can forget that. A bartender can (and should) refuse service to a guest who has had too much to drink, which can be viewed as an insult. The bartender should notify the party manager or caterer (if present), and then the host should be informed. If the host objects, let the host take over as the bartender. This issue is always the bartender's call, in my opinion. You don't want to find out how the law views the situation in its worst-case scenario.

Smoked Salmon with Pumpernickel and Lively Mustard Dill Sauce

MAKES ABOUT 25 APPETIZER SERVINGS

A most impressive presentation can be made with a velvety whole fillet of cold-smoked salmon. Fish can be cooked using a cold or hot technique, and is smoked or cured with brine. Cold-smoked salmon, also known as lox, is cooked no hotter than 75F (25C). The end product has a glossy texture and rich orange color. Ask your local fishmonger to order a 3-pound fillet for you, which yields approximately 25 appetizer servings.

Pumpernickel baguettes are usually available by special order from a bakery. Ask the bakery to slice it for you.

1 CUP DIJON MUSTARD	1 LARGE RED ONION, FINELY CHOPPED
⅓ CUP HONEY	1 (32-OUNCE) JAR CAPERS, DRAINED
2 TEASPOONS WHITE WINE	20 LEMON WEDGES
2 TABLESPOONS CHOPPED FRESH DILL	2 PUMPERNICKEL BAGUETTES, THINLY SLICED
1 (ABOUT 3-POUND) COLD-SMOKED SALMON FILLET, THINLY SLICED	

Whisk together the mustard, honey, wine, and dill in a small bowl until blended.

Place the salmon on a large, oblong serving platter or a nice wood cutting board. Slice salmon in half lengthwise. Part salmon halves, leaving 2 inches between them. Fill half of gap, from salmon end to middle, with the red onion, and the remaining half with the capers. Arrange the lemon wedges around outer edge of salmon on serving tray.

Place the pumpernickel bread in a lined basket and serve with a bowl of Lively Mustard Dill Sauce next to salmon on table.

NOTES: Consider the length of time that the salmon will be on the buffet. I don't leave salmon at room temperature for more than 2 hours without chilling it somehow. You can set an oblong silver tray or platter on risers and place a small bag of ice underneath, touching the tray. Mask the bag with greenery and make sure it doesn't have any leaks. Or set half of the salmon fillet out at one time and leave the other half refrigerated, replenishing the tray as necessary.

Look for smaller portions of lox or cold-smoked salmon in the deli section of the grocery store. For some reason, I always seem to find the prepackaged lox near the hot dogs.

Frequently Asked Questions about Parties

Q: How do I find people to work at my party, and what do I tell them?

A: Start with the Yellow Pages. Look under the headings Party Staff, Party Planning or Event Planning, or Temporary Staff. No luck? Call a local restaurant, which you frequent and trust, and ask if someone would be willing to work a private party.

- Generally, most buffet parties with a guest list of 50 require about 4 people: 1 bartender, 1 food/kitchen person, 2 busers/helpers to pass trays during cocktails, pick up glasses and plates, and replenish the buffet.

- Phone the staff to confirm the date and give information.
   Date and Time: Two people should arrive 2½ hours before the guests and 2 people 45 minutes before the guests.
   Location and Phone Number: Give directions!

Dress: Nice white shirt, nice black pants, black shoes, and black bow tie for both male and female servers.

- It's customary to pay each person at the end of the night or when you let each person go. In Los Angeles and New York, staff earns about $20.00 an hour. I wouldn't go below $10.00 because waiters are used to an hourly wage plus tips. You may pay a gratuity on top of the hourly wage if you are happy at the evening's end.

- Call the day before the party to confirm and have a backup staff person in mind in case of an emergency. Expect the staff to clean dishes, but don't expect them to clean your house. Treat the staff courteously, and your party should be a success. A verbal "thank you" is greatly appreciated.

Parties in a Pinch
and Timesavers

THE EASY COCKTAIL PARTY FOR 25

Hot Artichoke and Cheese Dip

Sweet and Sour Drunken Drumettes

Blini with Caviar and Spiked Sour Cream

Gourmet Pizza Bites

MAKE-AHEAD HORS D'OEUVRES FOR 50

Easy Hors d'Oeuvre Cups with Gourmet Fillings

Sweet Curry Dip with Crudités

Mediterranean Tricolor Terrine

THE EASY COCKTAIL PARTY FOR 25

I call these quick and easy nibblers my "talk show menu." Recently, I've been appearing on *The X Show*, a guy-oriented television show "for men and the women who put up with them." I've had a blast, mainly because the preparation involved in the food segments is a no-brainer and the four male hosts are all great.

I feel blessed by the men in my life, as all of them can cook as well as, if not better than, I can. The sweet exception is my brother Daniel, who, when asked to boil water for pasta, set the metal pot in the microwave and almost blew us all to bits. This menu is just right for bachelors and freshman foodies; it is microwave-friendly and full of convenient, commercially prepared products.

———

Hot Artichoke and Cheese Dip

Sweet and Sour Drunken Drumettes

Blini with Caviar and Spiked Sour Cream

Gourmet Pizza Bites

———

FOOD AND DRINK PLANNER

ONE DAY BEFORE: Make Spiked Sour Cream.

PARTY DAY: Prepare Gourmet Pizza Bites. Make Sweet and Sour Drunken Drumettes. Make Hot Artichoke and Cheese Dip.

DURING PARTY: Heat and assemble blinis. Cook Gourmet Pizza Bites.

COCKTAIL SUGGESTION: Offer full bar (see "Proportion Chart for Beverages," pages 361).

WINE SUGGESTIONS: 1998 Glen Ellen Proprietor's Reserve Chardonnay, 1998 Glen Ellen Proprietor's Reserve Cabernet Sauvignon, 1998 Glen Ellen Proprietor's Reserve Gamay Beaujolais (see "The Wine List," page 23, for more information).

TIMESAVER: Substitute prepared buffalo chicken wings, available in the frozen food section of your grocery store.

TABLE SETTING AND DECORATING IDEAS: Quaint Designer Daisies (see "Floating Flowers and Candles," page 4.)

TABLE LINEN: Use colors compatible with Gerbera daisies; check "Color Families and Complementary Shades" (see page 6).

Designer Candle and Potted Gerbera Daisies

Place a cloth on the table. Set one thick, tall designer candle in a decorative holder and place in center of table. Line small, about 4-inch-tall terra-cotta pots with plastic liners and place green floral foam in pots. Add water to foam and insert different colored Gerbera daisies into each pot. Cover top of foam in pot with green moss. Set pots around table, between food platters.

Votive Candles

Place small votive candles, in holders, around the table. Make sure guests don't have to reach over them when helping themselves to food.

Hot Artichoke and Cheese Dip

MAKES ABOUT 3 CUPS; 25 SERVINGS

*C*hances are you received a fondue pot as a wedding gift. If you are happily single or found that you could live without the famed Swiss pot, see the recipe variation below.
Serve with a bowl of carrot and celery sticks or baguette slices.

---

1 (8½-OUNCE) CAN ARTICHOKE HEARTS, COARSELY CHOPPED

¾ CUP MAYONNAISE

1 CUP (4 OUNCES) SHREDDED SWISS CHEESE

½ CUP FRESHLY GRATED PARMESAN CHEESE

1 TABLESPOON CHARDONNAY

1 TABLESPOON FRESH LEMON JUICE

Place the ingredients in a fondue pot. Heat over a low flame, stirring occasionally, until cheese is melted and mixture is blended, about 15 minutes. Place a spoon in the dip and serve.

VARIATION

Place ingredients in a microwave-safe bowl and heat on high, about 2 minutes. Stir, and heat in 1-minute increments until cheese is melted and blended, then serve. Reheat throughout party as necessary.

Sweet and Sour Drunken Drumettes

MAKES 25 SERVINGS

*A*t every cocktail party, Mom made the best sweet and sour meatballs with this simple, tangy sauce. Try it on beef or spareribs at your next barbecue.

8 POUNDS MINIATURE CHICKEN DRUMSTICKS

¼ CUP VODKA

3 (12-OUNCE) BOTTLES HEINZ CHILI SAUCE

1 (1-POUND) JAR GRAPE JELLY

1 TEASPOON SALT

½ TEASPOON BLACK PEPPER

Place the chicken in a large stockpot. Pour the vodka, chili sauce, and jelly over the chicken. Cook, uncovered, over medium heat, stirring occasionally, until chicken is done, 45 to 60 minutes. Skim the fat from top of sauce with a spoon and stir in the salt and pepper. Arrange the chicken on a platter and spoon sauce over the top.

Blini with Caviar and Spiked Sour Cream

MAKES 48 TO 50 BLINIS

My small son Dylan's taste preferences have introduced me to the wonderful world of frozen food. Mini pancakes, which can easily pinch-hit for blini, can be found in the frozen breakfast food section of your grocery store. This shortcut version of a gourmet favorite will be a big hit.

1 (15-OUNCE) PACKAGE FROZEN MINI PANCAKES	1 TABLESPOON VODKA
1 CUP SOUR CREAM	1 TABLESPOON FRESH LEMON JUICE
2 TABLESPOONS MINCED FRESH CHIVES	2 (2-OUNCE) JARS CAVIAR OR BLACK LUMPFISH ROE

Remove the pancakes from plastic wrapper. Place on a microwave-safe dish and heat according to package instructions until pancakes are thawed. Mix together sour cream, chives, vodka, and lemon juice.

Bring the pancakes to room temperature and arrange on a serving platter. Place a small dollop of sour cream mixture on each pancake and dot with caviar. Serve immediately.

NOTE: I like to use Krusteaz frozen mini pancakes for this recipe. They are a bit sweet and vary slightly in shape, making them appear homemade. However, they may not be available in your area, so check for other brands.

Gourmet Pizza Bites

MAKES ABOUT 50 BITES

*G*ourmet pizza's popularity has boomed over the last 10 years. There are a variety of ready-made pizza crusts on the market. I prefer to start with a raw dough crust, but you can use an oblong prebaked crust like the Boboli brand. The sophistication of a pizza can be gauged by its topping. Shrimp will always raise the level of a snack to an hors d'oeuvre, as will the topping variations suggested below.

---

1 (10-OUNCE) CAN REFRIGERATED PIZZA CRUST OR OTHER UNBAKED PIZZA CRUST

1/2 CUP PURCHASED PESTO

1 CUP COOKED BAY SHRIMP

1 CUP (4 OUNCES) SHREDDED MOZZARELLA CHEESE

1 CUP (4 OUNCES) SHREDDED FONTINA CHEESE

Preheat the oven to 425F (220C). Lightly oil a 13 × 9-inch baking pan. Place dough on pan. Unroll the dough and, starting in center, press to edges until evenly distributed over pan. Bake for 8 to 10 minutes or until lightly browned.

Spread the pesto over the crust. Scatter the shrimp over pesto and sprinkle with the cheese. Bake for 10 minutes or until cheese is melted and edges of crust are golden brown.

Cut the pizza into 1 1/2-inch squares and arrange on a platter. Serve warm.

NOTE: Pillsbury's Refrigerated All-Ready Pizza Crust is one of my favorites for this recipe.

VARIATIONS

Try these topping combinations and layer them on the crust as indicated in each recipe, starting with sauce and ending with cheese.

BARBECUE CHICKEN PIZZA

1 CUP BARBECUE SAUCE

1 CUP CHOPPED, COOKED CHICKEN

½ CUP SLICED RED ONION

¼ CUP CHOPPED FRESH CILANTRO

2 CUPS (8 OUNCES) SHREDDED
MOZZARELLA CHEESE

THAI CHICKEN PIZZA

1 CUP SPICY PEANUT SAUCE OR
PEANUT SAUCE SALAD DRESSING

1 CUP CHOPPED COOKED CHICKEN

¼ CUP CHOPPED FRESH CILANTRO

2 CUPS (8 OUNCES) SHREDDED
MOZZARELLA CHEESE

MEXICAN PIZZA

1 CUP OLD EL PASO THICK 'N'
CHUNKY SALSA

1 CUP CHOPPED COOKED CHICKEN
OR COOKED GROUND MEAT

1 CUP (4 OUNCES) SHREDDED
MONTEREY JACK CHEESE

1 CUP (4 OUNCES) SHREDDED
CHEDDAR CHEESE

MAKE-AHEAD HORS D'OEUVRES FOR 50

*O*ne of the main reasons hosts don't enjoy their own parties is that they work through them. I am forever guilty of this, because I try to make at least one fabulous, hot hors d'oeuvre every time my husband and I throw a party. With the appetizers listed in this menu, you may have to pop into the kitchen to take a tray out of the oven, but you will be able to attend your own party.

This menu includes Easy Hors d'Oeuvre Cups with Gourmet Fillings. As you become more familiar with the filling recipes, you may notice that I follow a formula. Almost all my hot hors d'oeuvres contain cheese. Cheese is a perfect ingredient binder and, simply put, it just tastes good. I rarely substitute low-fat dairy products for the real thing. A party is hardly the time to scrimp on taste in the interest of watching one's waist.

———

Easy Hors d'Oeuvre Cups with Gourmet Fillings

Sweet Curry Dip with Crudités

Mediterranean Tricolor Terrine

———

FOOD AND DRINK PLANNER

ONE DAY BEFORE: Make hot hors d'oeuvre cups. Make cold hors d'oeuvre cups. Make Sweet Curry Dip. Cut vegetables for crudités (See "Notes" for Sweet Curry Dip). Make Tri-Color Terrine.

PARTY DAY: Cut additional vegetables for crudités and assemble. Prepare cold hors d'oeuvre fillings and fill cups.

DURING PARTY: Reheat hot hors d'oeuvres.

COCKTAIL SUGGESTION: Offer full bar (see Proportion Chart for Beverage, page 361).

WINE SUGGESTIONS: 1997 Estancia Chardonnay, 1998 Fetzer Eagle Peak Merlot (see "The Wine List," page 23, for more information).

TIMESAVERS: Purchase pre-cut vegetables for crudités. Substitute prepared vegetable dip for Sweet Curry Dip.

TABLE SETTING AND DECORATING IDEAS: Natural Rock and Flowering Mountainside Station (see "Practical Tips and Ideas for Food Stations," page 10).

TABLE LINEN: Use forest green table linen.

Rock and Flower Station Display

Place cloth on table that is against a wall. Set plastic milk crate in back center of tabletop. Place varying heights of risers on side and in front of crate. Use large books or small crates for risers; they must be very sturdy and level. Place another cloth of the same color over risers, allowing cloth enough slack to lie flat on each riser. Fold under cloth ends on top of table.

Place potted green plants with large leaves on crate, on some risers, and on table along wall. Plants will create a backdrop for display. Place whole and large, broken pieces of clean, natural-looking tile, such as terra-cotta and slate, flat on risers. Check tiles for sharp edges and rearrange them if necessary. Fill in display with flowering plants, green moss, and Spanish moss. Spanish moss can hang from risers as long as it doesn't touch food or a candle flame.

Place Mediterranean terrine directly on table in front of display with tilted cracker basket nearby. Place crudités basket on large flat riser with dip nearby. Place hors d'oeuvres directly on top of tiles, as if they were serving trays. Some tiles may have food and some may have plants or décor. Garnish food tiles with loose flowers and stones. Replenish hors d'oeuvres from a silver tray, using tongs to place food on tile instead of removing tiles from display. Wipe tile clean occasionally when replenishing.

Easy Hors d'Oeuvre Cups with Gourmet Fillings

*P*reparing cocktail appetizers is a breeze when all you have to do is spoon delicious fillings into pre-made hors d'oeuvre cups. Some of these ingredients are new and some we've seen time and again in books on entertaining, but these (edible gems) are worth repeating.

Following the preparation instructions for the types of cups are filling suggestions. Make cups for cold hors d'oeuvres a couple of days before your party and fill on the party day. For hot hors d'oeuvres, it is best to bake the cups filled and serve immediately or reheat just before serving. Vegetable cups should be prepared on the party day for maximum freshness.

Flour and Corn Tortilla Cups

ABOUT 1 DOZEN CORN OR 6 FLOUR TORTILLAS

SUGGESTED HOT FILLINGS

BARBECUE CHICKEN, PICADILLO, CHILE CON QUESO, SOUTHWEST STEAK (SEE PAGES 118–123)

SUGGESTED COLD FILLINGS

BARBECUE CHICKEN, SOUTHWEST STEAK (PAGES 118–123)

Use a 2-inch cookie cutter shaped like a star, flower, or circle to cut 24 shapes from tortillas. Spray cups of a mini muffin pan with nonstick cooking spray. Set tortilla shapes into mini muffin cups so they form cups.

To serve hot: Spoon 1 tablespoon filling into each cup. Bake at 400F (205C) for 8 minutes or until crisp. Remove from oven and cool in pan for 5 minutes to allow filling to set before serving. (To make ahead, cool, cover with plastic wrap, and store in the refrigerator for up to 1 day in advance. Just before serving, reheat at 350F [175C] for 5 minutes or until warm.)

To serve cold: Bake cups without filling at 400F (205C) for 18 minutes or until crisp. Cool, spoon 1 tablespoon filling into each cup, and serve immediately. (To make ahead, store unfilled cups covered in plastic wrap at room temperature for up to 2 days. Store filled cups in refrigerator for up to 4 hours.)

Wonton Cups

24 (3-INCH-DIAMETER) WONTON SKINS	SUGGESTED COLD FILLINGS
	ASIAN CHICKEN BLEND, CHINESE DUCK, SWEET CURRIED CHICKEN SALAD, PACIFIC RIM SHRIMP (PAGES 121–122)
SUGGESTED HOT FILLINGS	
SEAFOOD MELT, CHINESE DUCK, (PAGES 120, 121)	

Spray cups of a mini muffin pan with nonstick cooking spray. Set wontons in muffin pan so they form cups.

To serve hot: Bake at 350F (175C) for 8 minutes or until golden brown. Remove from oven and cool in pan for 5 minutes to allow filling to set before serving.

To serve cold: Bake cups without filling at 350F (175C) for 8 minutes or until golden brown. Cool, spoon 1 tablespoon filling into each cup, and serve immediately. (To make ahead, store unfilled cups, covered in plastic wrap, at room temperature for up to 2 days. Store filling in the refrigerator for up to 2 hours.)

Phyllo Cups

A trendy dessert cup in restaurants, this flaky Greek pastry makes a perfect appetizer shell. Phyllo dough can be found near the puff pastry in the freezer section of most grocery stores.

4 (17 × 12-INCH) SHEETS PHYLLO DOUGH, THAWED	CHEESE BAKE, SWEET POTATO PECAN PLEASER (PAGES 117–124)
¼ CUP (½ STICK) BUTTER, MELTED	SUGGESTED COLD FILLINGS (2 RECIPES)
SUGGESTED HOT FILLINGS (2 RECIPES)	GREEK TREAT, CAPRESE CANAPE, PACIFIC RIM SHRIMP, FUDGY LUXURY, FRUIT PUDDING PASSION (PAGES 117–124)
GREEK TREAT, CAPRESE CANAPE, PICADILLO, SEAFOOD MELT, APPLE	

Lay 4 dough sheets directly on top of each other on a flat surface and lightly brush with melted butter. Cut sheets into 48 (2-inch) squares. Set squares into cups of an ungreased mini muffin pan so they form a cup.

To serve hot: Spoon 1 tablespoon filling into each cup. Bake at 400F (205C) for 8 minutes or until crisp. Remove from oven and cool in pan for 5 minutes for filling to set before serving. (To make ahead, cool, cover with plastic wrap, and store in the refrigerator for up to 1 day. Just before serving, reheat at 350F [175C] for 5 minutes or until warm.)

To serve cold: Bake cups without filling at 400F (205C) for 10 minutes until crisp. Cool, spoon 1 tablespoon filling into each cup, and serve immediately. Or store unfilled cups, covered in plastic wrap, at room temperature for up to 2 days. Store filled cups in refrigerator for up to 4 hours.

Mini Pie Shell Cups

Purchase unbaked dough found in the refrigerator section.

---

1 (2-CRUST) PACKAGE REFRIGERATED PASTRY DOUGH, PREFERABLY PILLSBURY	BAKE, SWEET POTATO PECAN PLEASER (PAGE 117–124)
SUGGESTED HOT FILLINGS	SUGGESTED COLD FILLINGS
AMERICAN CLASSIC QUICHE, MUSHROOM QUICHE, SMOKED OYSTER AND CAMEMBERT QUICHE, ANTIPASTO MEDLEY, APPLE CHEESE	FUDGY LUXURY, FRUIT PUDDING PASSION (PAGE 124)

Bring the dough to room temperature and unfold on a flat surface. Cut 24 shapes from the dough with 2-inch round cookie cutters. Set rounds into cups of an ungreased mini muffin pan so they form cups.

To serve hot: Spoon 1 tablespoon filling into each cup. Bake at 425F (220C) for 8 minutes or until light brown. Remove from oven and let cool in pan for 5 minutes for filling to set before serving. (To make ahead, cool, cover with plastic wrap, and store in the refrigerator for up to 1 day. Just before serving, reheat at 350F [175C] for 5 minutes or until warm.)

To serve cold: Bake cups without filling at 400F (205C) for 10 minutes until light brown. Cool; spoon 1 tablespoon of filling into each cup, and serve immediately. (To make ahead, store unfilled cups, covered in plastic wrap, at room temperature for up to 2 days. Store filled cups in refrigerator for up to 4 hours.)

Flaky Biscuit Layer Puffs

Biscuits are found in the refrigerator section of your grocery store. These are not recommended for cold hors d'oeuvres.

2 (12-OUNCE) CANS HUNGRY JACK
FLAKY BISCUITS

SUGGESTED HOT
FILLINGS

ARTICHOKE DELIGHT, BARBECUE
CHICKEN, SOUTHWEST STEAK,
ANTIPASTO MEDLEY, PHILLY CHEESE
STEAK (PAGES 117–123)

Pull apart flaky layers of biscuits into thin dough rounds. Each biscuit makes about 3 rounds. Spray 24 muffin cups with a nonstick cooking spray. Lay rounds in the bottom of muffin cups.

To serve: Spoon 1 tablespoon filling into each cup. Bake at 400F (205C) for 8 minutes, until puffy and edges of biscuit are golden brown. Remove from oven and let stand for 5 minutes to allow filling to set before serving. (To make ahead, cool, cover with plastic wrap, and store in the refrigerator for up to 1 day. Just before serving, reheat at 350F [175C] for 5 minutes or until warm.)

Small Whole Potato Cups

My favorite filling for these is sour cream topped with caviar.

---

36 BABY POTATOES

SUGGESTED HOT FILLINGS (½ RECIPE)

GREEK TREAT, ARTICHOKE DELIGHT, CHILE CON QUESO, PHILLY CHEESE STEAK (PAGES 117, 120, 123)

SUGGESTED COLD FILLINGS (½ RECIPE)

ARTICHOKE DELIGHT (PAGE 117), SOUR CREAM AND CAVIAR, SOUR CREAM, CHIVES, AND CRUMBLED BACON

Wash potatoes and boil, covered in water, over medium-high heat for 15 minutes or until tender. Remove from heat and drain. When cool, cut a very thin slice from one end of each potato so it stands level. Scoop out centers of potatoes from unsliced ends, using a small melon baller.

To serve hot: Spoon 1 teaspoon filling in each cup. Bake at 350F (175C) for 5 minutes or until warm. Remove from heat and serve immediately. (To make ahead, store unfilled potatoes, covered in plastic wrap, in the refrigerator for up to 4 hours. To serve, fill and bake for about 10 minutes or until warm.)

To serve cold: Cool potatoes. Spoon 1 teaspoon filling in each cup and serve immediately. (To make ahead, store unfilled potatoes, covered in plastic wrap, in the refrigerator for up to 4 hours. Fill and serve.)

Zucchini and Pattypan Squash Cups

---

6 TO 7 (6-INCH) ZUCCHINI OR 36 BABY PATTYPAN SQUASH

SUGGESTED HOT FILLINGS (½ RECIPE)

ARTICHOKE DELIGHT, ANTIPASTO MEDLEY, BARBECUE CHICKEN, CAPRESE CANAPE, SEAFOOD MELT (PAGES 117, 118, 120)

SUGGESTED COLD FILLINGS (½ RECIPE)

ARTICHOKE DELIGHT, ANTIPASTO MEDLEY, BARBECUE CHICKEN, CAPRESE CANAPE (PAGES 117, 118)

Wash zucchini and cut crosswise into ¾-inch-thick slices. Wash pattypan squash and slice off the top. Use a melon baller to scoop out the center of zucchini slices and pattypans to form a cup for filling.

To serve hot: Spoon 1 teaspoon filling into each cup. Bake at 350F (175C) for 5 minutes, or until warm. Remove from heat and serve immediately. (To make ahead, store unfilled cups, covered in plastic wrap, in the refrigerator for up to 4 hours. To serve, fill and bake for about 10 minutes or until warm.)

To serve cold: Spoon 1 teaspoon filling into each cup and serve immediately. (To make ahead, store unfilled cups, covered in plastic wrap, in the refrigerator for up to 4 hours. Fill and serve.)

Cucumber Cups

These are not recommended for hot hors d' oeuvres.

ABOUT 3 ENGLISH CUCUMBERS OR 5
REGULAR CUCUMBERS

SUGGESTED COLD
FILLINGS (½ RECIPE)
GREEK TREAT, ARTICHOKE
DELIGHT, ASIAN CHICKEN BLEND,
SWEET CURRIED CHICKEN SALAD,
PACIFIC RIM SHRIMP (PAGES 117, 121,
122)

Peel cucumbers if using regular cucumbers. Cut crosswise into 36 (¾-inch-thick) slices. Use a melon baller to scoop out the center of each slice, forming a cup for the filling.

To serve: Spoon 1 teaspoon filling into each cup and serve immediately. (To make ahead, store unfilled cups, covered in plastic wrap, in the refrigerator for up to 4 hours. Fill and serve.)

Cherry Tomato Cups

These are not recommended for hot hors d'oeuvres.

---

36 CHERRY TOMATOES

SUGGESTED COLD
FILLINGS ($^{1}/_{2}$ RECIPE)

GREEK TREAT, ANTIPASTO MEDLEY,
CAPRESE CANAPE, SOUTHWEST
STEAK (PAGES 117, 118, 123)

Wash tomatoes and remove stem. Slice top off tomatoes and scoop out pulp.

To serve: Spoon 1 teaspoon filling into each tomato and serve immediately. (To make ahead, store unfilled cups, covered in plastic wrap, in the refrigerator for up to 4 hours. Fill and serve.)

Radicchio and Belgian Endive Leaves

These naturally curved vegetables make delicate edible cups. These are not recommended for hot hors d'oeuvres.

ABOUT 4 HEADS RADICCHIO OR
BELGIAN ENDIVE

SUGGESTED COLD
FILLINGS

GREEK TREAT, ARTICHOKE
DELIGHT, ASIAN CHICKEN BLEND
(PAGES 117, 121)

Separate the leaves, wash in cold water, and pat dry with paper towels.

To serve: Spoon 1 tablespoon filling on each leaf and serve immediately. (To make ahead, store in the refrigerator, loosely covered in plastic, for up to 2 hours. Fill and serve.)

Hen and Quail Egg Cups

Hard-boiled hen and quail egg cups are a staple in the hors d'oeuvre world. Quail eggs are available canned in many grocery stores or can be special ordered.

These are not recommended for hot hors d'oeuvre.

12 HEN EGGS OR 36 CANNED QUAIL
EGGS

SUGGESTED COLD
FILLINGS (½ RECIPE)

ARTICHOKE DELIGHT, ASIAN
CHICKEN BLEND, SWEET CURRIED
CHICKEN SALAD, PACIFIC RIM
SHRIMP (PAGES 117, 121, 122)

To cook the hen eggs, cover eggs with water and boil over medium-high heat for 15 minutes. To cook the quail eggs, cover eggs with water and boil over medium-high heat for 5 minutes. Remove from heat and immediately run cold water over the eggs. When cool, peel shells off eggs and slice in half lengthwise. If using canned quail eggs, drain and rinse; cut in half lengthwise. Remove yolks and mix with filling.

To serve: Spoon filling mixed with cooked egg yolk into centers of cooked egg whites. Serve immediately. (To make ahead, store filled eggs, covered in plastic wrap, in the refrigerator for up to 1 day.)

Hot and Cold Gourmet Fillings

Many fillings can be served either hot or cold, depending on what type of cup they will fill.

Greek Treat

MAKES ABOUT 1 ½ CUPS (24 TABLESPOONS)

¾ CUP CRUMBLED FETA CHEESE	1 TEASPOON WHITE WINE
¾ CUP DICED TOMATO	¼ TEASPOON SALT
1 TABLESPOON FRESH LEMON JUICE	⅛ TEASPOON BLACK PEPPER
½ CUP FINELY CHOPPED COOKED SPINACH, DRAINED	

Combine all the ingredients in a medium bowl.

Artichoke Delight

MAKES ABOUT 1 ½ CUPS (24 TABLESPOONS)

¾ CUP (3 OUNCES) SHREDDED SWISS CHEESE	¼ CUP FRESHLY GRATED PARMESAN CHEESE
½ CUP CHOPPED CANNED ARTICHOKE HEARTS	1 TEASPOON WHITE WINE
½ CUP MAYONNAISE	¼ TEASPOON SALT
	⅛ TEASPOON BLACK PEPPER

Combine all the ingredients in a medium bowl.

Antipasto Medley

MAKES ABOUT 1 ½ CUPS (24 TABLESPOONS)

¾ CUP (3 OUNCES) SHREDDED MOZZARELLA	½ TEASPOON RED WINE
½ CUP MINCED HARD SALAMI	½ TEASPOON CHOPPED FRESH OREGANO
¼ CUP FRESHLY GRATED PARMESAN CHEESE	2 TEASPOONS OLIVE OIL
¼ CUP CHOPPED BLACK OLIVES	1 TEASPOON RED WINE VINEGAR
¼ CUP DICED TOMATO	¼ TEASPOON SALT
	⅛ TEASPOON BLACK PEPPER

Combine all the ingredients in a medium bowl.

Barbecue Chicken

¾ CUP DICED COOKED CHICKEN

½ CUP (2 OUNCES) SHREDDED
MOZZARELLA CHEESE

½ CUP (2 OUNCES) SHREDDED
FONTINA CHEESE

2 TABLESPOONS CHOPPED RED
ONION

1 TEASPOON BEER

3 TABLESPOONS BARBECUE SAUCE

¼ TEASPOON SALT

⅛ TEASPOON BLACK PEPPER

Combine all the ingredients in a medium bowl.

Caprese Canape

1 CUP DICED BUFFALO MOZZARELLA

¾ CUP DICED ROMA TOMATO

2 TABLESPOONS SHREDDED FRESH
BASIL

1 TABLESPOON CAPERS

½ TEASPOON RED WINE

2 TEASPOONS OLIVE OIL

1 TEASPOON BALSAMIC VINEGAR

¼ TEASPOON SALT

⅛ TEASPOON BLACK PEPPER

Combine all the ingredients in a medium bowl.

American Classic Quiche

1 CUP (4 OUNCES) SHREDDED
CHEDDAR CHEESE

2 EGGS, LIGHTLY BEATEN

½ CUP HALF-AND-HALF

½ CUP FINELY CHOPPED COOKED
BACON

1 TEASPOON WHITE WINE

¼ TEASPOON SALT

⅛ TEASPOON BLACK PEPPER

Combine all the ingredients in a medium bowl.

Mushroom Quiche

1 CUP (4 OUNCES) SHREDDED SWISS CHEESE	1 TEASPOON SHERRY
2 EGGS, LIGHTLY BEATEN	1 TABLESPOON MINCED FRESH TARRAGON
½ CUP HALF-AND-HALF	¼ TEASPOON SALT
½ CUP SLICED COOKED MUSHROOMS	⅛ TEASPOON BLACK PEPPER

Combine all the ingredients in a medium bowl.

Smoked Oyster and Camembert Quiche

½ CUP CAMEMBERT	½ CUP FINELY CHOPPED SMOKED OYSTERS
¼ CUP SHREDDED MONTEREY JACK CHEESE	1 TEASPOON WHITE WINE
2 EGGS, LIGHTLY BEATEN	¼ TEASPOON SALT
½ CUP HALF-AND-HALF	⅛ TEASPOON BLACK PEPPER

Combine all the ingredients in a medium bowl.

Picadillo

½ CUP CHILI SAUCE	2 TABLESPOONS MINCED COOKED ONION
2 TABLESPOONS GRAPE JELLY	1 TEASPOON CREAM SHERRY
¾ CUP CRUMBLED COOKED GROUND BEEF	½ TEASPOON GROUND CUMIN
¼ CUP RAISINS	¼ TEASPOON SALT
¼ CUP SLIVERED ALMONDS	⅛ TEASPOON BLACK PEPPER

Combine all the ingredients in a medium bowl.

Chile con Queso

MAKES ABOUT 1 ½ CUPS (24 TABLESPOONS)

½ CUP VELVEETA PROCESSED
CHEESE FOOD

½ CUP (2 OUNCES) SHREDDED
CHEDDAR CHEESE

½ CUP DICED TOMATO

¼ CUP MINCED ONION

1 TABLESPOON MINCED GREEN CHILI

1 TEASPOON BEER

1 TABLESPOON MINCED FRESH
CILANTRO

¼ TEASPOON SALT

⅛ TEASPOON BLACK PEPPER

Combine all the ingredients in a medium bowl.

Seafood Melt

MAKES ABOUT 1 ½ CUPS (24 TABLESPOONS)

¾ CUP (3 OUNCES) SHREDDED SWISS
CHEESE

2 TABLESPOONS FRESHLY GRATED
PARMESAN CHEESE

¼ CUP MAYONNAISE

¾ CUP SHREDDED COOKED
CRABMEAT

¼ CUP PREPARED COLESLAW

1 TEASPOON WHITE WINE

¼ TEASPOON SALT

⅛ TEASPOON BLACK PEPPER

Combine all the ingredients in a medium bowl.

Asian Chicken Blend

¾ CUP FINELY SHREDDED COOKED CHICKEN

½ CUP FINELY SHREDDED GREEN CABBAGE

¼ CUP FINELY SHREDDED CARROT

2 TABLESPOONS MINCED GREEN ONION

¼ CUP FINELY CHOPPED FRIED WONTONS

1 TEASPOON GRAND MARNIER

1 TABLESPOON FRESH ORANGE JUICE

½ TABLESPOON SESAME OIL

2 TEASPOONS RICE VINEGAR

2 TEASPOONS PLUM SAUCE

1 TEASPOON SESAME SEEDS

¼ TEASPOON SALT

Combine all the ingredients in a medium bowl.

Chinese Duck

2 TABLESPOONS HOISIN SAUCE

3 TABLESPOONS PLUM SAUCE

1 CUP FINELY SHREDDED COOKED DUCK

½ CUP THINLY SLICED COOKED MUSHROOMS

2 TABLESPOONS MINCED GREEN ONION

¼ TEASPOON SALT

⅛ TEASPOON BLACK PEPPER

1 TEASPOON CREAM SHERRY

Combine all the ingredients in a medium bowl.

Sweet Curried Chicken Salad

MAKES ABOUT 1 ½ CUPS (24 TABLESPOONS)

½ CUP SOUR CREAM

1 TABLESPOON ORANGE
MARMALADE

1 CUP DICED COOKED CHICKEN

3 TABLESPOONS RAISINS

2 TABLESPOONS CHOPPED ALMONDS

1 TABLESPOON SHREDDED
COCONUT

1 TEASPOON GRAND MARNIER

1 TEASPOON YELLOW CURRY

⅛ TEASPOON SALT

Combine all the ingredients in a medium bowl.

Pacific Rim Shrimp

MAKES ABOUT 1 ½ CUPS (24 TABLESPOONS)

¾ CUP COOKED BAY SHRIMP

¼ CUP MINCED WATER CHESTNUTS

¼ CUP CRUSHED PINEAPPLE,
DRAINED

2 TABLESPOONS MINCED GREEN
ONION

1 TABLESPOON GRAND MARNIER

½ TABLESPOON SESAME OIL

1 TEASPOON SOY SAUCE

1 TEASPOON FRESHLY GRATED
ORANGE ZEST

Combine all the ingredients in a medium bowl.

Southwest Steak

MAKES ABOUT 2 CUPS (32 TABLESPOONS)

¼ CUP SOUR CREAM

¼ CUP SHREDDED MONTEREY JACK CHEESE

¼ CUP SHREDDED CHEDDAR CHEESE

½ CUP DICED COOKED BEEFSTEAK

¼ CUP COOKED BLACK BEANS

¼ CUP COOKED CORN KERNELS

¼ CUP DICED TOMATO

2 TABLESPOONS MINCED GREEN ONION

1 TEASPOON TEQUILA

½ TEASPOON DRY FAJITA MIX

1 TABLESPOON MINCED FRESH CILANTRO

¼ TEASPOON SALT

⅛ TEASPOON BLACK PEPPER

Combine all the ingredients in a medium bowl.

Philly Cheese Steak

MAKES ABOUT 2 CUPS (32 TABLESPOONS)

¾ CUP FINELY CHOPPED COOKED FLANK STEAK

⅔ CUP CHEEZ WHIZ

½ CUP DICED COOKED ONION

¼ CUP DICED COOKED GREEN BELL PEPPER

1 TEASPOON BEER

¼ TEASPOON SALT

⅛ TEASPOON BLACK PEPPER

Combine all the ingredients in a medium bowl.

Apple Cheese Bake

MAKES ABOUT 1½ CUPS (24 TABLESPOONS)

8 OUNCES CREAM CHEESE, SOFTENED

1 TABLESPOON UNSALTED BUTTER, MELTED

¾ CUP DICED COOKED APPLES

2 TABLESPOONS BROWN SUGAR

1 TEASPOON CALVADOS

Combine all the ingredients in a medium bowl.

Sweet Potato Pecan Pleaser

MAKES ABOUT 1 ½ CUPS (24 TABLESPOONS)

1 EGG, LIGHTLY BEATEN	½ CUP CHOPPED PECANS
1 TABLESPOON UNSALTED BUTTER, MELTED AND COOLED	⅓ CUP PACKED LIGHT BROWN SUGAR
1 CUP MASHED COOKED SWEET POTATO	½ TEASPOON BOURBON

Combine all the ingredients in a medium bowl.

Fudgy Luxury

MAKES ABOUT 1 ½ CUPS (24 TABLESPOONS)

⅔ CUP PREPARED FUDGE SAUCE	1 TEASPOON GRAND MARNIER
⅓ CUP PREPARED MARSHALLOW CREME	1 TEASPOON ORANGE ZEST
½ CUP CHOPPED WALNUTS OR ANY NUT	

Combine all the ingredients in a medium bowl.

Fruit Pudding Passion

MAKES ABOUT 1 ½ CUPS (24 TABLESPOONS)

1 CUP PREPARED VANILLA PUDDING	1 TEASPOON GRAND MARNIER
1 CUP FRESH BERRIES OR SLICED STRAWBERRIES	

Combine all the ingredients in a medium bowl.

Sweet Curry Dip with Crudités

MAKES 50 SERVINGS

I'm always surprised at the overwhelming reaction from guests when they taste this dip because it is so effortless. With all the intricate dishes I serve, I guess I expect the big applause only when I've slaved in the kitchen for hours.

The term "crudité" refers to a platter of raw vegetables. Recent health reports have suggested that broccoli and cauliflower should not be consumed raw, and almost all of my clients request that these vegetables be blanched. Personally, I dismiss these reports, but have sided with the majority in their preparation below.

4 CUPS (1 QUART) SOUR CREAM	5 LARGE CARROTS, PEELED
½ CUP ORANGE MARMALADE	1 LARGE BUNCH CELERY
1 TEASPOON GRAND MARNIER	4 CUCUMBERS, PEELED
2 TABLESPOONS CURRY POWDER	1 (8-OUNCE) PACKAGE WHOLE BUTTON MUSHROOMS
1 POUND BROCCOLI	1 (8-OUNCE) PACKAGE CHERRY TOMATOES
1 POUND CAULIFLOWER	

Mix the sour cream, marmalade, Grand Marnier, and curry powder in a medium bowl until smooth and combined. Cover and refrigerate until chilled or make up to 24 hours ahead.

Cut florets from broccoli and cauliflower and then cut into bite-size pieces. Bring 2 small pots of water to a boil over medium-high heat. Place broccoli in one pot and cauliflower in the other, and cook for 3 minutes, until blanched. Pour each into a colander and run cold water over vegetables to stop the cooking process. Allow all water to drain.

Trim carrots and celery. Cut carrots and celery stalks in half lengthwise and then cut into 3-inch sticks. Cut cucumbers crosswise into ½-inch rounds.

Arrange vegetables in a lined basket or on a large platter. Place cherry tomatoes in center or scatter over top of all vegetables. Place half of the Sweet Curry Dip in a medium bowl and serve chilled alongside vegetables. Replenish dip as needed.

NOTES: Many grocery stores sell pre-cut vegetables for crudités, a great time-saver.

You can prepare some of the vegetables a day in advance. Keep carrots and celery fresh by storing in an airtight container of water in the refrigerator. Refrigerate broccoli and cauliflower, each in its own airtight container, without water. Mushrooms will brown if washed too early and cucumbers may become mushy if cut too soon, so prepare them just before serving.

Mediterranean Tricolor Terrine

MAKE 2 TERRINES FOR A PARTY OF 50. MAKES 25 SERVINGS
AS PART OF AN APPETIZER SELECTION

*M*any hosts offer a layered cheese spread at larger parties. A terrine can be either a pan used as a mold or the food that takes the mold's shape. I've seen many commercially prepared cheese molds on the market, but they seem to serve only a few. This terrine, with three vivid layers of red bell pepper, green pesto, and eggplant, looks as good as it tastes.

PESTO LAYER

1 CLOVE GARLIC, MINCED

1 CUP FRESH BASIL LEAVES

2 TABLESPOONS CHIVES

¼ CUP PINE NUTS

¼ CUP FRESHLY GRATED PARMESAN CHEESE

¼ CUP OLIVE OIL

2 TABLESPOONS FRESH LEMON JUICE

12 OUNCES CREAM CHEESE, SOFTENED

RED PEPPER LAYER

1 TABLESPOON OLIVE OIL

1 RED BELL PEPPER, COARSELY CHOPPED

2 TABLESPOONS WHITE WINE

1 TABLESPOON FRESH LEMON JUICE

1 TEASPOON CUMIN SEEDS

½ TEASPOON SALT

12 OUNCES CREAM CHEESE, SOFTENED

EGGPLANT LAYER

3 TABLESPOONS OLIVE OIL

1 LARGE EGGPLANT, PEELED AND CUT IN 1-INCH CUBES

4 TEASPOONS CUMIN SEEDS

2 TABLESPOONS WHITE WINE

1 TABLESPOON LEMON JUICE

½ TEASPOON SALT

12 OUNCES CREAM CHEESE, SOFTENED

2 TABLESPOONS SLICED RIPE OLIVES

CRACKERS OR FRENCH BAGUETTE, THINLY SLICED

Completely line a 9 × 5-inch loaf pan with long sheets of plastic wrap extending down one side, over bottom, and up other side of pan. Leave 6 inches of plastic wrap on either side to fold over top of terrine.

To make the pesto layer: Put the garlic, basil, chives, pine nuts, Parmesan cheese, olive oil, and lemon juice in a blender jar and puree until ingredients are finely minced. Add cream cheese and blend until smooth and combined. Spread mixture in an even layer in bottom of prepared pan. Chill for 30 minutes or until firm.

To make the red pepper layer: Heat the oil in a large skillet over medium-high heat. Add bell pepper and wine. Cook, stirring occasionally, until tender, about 10 minutes. Remove from heat and cool for 10 minutes. Put bell pepper, lemon juice, cumin seeds, and salt in clean blender jar and puree until smooth. Add cream cheese and blend until combined. Spread red pepper mixture in an even layer over pesto mixture in pan. Chill for 30 minutes or until firm.

To make the eggplant layer: Heat the oil in a large skillet over medium-high heat. Add eggplant, 2 teaspoons cumin seeds, and wine. Cook, stirring occasionally, until translucent, about 15 minutes. Add more oil, if necessary, to prevent eggplant from sticking to the pan. Remove from heat and cool 10 minutes. Put the eggplant, remaining 2 teaspoons of cumin seeds, lemon juice, and salt in clean blender jar and puree until smooth. Add cream cheese and blend until combined. Spread mixture in an even layer over pepper layer in pan. Fold extra plastic wrap over top of terrine to cover completely and refrigerate for 2 hours or until set.

Just before serving, unfold top plastic wrap and place a large platter, facedown, on loaf pan. Invert pan to unmold terrine on platter, using plastic wrap to help pull terrine away from pan. Remove plastic wrap and smooth edges of terrine if necessary. Arrange a row of sliced olives along the center of the top. Serve cool with crackers or sliced baguette.

Hearty Fare

POUR ME A STIFF ONE! FOR 4

Scotch and Caramelized Onion Orzo

T-Bone Steak with Scotch and Mushroom Sauce

Pearl Onion, Pea, and Parsnip Gratin

Scotch Chocolate Chip Cookies

A SHOT FOR THE SOUTHERN SOUL FOR 6

Creamy Cheese Grits

Pepper Vodka Fried Catfish

Spicy Spiked Greens

Peach Brandy Cobbler

WARM WINTER ELIXIRS FOR 8

Brandied Pumpkin and Hazelnut Soup

Roast Pork Stuffed with Sherried Tarragon Mushrooms

Port Wine Carrots

Chocolate Biscotti and Pear Brandy Betty

POUR ME A STIFF ONE! FOR 4

I wonder how the term "stiff" became associated with a shot of booze. I imagine it has to do with the hair on the back of one's neck standing straight up after taking a healthy swig of scotch. There are a lot of vivid catch phrases associated with the world of liquor, with "shaken, not stirred" a line for the upper crust and "I'll have the usual" being the barfly's mantra.

The offbeat "Table Setting and Decorating Ideas" for this menu were designed for the Hemingwayesque man or the crusty old newspaper editor. He may blow cigar smoke through the flower arrangement but he'll get a kick out of the headline place mats.

———

Scotch and Caramelized Onion Orzo

T-Bone Steak with Scotch and Mushroom Sauce

Pearl Onion, Pea, and Parsnip Gratin

Scotch Chocolate Chip Cookies

———

FOOD AND DRINK PLANNER

ONE DAY BEFORE: Make Scotch Chocolate Chip Cookies.

PARTY DAY: Make Scotch and Caramelized Onion Orzo. Make Pearl Onion, Pea, and Parsnip Gratin.

JUST BEFORE SERVING: Reheat Pearl Onion, Pea, and Parsnip Gratin. Make T-Bone Steak with Scotch and Mushroom Sauce.

COCKTAIL SUGGESTION: Rob Roy: Add 1 ounce scotch and a splash of sweet vermouth to ice in a cocktail shaker. Shake and strain into a short glass. Use a quality scotch like Glenlivet.

WINE SUGGESTION: 1997 Firestone Cabernet Sauvignon (see "The Wine List," page 23 for more information).

TIMESAVER: Purchase prepared chocolate chip cookies.

MENU EXTRA: Serve a green salad or steamed nonstarchy vegetable.

TABLE SETTING AND DECORATING IDEAS: editor-in-chief newsroom dinner

TABLE LINEN: Use black or white table linen.

Headline Place Mats

During the week before your party, scan the newspapers for headlines that relate to your guests. For example, if one of your guests is blonde, a headline reading "Blondes Have More Fun" would be perfect for him or her. Or if a guest has a passion for a music group, choose "Springsteen to Tour in Fall." Neatly cut out headlines and any artwork that could relate to your guests. Purchase black, white, or red poster board at a craft or stationery store. Cut poster board into 17 X 3-inch rectangles, making one rectangle per person. Lay out headline, artwork, and a photo of guest on poster board rectangle to resemble a newspaper. Spray an adhesive spray on back of headline and other elements, and press them on rectangle. Liquid glue may make newspaper too soggy and will tear.

Go to a large stationery store or copy center and have the place mats laminated with plastic sheeting. Set the place mats on the table and have guests find where they are sitting by the headlines. Let guests keep the place mats.

Comics Vase of Tulips

Save the Sunday comics section. Clean a large coffee can or a large square olive oil can. Make sure the can doesn't leak when filled with water. Trim a comic page so that it wraps around the can and covers can from top to bottom. Spray an adhesive spray on back of the comic page and apply to dry can. Purchase a clear acrylic spray from a hardware or craft store. In a well-vented outdoor area, spray comic-covered can with acrylic to give it a finished look. Allow acrylic to dry at least 24 hours or length of time suggested by manufacturer. Fill can halfway with water, and place a bunch of red tulips in can. Set arrangement in center of dinner table.

Personal Ad Napkin Rings

Cut a cardboard paper towel roll into 1½-inch-wide rings, making one ring per person. Cut out personal ads or classified ads from a newspaper to fit around the cardboard ring. Spray an adhesive spray on back of ads and apply neatly around cardboard ring. Finish off ring by applying a 2-inch-wide strip of clear mailing tape around ring. Trim tape and paper edges around ring top and bottom. Slide rings over napkins.

Inkwell Candleholders

Inkwells as candleholders are my first choice for this theme, though they may be hard to find. Since the hole in most inkwells is very small, you will need to purchase pencil-thin candles, found in many specialty candle and gift shops. Or you may have fun or gimmicky candleholders which would work on this table.

Scotch and Caramelized Onion Orzo

*O*rzo, also known as riso and Rosa Marina, is a rice-shaped pasta. I prefer the lighter, smoother texture of orzo to rice with most dishes.

3 TABLESPOONS BUTTER	5 CUPS WATER
1 LARGE BROWN ONION, COARSELY CHOPPED	1½ TEASPOONS SALT
2 TABLESPOONS J&B SCOTCH WHISKY	1 TEASPOON OLIVE OIL
¼ CUP PACKED LIGHT BROWN SUGAR	1½ CUPS ORZO

Melt 1 tablespoon of the butter in a large skillet over medium-high heat. Add the onion and cook, stirring occasionally, until translucent, about 5 minutes. Add the scotch and cook until liquid reduces completely, about 1 minute. Add the brown sugar and remaining 2 tablespoons butter and cook, stirring occasionally, until sugar caramelizes, about 2 minutes.

Meanwhile, combine the water, 1 teaspoon of the salt, and oil in a large pot and bring to a boil over high heat. Add the orzo and cook until tender, about 10 minutes. Drain in a colander and pour into a large bowl. Stir in the caramelized onion and remaining ½ teaspoon salt. Serve warm.

T-Bone Steak with Scotch and Mushroom Sauce

MAKES 4 SERVINGS

*M*any cooking schools teach an interesting technique to test a steak's degree of doneness. Use the index finger and thumb of one hand to press the triangle of flesh between the index finger and thumb of the other hand. Compare the feel of the hand being pressed with the surface of the steak. If the pressed hand is relaxed, it should feel soft and a little firm, like a rare steak; if the hand is stretched, it will feel a bit firmer, like a medium-rare steak. For well-done steak, compare its surface with the firm cartilage at the tip of your nose. I prefer to use a meat thermometer.

2 CLOVES GARLIC, MINCED	½ TEASPOON SALT
2 TABLESPOONS SCOTCH	½ TEASPOON BLACK PEPPER
½ CUP VEGETABLE OIL	4 (12-OUNCE) BEEF T-BONE LOIN STEAKS, 1½ INCHES THICK
2 CUPS BEEF BROTH	
¼ CUP WORCESTERSHIRE SAUCE	1 POUND SLICED MUSHROOMS

Whisk together the garlic, scotch, oil, broth, Worcestershire sauce, salt, and pepper in a medium bowl until combined. Arrange steak in a 13 × 9-inch baking pan. Pour mixture over steaks and marinate, covered, in the refrigerator for 1 hour.

Preheat the broiler to high. Remove the steaks from the marinade, reserving marinade, and arrange on a rack in a broiler pan 4 to 6 inches from heat. Broil 5 minutes on one side, then flip steaks and broil 5 minutes on other side for medium.

Meanwhile, put the marinade and mushrooms in a large skillet. Cook over medium-high heat, stirring occasionally, until liquid reduces by half, 12 to 15 minutes.

Place steaks on dinner plates and spoon sauce over top.

Pearl Onion, Pea, and Parsnip Gratin

MAKES 4 TO 6 SERVINGS

Pearl onions and peas was a traditional winter dish in my childhood. As I dined at the home of other Irish folk, I realized the combination was served in various forms at their tables as well. The addition of parsnips in a gratin is for my root vegetable–loving husband.

1 TABLESPOON OLIVE OIL

1 TABLESPOON BUTTER

½ POUND PARSNIPS, PEELED AND THINLY SLICED CROSSWISE

2 CLOVES GARLIC, MINCED

1 CUP SHELLED FRESH OR FROZEN GREEN PEAS

½ CUP PEARL ONIONS, PEELED AND SLIVERED

¾ CUP (3 OUNCES) SHREDDED MONTEREY JACK CHEESE

½ CUP HEAVY CREAM

⅓ CUP SOUR CREAM

1 EGG

1 TABLESPOON DRY VERMOUTH

½ TEASPOON SALT

½ TEASPOON WHITE PEPPER

Heat the oil and butter in a large skillet over medium-high heat. Add the parsnips and cook, stirring occasionally, until tender, 8 to 10 minutes. Remove from heat and set aside.

Preheat oven to 375F (190C). Butter bottom and sides of an 8-inch round cake pan.

Scatter garlic over bottom of prepared pan. Place half of the parsnips in an even layer over bottom of pan. Scatter half of the onions, and half of the peas over the parsnips. Scatter half of cheese over the top. Repeat layers with remaining parsnips, onions, peas, and cheese.

Whisk together the creams, egg, vermouth, salt, and pepper until creamy. Pour evenly over top of ingredients in pan.

Bake for 40 to 45 minutes or until top is golden brown and bubbly. Remove from heat and cool for 5 minutes. Cut into wedges and serve hot.

Scotch Chocolate Chip Cookies

Scotch is a chancy baking ingredient. Its sophisticated blend will be compatible with few flavors, so the simpler the baked good, the better. Experiment, using your favorite scotch in basic cakes, shortbread, and the classic chocolate chip cookie.

1 CUP UNSALTED BUTTER, ROOM TEMPERATURE	2¼ CUPS ALL-PURPOSE FLOUR
¾ CUP GRANULATED SUGAR	1 TEASPOON BAKING POWDER
¾ CUP PACKED LIGHT BROWN SUGAR	1¼ CUPS SEMISWEET CHOCOLATE CHIPS
2 EGGS	1 CUP WALNUTS, COARSELY CHOPPED
2 TABLESPOONS SCOTCH	

Preheat oven to 350F (175C). Lightly spray a baking sheet with nonstick cooking spray.

Beat the butter and sugars in a large bowl until fluffy. Add the eggs and scotch, and beat until creamy. Sift together the flour and baking powder, and beat into mixture until combined. Stir in the chocolate chips and walnuts.

Drop dough by heaping tablespoons 2 inches apart on prepared baking sheet and flatten out to 3 inches in diameter using the back of a spoon. Bake for 10 minutes or until golden brown. Store in an airtight container at room temperature up to 1 week.

A SHOT FOR THE SOUTHERN SOUL FOR 6

When I told my many Southern-born friends about this menu, they beat on my front door, begging for samples. I felt an obligation, and a tiny bit of pressure, to do this menu justice for my harsh critics. The goal was to create traditional foods with a twist that would remind my tasters of their home.

This whole menu was a big hit, but I was toasted for the Pepper Vodka Catfish. It's incredibly easy because pepper vodka, without the addition of anything else, is the catfish marinade. A close cousin to Southern food is "soul food." A number of gourmet restaurants serving this style of home cooking are popping up in Los Angeles. They have hooked celebrities who savored this food in their youth, and have enticed many new converts as well.

———

Creamy Cheese Grits

Pepper Vodka Fried Catfish

Spicy Spiked Greens

Peach Brandy Cobbler

———

FOOD AND DRINK PLANNER

ONE DAY BEFORE: Make Peach Brandy Cobbler. Make Creamy Cheese Grits.

PARTY DAY: Make Spicy Spiked Greens.

JUST BEFORE SERVING: Make Pepper Vodka Fried Catfish.

COCKTAIL SUGGESTION: Vodka Lemonade: Pour 1 ounce vodka over ice in a tall glass; fill glass with lemonade. Float star shapes cut from lemon peel in glasses (see "Floating Candles with Lemon Fish," below).

WINE SUGGESTION: 1997 Kendall-Jackson Vintner's Reserve Chardonnay or Sauvignon Blanc (See "The Wine List," page 23, for more information).

TIMESAVER: Substitute canned corn for Creamy Cheese Grits.

TABLE SETTING AND DECORATING IDEAS: The Happy Sunflower and
Lemon Fish Table

TABLE LINEN: Use Summer Brights suggested in "Color Families and Complementary Shades" (see page 6).

Happy Sunflower and Lemon Centerpiece

Use a wide, cylindrical glass vase about 1 foot high with smooth (not etched) sides.
Layer lemon leaves and whole lemons in vase up to the top. Fill vase with water and
insert about 6 sunflowers. Place in center of table.

Floating Candles with Lemon Fish

Cut lemons in half and scrape out pulp. Using clean scissors, cut small goldfish shapes
from lemon peel. Give the fish a little smile by cutting a notch where the lips would
be. Fill a small glass bowl with 1 inch of water. Place a small lemon leaf in the bottom
of the bowl and place a votive candle in the center to weigh down the leaf. Float 2
lemon fish, yellow side up, in the bowl around the candle. Fill a total of 4 bowls and
place them around the table. Do not use live fish.

Creamy Cheese Grits

*M*s. *Southern girl, Ruth Shure, has kindly shared another recipe from her Kentucky home. We've spiked these velvety cheese grits with Chardonnay, putting a California spin on this heartland favorite. I recommend regular or quick grits for this recipe; do not use instant grits.*

1 CUP HOMINY GRITS

2 TEASPOONS SALT

3 CUPS WATER

1 CUP CHARDONNAY

½ CUP (1 STICK) BUTTER

¼ POUND PROCESSED CHEESE, CUBED

½ CUP (2 OUNCES) SHREDDED SHARP CHEDDAR CHEESE

3 EGGS, LIGHTLY BEATEN

⅓ CUP MILK

1 TEASPOON WHITE PEPPER

Preheat oven to 350F (175C). Butter a 13 × 9-inch baking pan. Combine the grits, salt, water, and wine in a medium saucepan and bring to a boil over medium-high heat, stirring occasionally. Reduce heat to low. Cover and cook 5 to 6 minutes. (Check manufacturer's recommended cooking time on package.) Remove from heat.

Add the remaining ingredients to the saucepan and stir into grits until smooth. Pour mixture into prepared baking pan. Bake for 45 minutes or until grits are set and a knife inserted off-center comes out clean. Cut into 2-inch squares and serve immediately. (To make ahead, cover with plastic wrap and refrigerate up to 2 days. Reheat and cut into squares when ready to serve.)

Pepper Vodka Fried Catfish

MAKES 6 SERVINGS

*A*bsolut's Peppar vodka is out of this world! This liquid pepper is my first choice for Bloody Marys, and as a marinade for any spicy dish.

6 (8-OUNCE) CATFISH FILETS, DEBONED AND SKINNED

¾ CUP ABSOLUT PEPPAR VODKA

1½ CUPS ALL-PURPOSE FLOUR

½ CUP CHILI POWDER

¼ CUP SALT

2 TABLESPOONS BLACK PEPPER

OLIVE OIL

Place the catfish in a 13 × 9-inch baking pan. Pour vodka over fish and marinate, covered, for 1 hour in the refrigerator. Drain catfish and discard vodka.

Toss together the flour, chili powder, salt, and pepper, and place on a dinner plate. Coat the catfish in flour mixture.

Heat 1 tablespoon olive oil in a large skillet over medium-high heat. Cook 2 filets at one time until outer coating is a pinkish golden brown and fish flakes, about 8 minutes on each side. Repeat with remaining catfish, adding 1 tablespoon olive oil with each batch. Remove catfish from pan and drain on paper towels.

Place on a large platter or on individual plates and serve hot.

Spicy Spiked Greens

My fabulous galpal Raye Dowell shared this spicy greens recipe with me. "Greens" can be kale, mustard greens, or collard greens, among others. Most have a slightly bitter taste which contrasts with a sweet or spicy flavoring.

4 LARGE BUNCHES COLLARD GREENS, WASHED, STEMS AND RIBS REMOVED

2 BEEF BOUILLON CUBES

2 CUPS HOT WATER

2 TABLESPOONS OLIVE OIL

4 CLOVES GARLIC, MINCED

3 TABLESPOONS LIGHT BROWN SUGAR

1 TEASPOON HOT PEPPER SAUCE

1/3 CUP RED WINE VINEGAR

1/4 CUP ABSOLUT PEPPAR VODKA

1 TEASPOON SALT

Tear the greens into irregular pieces. Dissolve the bouillon cubes in hot water.

Heat the oil and garlic in a large pot over medium heat. Add the sugar, hot pepper sauce, and vinegar; cook until sugar dissolves, 1 to 2 minutes. Pour vinegar mixture into a small bowl. Alternately add the greens and vinegar mixture to pot. Pour the vodka and bouillon over the greens.

Cook the greens over medium heat until tender and they change from bright green to dark green, about 25 minutes. Turn greens over occasionally during cooking process.

Discard liquid from the greens and transfer them to a large bowl. Season with salt and serve hot.

Peach Brandy Cobbler

A cobbler is named for its appearance. Dough similar to that used for biscuits is crumbled over the surface of a fruit mixture. As the dessert bakes, the dough spreads and resembles a cobblestone street.

8 FRESH PEACHES (UNPEELED), RINSED AND CUT IN WEDGES, OR 4 CUPS SLICED FROZEN PEACHES, THAWED	1 CUP ALL-PURPOSE FLOUR
	1/2 CUP PACKED LIGHT BROWN SUGAR
1/4 CUP GRANULATED SUGAR	1/2 CUP (1 STICK) PLUS 1 TABLESPOON UNSALTED BUTTER, SOFTENED
1 TEASPOON GROUND CINNAMON	
1/4 CUP PLUS 1 TABLESPOON PEACH BRANDY	1/8 TEASPOON SALT
	1 EGG
2 TEASPOONS FRESH LEMON JUICE	

Combine the peaches, granulated sugar, cinnamon, 1/4 cup peach brandy, and lemon juice in a medium saucepan. Cook over medium-low heat, stirring frequently, until mixture thickens into a heavy syrup, 15 to 20 minutes. Remove from heat and set aside.

Preheat oven to 400F (205C). Combine the flour, brown sugar, 1/2 cup butter, and salt in a food processor and process until mixture resembles coarse meal. Add the egg and the 1 tablespoon of brandy, and pulse until dough just begins to hold together.

Pour the peach mixture into an 8-inch-square glass baking dish. Dot top of peach mixture with the 1 tablespoon butter. Crumble the dough over the peaches.

Bake for 20 minutes or until the crust is golden brown. (To make ahead, store, covered in plastic wrap, in the refrigerator for up to 2 days.) Spoon onto dessert plates and serve warm.

VARIATION

Rhubarb-Peach Crumb Cobbler

Substitute 2 cups chopped fresh or frozen rhubarb for 4 peaches. Cut off woody ends and leaves. Rinse rhubarb clean of any dirt and drain well. Coarsely chop stalks into 1/2-inch pieces.

WARM WINTER ELIXIRS FOR 8

*R*oast pork conjures up images of dining on a blustery winter night after a day of chopping wood for a fire. You can use the logs to craft the rustic centerpiece suggested in "Table Setting and Decorating Ideas" (below). A versatile meat, pork is on most Americans' breakfast tables as bacon, and is prepared mainly as pork chops for dinner. Just as the chops are perfectly partnered with a sweet applesauce, so a pork roast is absolutely delicious with a winter menu featuring fruit, pumpkin, and Port.

Brandy is another cold weather favorite when enjoyed by a toasty fire. Pull out your best after-dinner spirits and play a game of cards while sipping from a snifter. Or spend time with good friends, reminiscing about old times over photos. This menu is a real soul warmer meant for nostalgic occasions with loved ones.

———

Brandied Pumpkin and Hazelnut Soup

Roast Pork Stuffed with Sherried Tarragon Mushrooms

Port Wine Carrots

Chocolate Amaretto Biscotti and Pear Brandy Betty

———

FOOD AND DRINK PLANNER

ONE DAY BEFORE: Make Chocolate Amaretto Biscotti and Pear Brandy Betty.

PARTY DAY: Make Brandied Pumpkin and Hazelnut Soup.

JUST BEFORE SERVING: Reheat Brandied Pumpkin and Hazelnut Soup. Make Roast Pork Stuffed with Sherried Tarragon Mushrooms. Make Port Wine Carrots. Reheat Chocolate Amaretto Biscotti and Pear Brandy Betty.

COCKTAIL SUGGESTION: Orange Brandy Cocktail: Pour 1 ounce spiced brandy and 1 ounce Grand Marnier over ice in a short glass. Garnish with an orange twist.

WINE SUGGESTION: 1998 Niebaum-Coppola Talia Rosé (see "The Wine List," page 23, for more information).

TIME-SAVER: Substitute prepared fruit pie for Chocolate Amaretto Biscotti and Pear Brandy Betty.

TABLE SETTING AND DECORATING IDEAS: The Winter Wood Table

TABLE LINEN: Use Autumn Tones or Winter Hues suggested in "Color Families and Complementary Shades" (see page 6).

Woodpile Candle Centerpiece

Cut 2 (5-inch-diameter) wood logs crosswise into lengths ranging from 2 inches to 6 inches, using a circular saw, until you have six pieces. Cuts need to be smooth and level so each piece can stand sturdily on end. If you do not own or feel comfortable operating a circular saw, go to a large warehouse store like The Home Depot and ask them to cut the logs for you. They usually charge a nominal fee.

Lay a bed of freshly picked, clean lemon or autumn leaves in center of table. Place log pieces on end in a group on leaves. Purchase raffia string at a florist shop or craft store. Wrap raffia around the logs, binding them together like wooden pilings to make them more secure. Scatter extra leaves and acorns around base of logs and around table. Logs will be at varying heights and may resemble the pipes of an organ. Arrange about 4 votive candles on surfaces of most level and sturdy log pieces. Secure candles by lighting a candle and dripping wax where candles will be placed. Set candles in warm wax, pressing firmly.

Wood Slice Place Cards

Saw a 3-inch-diameter log crosswise into ½-inch-thick round slices, making 1 wood round per person. Glue acorns, a few whole cloves or nutmegs, and a small raffia bow in a little bunch on one side of wood round. Write each person's name across the center of wood round, on decorated side, with a thin felt-tip pen. Place the wood round flat on a small bed of clean autumn leaves in the center of each place at the table.

Raffia and Cinnamon Stick Napkin Ties

Purchase raffia string at a florist shop or craft store. Roll napkins lengthwise and wrap a few raffia strings around the middle. Tie raffia in a bow and place 2 cinnamon sticks in bow center. Tie bow loops around cinnamon sticks.

Brandied Pumpkin and Hazelnut Soup

MAKES 8 SERVINGS

The great thing about this creamy soup is that I've eliminated the blender step by using pureed pumpkin. When making soup for a dinner party, I tend to avoid messy recipes that require pouring a mixture batch by batch into a blender. The preparation of this soup is nice and tidy.

1 CUP HAZELNUTS, SKINNED	¼ CUP SPICED BRANDY
3 TABLESPOONS BUTTER	6 CUPS VEGETABLE BROTH
1 TABLESPOON OLIVE OIL	2 TABLESPOONS LIGHT BROWN SUGAR
1 TEASPOON FRESH THYME LEAVES	1 TEASPOON GROUND CINNAMON
1 MEDIUM BULB FENNEL, MINCED	½ TEASPOON SALT
4 CUPS CANNED PUMPKIN PUREE	

Preheat oven to 450F (230C). Place the hazelnuts on a baking sheet and bake 5 minutes or until lightly toasted. Cool, then chop the hazelnuts into coarse bits.

Heat the butter and oil in a stockpot over medium-high heat. Add the thyme and fennel; cook, stirring occasionally, until tender, about 5 minutes. Reduce the heat to medium-low and stir in the pumpkin, brandy, broth, brown sugar, cinnamon, and salt. Cook, covered, until mixture thickens, about 20 minutes, stirring occasionally.

Ladle the soup into a large tureen or individual bowls and scatter hazelnuts over the top.

Roast Pork Stuffed with Sherried Tarragon Mushrooms

MAKES 8 SERVINGS

The rich overtones of bourbon add an exquisite dimension to the stuffing inside this pork.

---

1 TABLESPOON BUTTER	1 TEASPOON SALT
4 TABLESPOONS OLIVE OIL	1/8 TEASPOON WHITE PEPPER
4 CLOVES GARLIC, MINCED	1/4 TEASPOON BLACK PEPPER
1 POUND FRESH BUTTON MUSHROOMS, COARSELY CHOPPED	1 (4-POUND) PORK LOIN ROAST, BONED AND TIED
1/4 CUP FINELY CHOPPED TARRAGON	1 CUP BEEF BROTH
3/4 CUP CREAM SHERRY	

Preheat oven to 450F (230C).

Heat the butter, 1 tablespoon of the oil, and 1 tablespoon of the garlic in a large skillet over medium-high heat. Add the mushrooms, tarragon, and 1/2 cup of the sherry; cook until liquid reduces completely, about 10 minutes. Remove from heat and stir in 1/2 teaspoon of the salt and the white pepper.

Untie roast and place mushroom mixture evenly over its center. Retie roast and place in a roasting pan. Spread the remaining 3 tablespoons olive oil, remaining garlic, 1/2 teaspoon salt and black pepper over surface of pork. Insert a meat thermometer into the pork so that it is in the meat, not the stuffing. Pour remaining 1/4 cup sherry and beef broth into roasting pan. Cook, covered, for 20 minutes. Uncover and cook, basting occasionally, 30 to 40 minutes or until meat thermometer registers 160F (70C).

Remove strings from roast and cut crosswise into thick slices. Overlap slices on a large serving platter and drizzle the drippings over top.

Port Wine Carrots

Whenever I serve these rosy glazed carrots, I think of my dear friend Tom and his passion for Port. The beauty and simplicity of this recipe have made it a staple at many of my finer functions.

2 POUNDS CARROTS, WASHED AND PEELED	1 CUP PORT
¼ CUP PLUS 1 TABLESPOON BUTTER	½ TEASPOON SALT

Cut carrots into matchstick-size pieces.

Melt the ¼ cup butter in a large skillet over medium-high heat. Add the carrots and sauté, stirring occasionally, for 5 minutes. Add the Port and cook, stirring occasionally, until liquid reduces completely into a glaze on the carrots, 5 to 8 minutes more. Remove from heat; stir in the remaining 1 tablespoon butter and salt. Serve hot.

Chocolate Amaretto Biscotti and Pear Brandy Betty

Pear brandy may be called poire *on the bottle. The combination of chocolate and pear is absolutely delightful in this dessert.*

---

5 PEARS, PEELED, CORED, AND CUT INTO THIN WEDGES	⅓ CUP GRANULATED SUGAR
½ CUP PEAR BRANDY	¾ CUP PLUS 3 TABLESPOONS UNSALTED BUTTER
⅓ CUP APPLE CIDER	4 CUPS CHOCOLATE AMARETTO BISCOTTI CRUMBS (PAGE 150)
⅓ CUP PACKED LIGHT BROWN SUGAR	

Preheat oven to 350F (175C). Butter a 13 × 9-inch glass baking dish. Toss together the pears, brandy, cider, and sugars in a medium bowl until combined.

Melt the ¾ cup butter. Stir together the biscotti crumbs and melted butter until combined.

Scatter half of the biscotti crumbs in the bottom of prepared baking dish. Top with the pear mixture. Sprinkle remaining biscotti crumbs on top of pear mixture. Dot with remaining 3 tablespoons butter.

Bake for 1 hour or until pear mixture is thick and top is crusty. (To make ahead, store, covered in plastic wrap, in the refrigerator for up to 2 days; heat until warm before serving.)

Spoon the dessert onto individual plates and serve warm.

Chocolate Amaretto Biscotti

This biscotti recipe uses chopped almonds instead of the whole nuts traditionally found in this cookie. Because these cookies will be crumbled and used in the Chocolate Amaretto Biscotti and Pear Brandy Betty, the chopped nuts are a more suitable choice.

3 OUNCES UNSWEETENED BAKING CHOCOLATE	3 TABLESPOONS AMARETTO
1 CUP (2 STICKS) UNSALTED BUTTER, SOFTENED	3½ CUPS ALL-PURPOSE FLOUR
1½ CUPS GRANULATED SUGAR	1 TABLESPOON BAKING POWDER
4 EGGS	1 CUP CHOPPED ALMONDS

Put the chocolate in top of double boiler over simmering water and stir until melted. Cool 5 minutes. Place the butter and sugar in a mixing bowl and beat until fluffy. Beat in the chocolate. Add the eggs and amaretto; beat well. Sift together the flour and baking powder, then beat into chocolate mixture until thoroughly combined. Stir in the almonds until evenly distributed throughout. Cover with plastic wrap and chill for 1 hour or until firm.

Preheat oven to 350F (175C). Lightly spray a baking sheet with nonstick cooking spray. Divide dough in half. Form each half into a loaf that is 14 inches long and 4 inches wide. Place loaves on prepared baking sheet. Bake for 20 to 30 minutes or until a wooden pick inserted in center comes out clean (see Tip below).

Remove the loaves from oven and place on a rack to cool for 10 minutes. Place the loaves on a cutting board and, using a serrated knife, cut them on the diagonal into ½-inch-thick slices. Place the slices flat, on their side, 1 inch apart on the baking sheet. Bake for 10 minutes or until lightly toasted. Store in an airtight container at room temperature for up to 1 week.

TIP: A problem I sometimes have when making biscotti is baking the loaf evenly, especially in an oven where some spots are hotter than others. The ends of the loaf bake more quickly than the middle, leaving the ends too dark and the middle undone. Here's a tip! After about 15 minutes, remove the baking sheet from the oven and slice off each end. Be sure to slice on the diagonal. Using a spatula, transfer the baked ends to your cutting board and then cut them into ½-inch slices. Place the middle back in the oven and bake for another 5 to 7 minutes.

Latin Fiesta

ELEGANT MEXICAN DINNER FOR 6

Tequila Tortilla Soup

Gourmet Tamales with Tequila Tomatillo Sauce

Shrimp in a Tequila Cilantro Cream Sauce

Tequila Mexican Rice

Margarita Fried Ice Cream

MEXICALI GALA FOR 20

Margarita Chicken Skewers

Enchilada Beer Stew

Yucatan Salbute Bar

Salsa Borracha

Fruit-Filled Cookie Tacos

ELEGANT MEXICAN DINNER FOR 6

I'm always in the mood for Mexican food. The diversity of this cuisine seems end-less, mixing spicy and sweet flavors with the zest of citrus and tomatoes. Within the last seven years or so, dishes from south of the border have become more authentic and are being identified more by their region than by a general Mexican label.

The Yucatan Peninsula and the area inland from Cancún has a cuisine that blends those of Mexico and the Caribbean. You'll find dishes with black beans rather than pinto beans, and ingredients such as mangoes and pickled red onions. In more affluent areas, such as Mexico City, cream sauces are more prevalent because cream is a more expensive ingredient.

However, anyone who has traveled through Tijuana can appreciate that this marvelous cuisine was built on creativity and what the land had to offer.

Tequila Tortilla Soup

Gourmet Tamales with Tequila Tomatillo Sauce

Shrimp in a Tequila Cilantro Cream Sauce

Tequila Mexican Rice

Margarita Fried Ice Cream

FOOD AND DRINK PLANNER

ONE DAY BEFORE: Prepare Margarita Fried Ice Cream.

PARTY DAY: Make Tequila Tortilla Soup, Make Gourmet Tamales and Tequila Tomatillo Sauce. Make Tequila Mexican Rice.

JUST BEFORE SERVING: Make Shrimp in a Tequila Cilantro Cream Sauce. Fry Margarita Fried Ice Cream.

COCKTAIL SUGGESTION: Gold Tequila Sunrise: Pour 1 ounce Cuervo Gold tequila over ice in a short glass. Fill three-fourths full with orange juice and add ¾ ounce grenadine on top.

WINE SUGGESTION: 1998 Duckhorn Sauvignon Blanc (see "The Wine List," page 23, for more information.)

TIMESAVER: Substitute cooked black beans for Gourmet Tamales.

TABLE SETTING AND DECORATING IDEAS: Aztec Cactus Table (see "Traditional Candlesticks with Accents," page 4)

TABLE LINEN: Use white, cream, black, turquoise, or burnt orange table linen.

Cactus Terrarium Centerpiece

Purchase a fishbowl the size of a basketball at a pet store. Also purchase two small bags of fish tank gravel, one turquoise and the other burnt orange. Purchase four different varieties of miniature cacti and black Mexican pebbles or small black stones at a plant nursery. Place an even layer of turquoise gravel about 2 inches deep over the bottom of the fishbowl. Spread an even layer of black pebbles about 2 inches deep over the gravel. Arrange cacti in bowl and place orange gravel 2 inches deep over pebbles, covering base of cacti. Before guests arrive, add a few small white flowers sprinkled with water around the cacti.

Terra-Cotta Candleholders

Stand long, tapered candles in the centers of four small (8-ounce) terra-cotta pots. Fill pots with black pebbles to secure candles in upright position. Set around the table.

Personalized Charm Husk Napkin Ties

Find charms, meant for a charm bracelet, that relate to your guests. Often, drugstores or department stores have charms in the jewelry section. Soak dried cornhusks in hot water for 5 minutes to soften; pat dry. Tear husks into ¼-inch-wide strips. Twist five husk strips together into one strip. Feed a ¼-inch strip through metal loop on charm. Tie strip around napkin ring so charm dangles. Roll napkins lengthwise and slip rings over napkins. Have guests guess where they are sitting by the charms. If charms are not available, use tiny ceramic beads with large center holes, found at most craft or sewing stores.

Tequila Tortilla Soup

ortilla soup is one of those rustic dishes whose beauty is in its final slapdash preparation. My hunch is that it originated in an American restaurant—none of my Latin friends remember this soup from their homelands. Basically, it is plain old chicken soup dressed up Mexican style with tortilla chips, cheese, cilantro, and other toppings.

1 TABLESPOON OLIVE OIL	8 CUPS (2 QUARTS) CHICKEN BROTH
1 CLOVE GARLIC, MINCED	¼ CUP CUERVO GOLD TEQUILA
½ CUP FRESH CILANTRO LEAVES	¼ CUP FRESH LIME JUICE
1 SMALL JALAPEÑO CHILI PEPPER, FINELY MINCED	¾ CUP (3 OUNCES) SHREDDED MONTEREY JACK CHEESE
1 MEDIUM BROWN ONION, CHOPPED	¾ CUP (3 OUNCES) SHREDDED CHEDDAR CHEESE
1 CELERY STALK, CUT CROSSWISE INTO ½-INCH PIECES	36 CORN TORTILLA CHIPS
2 LARGE CARROTS, PEELED AND CUT CROSSWISE INTO ¼-INCH ROUNDS	1 AVOCADO, PEELED AND CUT INTO ¼-INCH-THICK SLICES
3 SKINLESS, BONELESS CHICKEN BREAST HALVES, CUT CROSSWISE INTO ½-INCH-WIDE STRIPS	3 TABLESPOONS MINCED RED BELL PEPPER

Heat the oil and garlic in a large stockpot over medium-high heat. Add the cilantro, chili pepper, onion, celery, and carrots; cook, stirring occasionally, for 8 minutes. Add the chicken strips, chicken broth, tequila, and lime juice; bring to a boil. Reduce heat to medium-low and simmer, covered, until chicken is tender, 5 to 6 minutes. Skim fat from top of soup.

Mix the cheeses until combined. Ladle soup into individual bowls, distributing ingredients evenly. Add 6 tortilla chips to each bowl and sprinkle ¼ cup of the cheese mixture over each serving. Garnish with avocado slices and minced red pepper. Serve hot.

Gourmet Tamales with Tequila Tomatillo Sauce

MAKES ABOUT 16 TAMALES

*G*ourmet tamales are standard fare at almost every outdoor Los Angeles event, whether it's a kids' carnival or a Malibu art show. Vendors offer these savory husk-wrapped corn cakes from the open side of a catering truck or under a pop-up booth. They're a far cry from the corn dogs and cotton candy I splurged on as a child at street fairs.

30 DRIED CORN HUSKS

½ CUP SUN-DRIED TOMATOES (DRY PACK)

¾ CUP LARD

3 CUPS MASA HARINA (SEE NOTE, PAGE 166)

1½ TEASPOONS SALT

1½ CUPS CHICKEN BROTH

½ CUP MINCED GREEN ONIONS

½ CUP PUMPKIN SEEDS, SHELLED AND FINELY GROUND

1 (6-OUNCE) PACKAGE GOAT CHEESE, SOFTENED

CUERVO GOLD TEQUILA

2 (7-OUNCE) CANS SALSA VERDE OR TOMATILLO SAUCE

Soak the corn husks, covered, in boiling-hot water for 10 minutes to soften. Tear a few corn husks into 16 strips to tie around wrapped tamales. Place sun-dried tomatoes in a small bowl of boiling-hot water until softened, about 5 minutes. Pat tomatoes dry with paper towels and finely chop them.

Beat ½ cup of the lard in a large bowl until fluffy. Combine the masa harina and salt in another bowl. Beat the masa into lard alternately with broth, mixing well after each addition until combined. As mixture thickens, it may be easier to use your clean hands to mix. Melt remaining ¼ cup lard and mix into masa mixture until blended. Mix in sun-dried tomatoes, green onions, and pumpkin seeds until evenly distributed throughout.

Spoon ¼ cup of the masa mixture into center of a corn husk. Spread 1 teaspoon goat cheese over masa. Fold corn husk around mixture on all sides, as if wrapping a gift. Tie a corn husk string around tamale, securing folded husk (see note below). Repeat with remaining masa and goat cheese. (To make ahead, cover tamales and refrigerate up to 1 day.)

Fill a large stockpot with 2 inches of water. Add tequila to pot until waterline is at 3 inches. Place a metal steamer basket in pot (water level must be below steamer basket). Lay tamales flat, seam side up, in steamer basket and piled on top of each other in flat layers. Cover tamales with remaining corn husks.

Cover pot with lid and cook over medium-high heat for 1 hour, or until tamales are firm and separate easily from husks. It will be necessary to replenish the water several times throughout the steaming process. As liquid evaporates, uncover pot and pour ½ cup water mixed with 2 tablespoons tequila into pot as close to side as possible, to avoid soaking tamales.

Meanwhile, mix salsa verde and 2 tablespoons tequila in a small bowl until combined.

Remove the tamales from basket and arrange them on a large serving platter or individual plates. Serve hot with a bowl of sauce on the side.

NOTES: If corn husks are not large enough to fit around tamales, use 2 overlapping husks. If corn husk strings are not long enough to wrap around tamales, knot 2 strings together to form a long string.

Salsa verde translates as "green sauce" and is basically crushed or pureed tomatillos. They are much tarter than red tomatoes and have a slight lime flavor. Look for canned salsa verde in the Mexican or Latin food section of your local grocery store. If salsa verde is unavailable, you can serve these tamales plain or with a mild red salsa or Salsa Borracha (page 167).

Shrimp in a Tequila Cilantro Cream Sauce

MAKES 6 SERVINGS

*G*ardens of the Taxco, a Mexican restaurant in my old neighborhood, served a version of this dish in individual oval casserole dishes. Its specialty is Mexico City–style cuisine with cream sauces, an outstanding sherried banana dessert, and guava margaritas. This third-generation cantina is owned and operated by one of the kindest families I've met in Los Angeles.

WARNING: Adding liquor with a high alcohol content, such as tequila, rum, and brandy, to a hot pan may cause the hot liquid to erupt into flames. Should this occur, cover immediately with a lid.

---

1 TABLESPOON OLIVE OIL	2 CUPS HEAVY CREAM
1 CLOVE GARLIC, MINCED	1/2 TEASPOON SALT
1 CUP CUERVO GOLD TEQUILA	1/8 TEASPOON BLACK PEPPER
3 TABLESPOONS FRESH LIME JUICE	1 1/2 POUNDS MEDIUM (50-COUNT) SHRIMP, PEELED AND DEVEINED
1/2 CUP CHOPPED FRESH CILANTRO LEAVES	TEQUILA MEXICAN RICE (PAGE 158)

Heat the oil and garlic in large skillet over medium-high heat. Add the tequila and lime juice; cook until liquid reduces to one-fourth, about 5 minutes. Reduce the heat to medium-low and stir in the cilantro, cream, salt, and pepper. Cook, stirring occasionally, for 5 minutes. Add shrimp and cook until shrimp are pink, about 8 minutes.

Place shrimp and sauce in a large bowl or on individual plates. Serve hot on a bed of Tequila Mexican Rice.

Tequila Mexican Rice

Tequila sweetens this staple dish, which is prepared less spicy than usual as a complement for Shrimp with a Tequila Cilantro Cream Sauce. You can spice it up after it is prepared with a dash or two of hot pepper sauce. Rice and refried or black beans are served as a side dish with most Mexican entrées.

2 TABLESPOONS OLIVE OIL	¼ TEASPOON CHILI POWDER
1 MEDIUM ONION, COARSELY CHOPPED	½ TEASPOON SALT
3 CUPS CHICKEN BROTH	1½ CUPS LONG-GRAIN RICE
2 TABLESPOONS CUERVO GOLD TEQUILA	1 CUP CHOPPED TOMATOES

Heat the oil in a medium saucepan over medium-high heat. Add the onion and cook, stirring occasionally, until translucent, 3 to 5 minutes.

Add the broth, tequila, chili powder, and salt; bring to a boil. Stir in the rice and tomatoes, cover, and reduce heat to low. Cook for about 15 minutes, until liquid is absorbed and rice is tender.

Remove from heat and place in a large serving bowl or on individual plates. Serve hot with Shrimp in a Tequila Cilantro Cream Sauce.

Margarita Fried Ice Cream

The secret ingredient, cornflakes, is added to the cookie crumbs and cinnamon sugar, giving this traditional Mexican dessert an extra crunch! You may wish to make a few extra ice cream balls in case a ball leaks during the frying process.

½ GALLON VANILLA ICE CREAM

1 CUP CRUSHED PLAIN COOKIE CRUMBS

1 CUP CRUSHED CORNFLAKES

1 TABLESPOON SUGAR

2 EGG WHITES, BEATEN

½ TEASPOON ROSE'S LIME JUICE

½ TEASPOON TEQUILA

½ TEASPOON TRIPLE SEC

VEGETABLE OIL

HOT FUDGE OR CARAMEL SAUCE OR WHIPPED CREAM, AND MARASCHINO CHERRIES

Scoop out 6 ice cream balls. Place the balls on a wax paper-lined baking sheet and freeze for 1 hour or until firm.

Toss together the cookie crumbs, cornflakes, and sugar. Roll frozen balls in crumb mixture and return to the freezer for 30 minutes.

Meanwhile, whisk together egg whites, Rose's lime juice, tequila, and Triple Sec.

Roll balls in egg white mixture and then in remaining crumb mixture, coating completely. Check for any uncovered portions and dab with egg white and crumb mixture to cover completely. If entire ball is not coated, the ice cream will melt while frying. Line a baking sheet with fresh waxed paper. Place balls on baking sheet and freeze until firm, about 2 hours. (Balls may be prepared to this point 1 day in advance.)

Fill a medium saucepan with enough oil for ice cream balls to be completely immersed, and heat for 10 minutes over medium heat. Using a slotted spoon or wok basket, immerse one ball at a time and fry until golden brown, 30 to 60 seconds. Drain on paper towels and return each fried ball to freezer while you fry remaining balls.

Serve immediately after last ball is fried. Place in individual bowls or ice cream dishes and top with hot fudge or whipped cream and a maraschino cherry.

MEXICALI GALA FOR 20

A Mexican theme party is a real crowd pleaser. Everything about a traditional fiesta is fun, from the music to the food to the piñata. I see at least one piñata bobbing from a tree branch in a public park every weekend. Piñatas are made from papier-mâché and filled with candy and small trinkets. The piñata is connected to a string, which is swung over a branch or hook. One person pulls the string, making the piñata go up and down as another person, wearing a blindfold, tries to break the piñata open with a stick or bat. The batter gets three tries, and then the next person tries. When the piñata is broken, everyone scrambles for the goodies inside.

Although this is usually a kid's game, it can be a blast at an adult affair, especially after a few margaritas. And it is not only for Mexicali gatherings; I've played it at a baby shower with a baby rattle piñata, and at a Super Bowl party with a football piñata.

———

Margarita Chicken Skewers

Enchilada Beer Stew

Yucatan Salbute Bar

Salsa Borracha

Fruit-Filled Cookie Tacos

———

FOOD AND DRINK PLANNER

ONE DAY BEFORE: Make Salbute dough. Bake cookies for Fruit-Filled Cookie Tacos.

PARTY DAY: Make Enchilada Beer Stew. Make Salsa Borracha. Prepare Chicken Skewers. Prepare salbute bar ingredients. Cut fruit and prepare ingredients for Fruit-Filled Cookie Tacos.

JUST BEFORE SERVING: Cook Salbutes. Cook Chicken Skewers. Reheat Enchilada Beef Stew (unless made in a slow cooker).

COCKTAIL SUGGESTION: Margarita Bar: Offer a variety of fruit-flavored blender margaritas.

WINE SUGGESTIONS: 1997 Geyser Peak Sauvignon Blanc, 1997 Santa Rita Merlot (see The "Wine List," page 23 for more information.)

TIMESAVER: Substitute soft flour or corn tortillas for salbutes. Heat purchased tortillas in a microwave or according to package instructions. For traditional tacos, heat purchased hard taco shells in the oven. Keep warm in a chafing dish or tortilla warmer on buffet.

TABLE SETTING AND DECORATING IDEAS: Mexican Fiesta with multiple station setup (see "Practical Tips and Ideas for Food Stations," page 10)

TABLE LINEN: Use Summer Brights suggested in "Color Families and Complementary Shades" (see page 6).

Margarita Blender Bar

Set a table near an electric outlet for blender. Place cloth on table. Tie brightly colored cloth ribbons on handles of baskets. Fill baskets with fruit to be used in margaritas and set on one side of table. Place margarita glasses on other side of table. Set blender, liquor, and margarita fixings in center of table.

Fiesta Food Station

If using a slow cooker for the Enchilada Beer Stew, place table near an electrical outlet. Set cloth on the table. Place a few tropical plants in back center of table. Wrap brightly colored accent cloth around plant pots to mask pots. Lay a Mexican blanket or serape over front center of table. Place a sombrero on right side of table. Pour tortilla chips into rim of sombrero and place a bowl of Salsa Borracha nearby. Set platter of Margarita Chicken Skewers and Enchilada Beer Stew pot or chafing dish in front of display on table. Set a few Mexican items, such as maracas, chili strings, or brightly colored flowers, around table.

Yucatan Salbute Bar Station

This setup is best constructed with books or wooden planks set on bricks. Place table against a wall. Leave a 2-foot long space on right side of table for salbute platter or chafing dish. Over the rest of table you will create two risers that extend from the end of the table to the beginning of the 2-foot space. Start at back of table and make one long riser that is 1 foot high and about 8 inches wide from stacks of books or a wooden plank set on bricks. Make a second riser 6 inches high and the same length and width as first. Place second riser directly in front of first. There should be a enough room on table in front of second riser to set bowls of food on the table. Think of the risers as bleacher seats at a school football field.

Place cloth over table, allowing enough slack for cloth to lie flat on risers. Set a large tropical plant on back right side of table, behind where salbute platter will be. Wrap brightly colored fabric around plant pot to mask it, and allow fabric to flow onto table. Add a chili string or Mexican items such as maracas to display. Set salbute platter on table in front of display.

Place salbute toppings in similar sized bowls and set in a row on risers. I use clean terra-cotta plant saucers with plastic wrap over the bottom. Brightly colored ceramic bowls from a 99-cent store also are great. Place sour cream and similar items, which may spoil if left unrefrigerated for too long, in a bowl set in a larger bowl of ice. Dress the bar by placing kale around the bowls, or weave flowers and greenery between the bowls.

Piñata Dessert Station

Place cloth on table. Place a large piñata (found in many craft stores) in center of table. Or, hang piñata over center of table toward the back. Set about 4 risers on other side of piñata toward front of table. Set platters of food in front of piñata and on risers. Scatter wrapped hard candy, party favors, noisemakers, and other items that would be inside a piñata over table.

Margarita Chicken Skewers

*O*ne boneless breast of chicken should yield about 6 nuggets, making 2 skewers for each person. Since this marinade contains a lot of lime juice, soak the chicken for no more than an hour. Extensive exposure to acidic ingredients will cause the chicken to break down into an unappetizing, pasty texture.

2 CUPS CUERVO GOLD TEQUILA	3 TABLESPOONS SALT
2 CUPS FRESH LIME JUICE	2 TABLESPOONS BLACK PEPPER
3 CUPS OLIVE OIL	20 BONELESS, SKINLESS CHICKEN
6 CLOVES GARLIC, MINCED	BREAST HALVES, EACH CUT INTO 6
1 CUP CHOPPED FRESH CILANTRO	NUGGETS

Soak 40 bamboo skewers in water for 1 hour.

Whisk together tequila, lime juice, olive oil, garlic, cilantro, salt, and pepper. Spear 3 chicken nuggets with each bamboo skewer. Place skewers in large baking pans. Pour tequila marinade over skewers. Cover and chill for 1 hour.

Prepare your barbecue grill according to manufacturer's instructions. Remove chicken from marinade, reserving marinade. Grill chicken, basting with marinade, until thoroughly cooked, 8 to 10 minutes. Serve hot.

Enchilada Beer Stew

My buddy Joe Barret serves this stew at all his parties. His nickname for this one-pot wonder is Siesta Stew, because you just pack a pot with wall-to-wall vegetables, beer, assorted spicy ingredients, and sleep until it's time to party. Gracias, José!

4 LARGE CARROTS, PEELED

3 POUNDS RUSSET POTATOES, SCRUBBED

4 CELERY STALKS

4 GREEN ONIONS

2 MEDIUM ONIONS

1 (1-POUND) CAN STEWED TOMATOES

1 POUND FRESH BUTTON MUSHROOMS

1 (15-OUNCE) CAN WHOLE-KERNEL CORN

1 CUP CHOPPED FRESH CILANTRO

3 CANNED CHIPOTLE CHILI PEPPERS, FINELY CHOPPED

1 (12-OUNCE) BOTTLE BEER

2 (1-POUND) CANS MILD LAS PALMAS ENCHILADA SAUCE

3 DROPS HOT PEPPER SAUCE

JUICE OF 4 LIMES

2 BAY LEAVES

¼ CUP CHOPPED FRESH PARSLEY

1 TEASPOON CRUSHED RED PEPPER FLAKES

2 BEEF BOUILLON CUBES, CRUSHED

2 TEASPOONS SALT

1 TEASPOON BLACK PEPPER

Cut carrots, potatoes, celery, and green onions into large chunks. Slice onions into rings.

Place vegetables and remaining ingredients in a large stockpot and stir until combined. Cook, uncovered, over medium-low heat for 3 hours.

During the party, keep the stew over a low flame on the stove and allow guests to help themselves. Or transfer it to a slow cooker or round chafing dish and set on the buffet table.

NOTE: Joe uses 1 drop of Dave's Insanity Sauce as his hot pepper sauce when he cooks up his brew. He claims that Dave's is the hottest sauce on the planet and warns that only the brave should add it.

Yucatan Salbute Bar

I'm surprised that the fast food gurus haven't fashioned a quick and easy salbute dish. I sampled salbutes for the first time in Cancún last summer. Salbutes are ¼-inch-thick, about 3-inch-diameter, handmade corn tortillas that are served with a variety of toppings. In the little Yucatan cantina where I enjoyed them, they were topped with shredded pork, avocado, and pickled red onions.

Panuchos are a variation of the salbute. They are two tortillas filled with refried or black beans and dressed with the toppings. A salbute bar is a fun and thrifty idea for larger parties. Guests love to build their own Mexican treats from the colorful bowls of ingredients displayed on the buffet bar (see "Yucatan Salbute Bar Station," page 162).

3½ CUPS MASA HARINA (SEE NOTE, BELOW)

2 CUPS LUKEWARM WATER

¼ CUP MEXICAN BEER

½ CUP ALL-PURPOSE FLOUR

2 TEASPOONS BAKING POWDER

1 TEASPOON SALT

¼ CUP SHORTENING OR LARD

½ CUP FINELY CHOPPED GREEN ONIONS

¾ CUP (3 OUNCES) SHREDDED CHEDDAR CHEESE

VEGETABLE OIL

SUGGESTED TOPPINGS FOR SALBUTE BAR

SALSA BORRACHA (PAGE 167), TEQUILA TOMATILLO SALSA (PAGE 155), SHREDDED LETTUCE, SHREDDED CHEDDAR AND MONTEREY JACK CHEESES, CONEJO CHEESE, CHOPPED TOMATOES, CHOPPED ONIONS, SOUR CREAM, COOKED CHORIZO, SHREDDED COOKED CHICKEN OR PORK, COOKED SHRIMP OR CRAB, BLACK BEANS MIXED WITH CORN, REFRIED BEANS, SLICED OLIVES

Combine the masa harina, water, and beer until blended. Sift together the flour, baking powder, and salt; stir into masa mixture. Add the shortening or lard and mix until combined. Moisten hands and knead in the green onions and cheese until distributed throughout mixture. (Unshaped dough can be stored in a plastic bag in the refrigerator up to 2 days.)

Using 1 tablespoon dough, form ¼-inch-thick disks, about 3 inches across. Cover the disks with a damp towel, wrap in plastic wrap, and refrigerate until ready to use. (Uncooked salbutes may be prepared up to 4 hours before serving.)

Heat 2 tablespoons oil in a large skillet over medium-high heat. Cook about 6 salbutes at a time until golden brown, 2 to 3 minutes on each side. Remove the salbutes from skillet and place on paper towels to absorb excess oil. Repeat with remaining salbutes, adding 2 tablespoons of oil to skillet for every batch. (Cooked salbutes can be stored, tightly wrapped, in the refrigerator for up to 2 days.)

Place the salbutes in a chafing dish set on the buffet next to the bowls of toppings. Or keep fried salbutes warm in the oven and place on a large platter just before serving.

NOTE Masa harina is a powdered corn mix distributed by the Quaker Oats Company. It can be found near the flour in the baking section of your grocery store.

Salsa Borracha

*O*n a recent visit to Rosarita Beach on the Baja Peninsula, I discovered this excellent salsa. Happily, its star ingredient is beer. In my broken Spanish, I asked our waiter, Roberto, for the ingredients. He went into game show mode, acting out food and mixing, and drawing a blender on the paper tablecloth. "And the meaning of borracha?" I asked. He chuckled and wrote "hangover" on our meal ticket. A later confirmation was humorously defined as "drunken or the guy with his head on the table the next morning."

---

1 MEDIUM DRIED CHIPOTLE OR ANCHO CHILI

4 CUPS DICED TOMATOES

1 CUP DICED BROWN ONION

1 BEEF BOULLION CUBE, MASHED

¼ CUP UGO MAGI OR OYSTER SAUCE (SEE NOTE, BELOW)

½ CUP BEER

½ CUP CHOPPED FRESH CILANTRO

1 TEASPOON SALT

Remove stem and seeds from chili and place in a small saucepan of water. Bring water to a boil for 5 minutes to soften chile. Cool until comfortable to touch and mince into tiny bits.

Cut tomatoes in half and remove seeds before dicing. Place chile, tomatoes, and remaining ingredients in a bowl and stir to combine. Cover salsa and let stand for 1 hour at room temperature before serving, to allow flavors to blend. (To make ahead, store in an airtight container in the refrigerator for up to 1 day.)

NOTE: Ugo Magi is a condiment found in Mexico, but I suspect it originated in the Far East, because it tastes exactly like oyster sauce. Oyster sauce can be found near the soy sauce in the Asian section of most grocery stores.

Fruit-Filled Cookie Tacos

MAKES 20 COOKIE TACOS

For a festive dessert presentation, set up a fruit taco bar where guests can fill Kahlua cookie tacos with a variety of fruits and whipped cream. Tuiles are wafer-thin cookies that are formed into shapes such as cookie cups or taco shells. They take only moments to bake, and you can chart their progress by the minute. The first minute, the cookies will spread a bit. The second minute, the tops become a little cakey. The third minute, the tops begin to bubble. At five or six minutes, the edges brown, and if you don't pull that baking sheet out of the oven, they're goners. For a guest count of 20, make at least 3 batches of cookies.

¼ CUP UNSALTED BUTTER, ROOM TEMPERATURE	COOKIE TACO FILLINGS
⅓ CUP SUGAR	SLICED BANANAS
2 EGG WHITES	SLICED STRAWBERRIES
1 TABLESPOON KAHLUA	SEMISWEET CHOCOLATE CHIPS
⅓ CUP ALL-PURPOSE FLOUR	SWEETENED WHIPPED CREAM OR PREPARED WHIPPED TOPPING
1 TABLESPOON UNSWEETENED COCOA POWDER	

Preheat oven to 400F (205C). Spray baking sheets with a nonstick cooking spray. Place the butter and sugar into a mixing bowl and beat until creamy. Add the egg whites and beat for 10 seconds. Add the Kahlua and beat well. Sift together flour and cocoa powder, then beat into mixture until blended.

Place level teaspoons of dough 3 inches apart on prepared baking sheet. Limit each baking sheet to 6 cookies, they will spread during baking process. Press them into very thin 2-inch circles.

Bake for 5 to 6 minutes, keeping a very watchful eye. When the cookies have a brown ring around the edges, remove from heat. Immediately slide cookies off baking sheet, using a thin spatula, and drape them over a suspended ½-inch-diameter dowel or rod (see Notes below). Hot cookies will drape over the dowel and harden into a taco shell shape. Cool thoroughly. (Store unfilled cookies in an airtight container in the refrigerator for up to 4 days.)

Place fresh fruits and toppings in small bowls on the buffet. Place cookies on a platter and serve cool.

NOTES: These cookies are challenging to make. If they do not harden within 1 to 2 minutes after removal from the oven, they are probably underdone. Put them back on the baking sheet and bake for another minute or so.

You will need to fashion your own device for cooling these cookies so they form a taco shell shape. I've found that the handle of a wooden spoon works well but will hold only 3 cookies. Hardware stores sell ½-inch-diameter dowels, which they will usually cut to any length you wish. Lay dowels 2 inches apart across a large pot or place each end on a soup can. Secure ends with masking tape so dowels won't roll. These cookies will harden very quickly once out of the oven, so prepare your cooling rack in advance.

Eye-Openers

AN ELEGANT CHAMPAGNE BRUNCH FOR 12

Artichoke, Leek, and Red Pepper Tart

Fresh Fruit Tossed with Champagne Citrus Sauce

Sweet Potato Waffles with Rum Maple Syrup

Caramel and Coffee Liqueur Ice Cream Crepes

BREAKFAST BASKET WITH A TWIST FOR 20

Cappuccino Mousse Muffins

Amaretto-Almond Croissants

Chocolate-Drizzled Apricot Squares

Cordial Pecan Nut Cake

AN ELEGANT CHAMPAGNE BRUNCH FOR 12

Brunch always feels like a special occasion. Perhaps it's the free-flowing Champagne or the spontaneity of eating an off-hour meal. Brunch on the restaurant circuit has gone a bit crazy over the years with chefs carving roast beef, 50-ingredient omelet bars, and yards of seafood on ice. I prefer the relaxed elegance of a few extravagant dishes as opposed to the pie-eating contest mentality found in many restaurants.

Guests never tire of quiche or its fashionable counterpart, the Artichoke, Leek, and Red Pepper Tart. I always serve an egg dish. Omelets are nice, but they mean more time in the kitchen, away from your guests. Fresh fruit is another must on a brunch table, along with some kind of starch. And for a sweet Sunday reward after a busy workweek, serve Caramel and Coffee Liqueur Ice Cream Crepes.

Artichoke, Leek, and Red Pepper Tart

Fresh Fruit Tossed with Champagne Citrus Sauce

Sweet Potato Waffles with Rum Maple Syrup

Caramel and Coffee Liqueur Ice Cream Crepes

FOOD AND DRINK PLANNER

ONE DAY BEFORE: Make Artichoke, Leek, and Red Pepper Tart. Make crepes. Make Rum Maple Syrup. Make caramel for Caramel and Coffee Liqueur Ice Cream Crepes.

PARTY DAY: Prepare orange peel for Mimosa Ultras (see below). Cut fruit and make Champagne Citrus Sauce.

JUST BEFORE SERVING: Reheat tart. Make Sweet Potato Waffles. Warm Rum Maple Syrup. Warm caramel for Caramel and Coffee Liqueur Ice Cream Crepes. Assemble Caramel and Coffee Liqueur Ice Cream Crepes.

COCKTAIL SUGGESTION: Mimosa Ultras: Combine ½ Champagne and ½ orange juice in a Mimosa Ultra glass (see below). Float Grand Marnier on top.

WINE SUGGESTION: 1988 Veuve Clicquot Champagne Brut Reserve, (see "The Wine List," page 23, for more information)

TIMESAVERS: Substitute bakery muffins for Sweet Potato Waffles. Substitute ice cream sundaes for Caramel and Coffee Liqueur Ice Cream Crepes.

TABLE SETTING AND DECORATING IDEAS: A Scented Table with Pastel Rose Topiaries (see below)

TABLE LINEN: Use Spring Pastels suggested in "Color Families and Complementary Shades" (see page 6).

Pastel Rose Topiary

Purchase a small (about 6 inches high and 6 inches in diameter) cement or ceramic planter without a drain hole from a nursery. Planter should be off-white and can be either circular or square with an embossed floral or Grecian pattern on outer sides. Place a block of green floral foam in planter and add water to foam. Gather stems of one dozen pastel, long-stem roses into a tight bunch. Insert stems into center of foam. Tightly wrap a French or sheer cloth ribbon around the stems several times just under the flower blooms, until 4 inches of stem are covered in ribbon. Tie a large bow to secure ribbon. Cover top of foam in pot with green moss and place topiary in center of table. Optional: place a few roses in moss at base of rose stems.

Gossamer Potpourri Place Mats

Purchase enough chiffon and taffeta to make the place mats. Any see-through fabric (I prefer chiffon) will work. I chose taffeta because of its grain design, but satin or cotton will work. For 12 place mats, you will need about 2 yards of each fabric, which is usually 45 inches wide. Fabric colors should match or complement each other as well as rose topiary.

Cut 12 (17 × 13-inch) rectangles from each fabric. Pin 2 rectangles, one of each fabric, together with right fabric sides facing each other. Using a sewing machine, stitch a seam, ¼ inch in from edge, around rectangle. At one end, leave 2 inches of seam unstitched. Gently pull fabric right side out through that opening. Iron seams flat with a cool iron on taffeta side (chiffon side may melt). Put a couple of tablespoons of mild-scented rose potpourri into each place mat through the 2-inch opening. Stitch opening closed. Set place mats, chiffon side up, with potpourri visible through fabric, at each place.

Floating Petal Scented Candles

Fill a small glass bowl with 1 inch of water. Place a small lemon leaf or rose leaf in bottom of bowl and set a votive candle in center to weigh down leaf. Float rose petals in the bowl around the candle. Make 4 candle bowls. Add a drop of rose-scented oil or rose water, sometimes found in the Asian or Indonesian section of grocery store, to water. Place candle bowls around table.

Mimosa Ultra Glasses

Slice ½ inch off the top and bottom ends of 12 oranges. Scoop or cut out pulp, leaving whole peel intact forming cylinders that are open at both ends. Place each orange peel in a wineglass or any glass just large enough to hold the whole peel snugly; peel should be about ½ inch below rim of the glass. Pour Champagne and orange juice inside peel cylinder and float Grand Marnier on top.

Artichoke, Leek, and Red Pepper Tart

*A*ny home chef who has dabbled in gourmet cuisine knows the star of the onion family, the leek. Many were introduced to the leek by the legendary chef Julia Child. However, leeks have been around for centuries; history records that they were served at the first Thanksgiving in 1621.

Although this recipe yields 12 servings, you may wish to make an extra tart; it is always a popular item for brunch. Any leftovers can be refrigerated and served for a lunch or light supper.

FILLING

1 TABLESPOON VEGETABLE OIL

1 TABLESPOON BUTTER

1 CLOVE GARLIC, MINCED

1 LARGE LEEK, WASHED, CUT CROSSWISE INTO THIN SLICES

1 RED BELL PEPPER, CUT INTO THIN SLIVERS

¼ CUP DRY VERMOUTH

1 (8½-OUNCE) CAN ARTICHOKE HEARTS, DRAINED AND CUT IN HALF LENGTHWISE

¼ CUP FINELY CHOPPED FRESH ITALIAN PARSLEY

½ CUP (1½ OUNCES) FRESHLY GRATED PARMESAN CHEESE

1 CUP (4 OUNCES) GRUYÈRE CHEESE

3 EGGS

¾ CUP HALF-AND-HALF

1 TABLESPOON DIJON MUSTARD

½ TEASPOON SALT

⅛ TEASPOON WHITE PEPPER

CRUST

2 CUPS ALL-PURPOSE FLOUR

¼ TEASPOON SALT

½ CUP BUTTER, CHILLED, CUT INTO TABLESPOONS

¼ CUP VEGETABLE SHORTENING

2 TO 3 TABLESPOONS COLD WATER

To make the crust: Combine the flour, salt, butter, and shortening in a food processor and process until combined. With processor running, slowly add cold water through feed tube until dough just holds together. Form dough into a thick disk, cover in plastic, and chill for 1 hour.

To make the filling: Heat the oil and butter in a large skillet over medium-high heat. Add the garlic and cook for 1 minute. Add the leek, bell pepper, and vermouth; cook until tender, about 10 minutes. Remove from heat; stir in artichokes and parsley until combined.

Preheat oven to 425F (220C). Roll out the pastry ¼ inch thick on a heavily floured surface. Line a 10-inch tart tin with removable bottom with pastry and trim edges. Pierce crust bottom several times with a fork. Bake crust for 10 minutes. Remove crust from oven and reduce oven temperature to 375F (190C).

Scatter half of each cheese over the crust. Arrange the vegetables in an even layer over cheese. Whisk together the eggs, half-and-half, mustard, salt, and pepper until blended. Pour mixture over vegetables. Top with remaining cheese. Bake for 40 to 45 minutes or until puffed. Remove from oven and cool for 5 minutes to allow tart to set. (To make ahead, cool and store, covered in plastic wrap, in the refrigerator for up to 2 days. Heat in a 375F [190C] oven for 15 to 20 minutes before serving.)

Cut into wedges and serve warm.

TIP: Here's an easy way to line a tart tin or pie plate to avoid the pastry's tearing. Roll out pastry to desired thickness. Then, starting at end of pastry nearest you, roll pastry around a rolling pin. Hold rolling pin over edge of pie plate and unroll pastry.

Fresh Fruit Tossed with Champagne Citrus Sauce

MAKES 12 SERVINGS

Elegant and light, this Champagne sauce is lovely on fruit at a summertime brunch. You may use 6 cups of any fruit medley you wish, which will yield 12 servings. Be sure to include a citrus fruit, such as oranges, with creamier fruits like papaya, and always add seasonal berries to the mix.

2 CUPS CHAMPAGNE	2 ORANGES, CUT INTO SEGMENTS
1 1/2 CUPS FRESH ORANGE JUICE	2 BANANAS, SLICED CROSSWISE
1/4 CUP GRAND MARNIER	1 CUP DICED FRESH PINEAPPLE
2 TABLESPOONS ORANGE ZEST	1 CUP CHOPPED APPLES
3 TABLESPOONS UNSALTED BUTTER	1 CUP FRESH SEASONAL BERRIES
1 CUP DICED SEEDLESS WATERMELON	

Heat the Champagne, orange juice, Grand Marnier, and zest in a medium saucepan over medium-high heat. Bring to a boil and cook until liquid reduces to half, 5 to 8 minutes. Remove from heat and whisk in butter 1 tablespoon at a time. Cool to room temperature.

Place fruit in a large bowl and pour Champagne Citrus Sauce over fruit. Toss lightly to coat and serve cool.

Sweet Potato Waffles with Rum Maple Syrup

MAKES 12 TO 15 SERVINGS

A unique waffle dish, such as the popular Belgian kind or this Southern version, always leaves your guests feeling as if their palates have been pampered. The special crafting of Vermont maple syrup is best left to the Vermonters. I've blended their secret brew with a little rum, which makes an excellent condiment for this breakfast treat.

1½ CUPS PEELED, DICED SWEET POTATOES

3 EGGS, LIGHTLY BEATEN

1½ CUPS BUTTERMILK

½ CUP COLD WATER

2 TABLESPOONS GOLDSCHLAGER CINNAMON SCHNAPPS

¼ CUP UNSALTED BUTTER, MELTED

3 CUPS ALL-PURPOSE FLOUR

2 TABLESPOONS BAKING POWDER

½ CUP SUGAR

1 CUP CHOPPED WALNUTS

RUM MAPLE SYRUP

2 CUPS VERMONT MAPLE SYRUP

3 TABLESPOONS DARK RUM

Place the potatoes in a medium pot and cover with water. Bring to a boil over medium-high heat and cook until tender, about 10 minutes. Drain the potatoes and mash until smooth.

Measure 1 cup of potatoes and place in a large bowl. Add the eggs, buttermilk, water, schnapps, and butter; beat until blended. Sift together flour, baking powder, and sugar; stir into potato mixture until combined.

Prepare and heat waffle iron according to manufacturer's instructions. Pour about ½ cup of batter over waffle iron surface and cook about 5 minutes or until crisp.

Meanwhile, to make the Rum Maple Syrup: Combine maple syrup and rum in a small saucepan. Heat on low heat, stirring occasionally, for 5 minutes, until rum is incorporated into syrup. Remove from heat and cool slightly. Pour into a serving vessel with a pour spout, such as a gravy boat.

Place walnuts in a small bowl. Arrange waffles on a large serving platter and serve hot with warm syrup and walnuts. Or place each waffle on an individual plate and top with syrup and walnuts

VARIATION

Banana Waffles

Substitute 1 cup uncooked, mashed bananas for 1 cup sweet potatoes.

Caramel Apple Ice Cream Crepes

MAKES 12 CREPES

The best crepes I've ever enjoyed were on my honeymoon in Mont Saint Michel, France. A small granite hilltop, this quaint islet has only one street, which spirals around the city up to a Gothic abbey. It is a magical place with delicious crepes.

2 EGGS	2 GOLDEN DELICIOUS APPLES, PEELED AND CUT INTO THIN SLIVERS
1 CUP MILK	
⅔ CUP ALL-PURPOSE FLOUR	1 GALLON VANILLA ICE CREAM
2 TABLESPOONS SUGAR	
1 TEASPOON GROUND CINNAMON	CARAMEL APPLE SAUCE
2 TABLESPOONS LAIRD'S APPLEJACK	2 CUPS SUGAR
¼ CUP WATER	2 CUPS HEAVY CREAM
3 TABLESPOONS BUTTER	2 TABLESPOONS LAIRD'S APPLEJACK

Beat the eggs and milk in a large bowl until frothy. Sift together the flour, sugar, and cinnamon; beat into egg mixture. Stir in applejack and water. Let batter rest for 15 minutes.

Lightly spray an 8-inch crepe pan or large skillet with nonstick cooking spray and heat over medium heat. Spoon 3 tablespoons batter into pan. Tilt pan to spread batter into a thin layer over entire surface. Cook until light brown on bottom, 1 to 2 minutes. Gently flip crepe with a thin spatula and cook until light brown on other side, about 30 seconds. Turn out onto a paper towel. Lightly spray pan with nonstick cooking spray for each crepe. Reduce heat to medium-low if crepes are browning too quickly. Roll each crepe, wrap it in plastic wrap, and refrigerate for 2 hours or up to 2 days.

Melt the butter in a large skillet over medium heat. Add the apples and cook, stirring occasionally, until apples soften, about 8 minutes. Cover and refrigerate until ready to use or up to 8 hours.

To make the Caramel Apple Sauce: Place the sugar in a medium saucepan and cook, stirring occasionally, over low heat until it dissolves. Increase heat to medium and add the cream. Cook, stirring constantly, until mixture is smooth, about 10 minutes. Reduce heat to low and simmer 5 minutes. Test caramel by adding a small drop to cold water; if caramel sinks to bottom, it is ready. If caramel does not sink, continue to cook, testing every 2 minutes, until ready. Remove from heat and stir in applejack. Cool slightly. Store, covered, in the refrigerator for up to 2 days.

To serve: Bring crepes and apples to room temperature. Warm caramel in a double boiler or small saucepan set over a simmering pot of water until it softens. Place a scoop of vanilla ice cream and some apple slivers in center of each crepe. Roll crepes around ice cream and place, seam side down, on serving plates. Spoon hot sauce on top of each crepe and serve.

BREAKFAST BASKET WITH A TWIST FOR 20

Not being a huge early morning eater, the Continental breakfast is my ideal way to start the day. European in origin, the Continental breakfast consist of a basket of baked goods, juice, and a pot of coffee, tea, or hot chocolate. Many hosts put so much focus on choosing the tastiest pastries that they lose sight of the other key element of this meal, the beverage.

Fortunately, outstanding coffee is available in most grocery stores, if not on every corner, and the choice of teas these days is staggering. Gourmet coffee can be pricey, but don't skimp on the beverage when you've prepared a fabulous array of edibles. There is a reason why all these java joints are so popular. People love their coffee, and a bad cup can ruin one's day along with one's breakfast. A superb cup of coffee is like liquid gold.

Cappuccino Mousse Muffins

Amaretto-Almond Croissants

Chocolate-Drizzled Apricot Squares

Cordial Pecan Nut Cake

FOOD AND DRINK PLANNER

ONE DAY BEFORE: Make Cappuccino Mousse Muffins. Make Chocolate-Drizzled Apricot Squares. Make Cordial Pecan Nut Cake.

PARTY DAY: Make Amaretto-Almond Croissants.

COCKTAIL SUGGESTION: Hot coffee drinks (see below)

TIMESAVER: Substitute Pillsbury's cinnamon rolls for any item; add 1 teaspoon Baileys Original Irish Cream to prepared icing in package.

Hot Coffee Drink Bar and Spiked Baked Goods Station

Set a couple of risers on one side of table. Place cloth over risers and table. Set baskets of baked goods on and around risers. Arrange coffee cups on other side of table. Place coffee urn or serving vessel next to cups toward center of table. Set bottles of liqueur and other ingredients in center of table, between urn and baked goods. Set shot glasses near liqueurs.

Create a decorative placard listing the easy recipes below for coffee drinks and stand it upright next to bottles on table. Instruct guests to place the ingredients in a coffee cup and then fill the cup with coffee. Place small bowls of coffee toppings, such as whipped cream, chocolate shavings, cocoa, cinnamon, sprinkles, and maraschino cherries, in front of liqueurs on table.

Hot Coffee Drinks

Baileys and Coffee: Add 1 ounce Baileys Original Irish Cream to 1 cup of coffee.

Café Royale: Add 1 sugar cube, 1 ounce brandy, and a whipped cream topping to 1 cup of coffee.

Irish Coffee: Add 1 sugar cube, 1 ounce Irish whiskey, and a whipped cream topping to 1 cup of coffee.

Italian Coffee: Add 1 ounce Amaretto di Saronno to 1 cup of coffee.

Jamaican Coffee: Add 1 ounce rum to 1 cup of coffee.

Mexican Coffee: Add 1 ounce Kahlua and ½ ounce tequila to 1 cup of coffee.

Cappuccino Mousse Muffins

MAKES 12 MUFFINS

*A*ny bakery item with cappuccino in its name is a big seller. Who can resist the sensory image of espresso with a creamy foam topping and a sprinkling of cocoa or cinnamon? All these ingredients, plus a splash of liqueur, make these muffin irresistible.

Make two batches for 20 guests.

2 TEASPOONS ESPRESSO POWDER	2 EGGS
2 TABLESPOONS KAHLUA	2 CUPS ALL-PURPOSE FLOUR
½ CUP (1 STICK) UNSALTED BUTTER, SOFTENED	1 TABLESPOON BAKING POWDER
	1 CUP HALF-AND-HALF
¾ CUP PACKED LIGHT BROWN SUGAR	¾ CUP SEMISWEET CHOCOLATE CHIPS

Preheat oven to 350F (175C). Line a 12-cup muffin pan with foil baking cups. Spray cups with nonstick cooking spray. Dissolve the espresso powder in Kahlua in a small bowl.

Beat the butter and sugar in a large bowl until fluffy. Beat in the eggs and Kahlua-espresso mixture until combined. Sift together the flour and baking powder. Beat the dry ingredients into mixture alternately with half-and-half until just combined. Fold in the chocolate chips. Pour the mixture into prepared muffin cups.

Bake for 20 minutes or until a knife inserted in the centers comes out clean. Cool in pan for 10 minutes. Serve warm or at room temperature. Store cooled muffins in an airtight container at room temperature up to 2 days.

Amaretto-Almond Croissants

*A*maretto-laced almond paste fills these light, flaky delights. The recipe for these croissants is always requested when they are served, and guests are thrilled to find out that they are made with a commercially prepared dough.

1½ CUPS PACKED (ABOUT 15 OUNCES) ALMOND PASTE	3 (8-OUNCE) CANS PILLSBURY'S CRESCENT DINNER ROLLS
9 TABLESPOONS AMARETTO DI SARONNO	ABOUT 1 CUP POWDERED SUGAR

Preheat oven to 400F (205C). Lightly spray 2 large baking sheets with nonstick cooking spray. With a fork, break up the almond paste in a medium bowl. Add the amaretto; and mix until smooth and thoroughly combined.

Separate crescent rolls and roll each one out on a flat surface into a triangle. Spoon 1 tablespoon almond paste in center of wide end of each triangle. Roll up triangle, starting at wide end to triangle tip, and form into a crescent. Pinch edges to seal. Repeat with remaining rolls and almond paste. Place crescents, with rolled tip facing down, on prepared baking sheet.

Bake for 10 to 12 minutes or until brown. Remove crescents from oven and dust with powdered sugar. Serve warm. Store any leftovers in an airtight container at room temperature up to 2 days.

Chocolate-Drizzled Apricot Squares

MAKES 16 COOKIES

A moist dough is the base for this fruity breakfast square. Using this dough as a crust, I can serve a variety of desserts at my catered events. This recipe is usually included in morning menus, and a raspberry-glazed bar cookie version is always on my dinner menus. Make two batches for 20 guests.

ALMOND CRUST	APRICOT GLAZE
1 CUP (2 STICKS) UNSALTED BUTTER, SOFTENED	½ CUP APRICOT JAM
	2 TABLESPOONS APRICOT BRANDY
⅓ CUP PACKED (ABOUT 3½ OUNCES) ALMOND PASTE	CHOCOLATE DRIZZLE
½ CUP POWDERED SUGAR	¼ CUP SEMISWEET CHOCOLATE CHIPS
2 CUPS ALL-PURPOSE FLOUR	½ TABLESPOON UNSALTED BUTTER
	1 TABLESPOON APRICOT BRANDY

Preheat oven to 350F (175C). Lightly spray an 8-inch-square baking pan with non-stick cooking spray.

To make the crust: Beat the butter and almond paste in a medium bowl until creamy. Beat in the sugar until smooth. Add the flour and beat until combined. Pat dough in an even layer on bottom of prepared pan. Bake for 15 minutes.

Meanwhile, make the Apricot Glaze. Heat apricot jam and brandy in top of a double boiler, stirring occasionally, until jam melts. Stir until blended. Remove from heat.

Remove cookie from oven and immediately pour glaze in an even layer over top surface. Cool to room temperature or until glaze sets.

To make the Chocolate Drizzle: Place chocolate, butter, and brandy in top of a double boiler. Stir constantly until chocolate and butter are melted, and mixture is smooth and combined. Dip a knife tip in the melted chocolate and drizzle chocolate over surface of apricot glaze. Allow chocolate to set.

Cut into 2-inch squares. Store in an airtight container in the refrigerator up to 2 days.

Cordial Pecan Nut Cake

MAKES 15 TO 20 SERVINGS

*M*oister than most coffeecakes, this pecan-packed treat is laced with Frangelico. This decadent morning starter is the ultimate in breakfast pleasure.

---

1 ½ CUPS CHOPPED PECANS

1 CUP (2 STICKS) UNSALTED BUTTER, MELTED AND COOLED

1 CUP GRANULATED SUGAR

1 CUP PACKED LIGHT BROWN SUGAR

5 EGGS

¼ CUP FRANGELICO

½ CUP MILK

½ CUP SOUR CREAM

¾ CUPS ALL-PURPOSE FLOUR

½ TEASPOON SALT

½ TEASPOON BAKING SODA

1 TABLESPOON BAKING POWDER

2 TEASPOONS GROUND CINNAMON

CORDIAL SOUR CREAM TOPPING

1 CUP FRANGELICO

¼ CUP SOUR CREAM

¼ CUP HEAVY CREAM

Preheat oven to 350F (175C). Heavily butter a 12-cup Bundt pan. Sprinkle ½ cup of the pecans on bottom and up sides of pan.

Beat the butter and sugars in a large bowl until combined. Add the eggs, Frangelico, milk, and sour cream; beat until smooth. Sift together dry ingredients and beat into mixture until blended. Stir in remaining pecans until distributed throughout batter. Pour into prepared pan.

Bake for 45 to 50 minutes or until knife inserted in center of cake comes out clean. Cool in pan for 5 minutes and invert cake onto a wire rack. Cool completely.

Meanwhile, to make the Cordial Sour Cream Topping: Bring the Frangelico to a boil in a small saucepan over medium-high heat. Cook until mixture foams and quickly reduces by half into a thick syrup, about 3 minutes. Remove from heat and cool 10 minutes. Combine sour cream and heavy cream in a medium bowl. Stir in liqueur syrup until blended.

Spoon topping over cooled cake. Store, covered, in the refrigerator for up to 1 week. To serve, slice cake and arrange on a serving plate.

Hazelnut Liqueur Glaze

The Cordial Sour Cream Topping on this cake requires that it be refrigerated. For a tasty glaze that does not require refrigeration, mix together 1 cup powdered sugar and 4 teaspoons Frangelico in a small bowl until blended. Drizzle half of the glaze over top of the cooled cake. Allow the glaze to set for 10 minutes and drizzle remaining glaze over cake. Store, covered, at room temperature for up to 1 week.

Eastern Exotic Cuisine

COCONUT RUM AND INDO-ECLECTIC CUISINE FOR 6

Coconut Rum and Lime Shrimp Soup

Coconut Rum Chicken Curry

Coconut Rum Basmati Rice with Roasted Cashews

Coconut Rum Pudding on a Banana Leaf

CHINESE POTABLES FOR 8

Orange Liqueur Pork Dumplings

Oyster Bourbon Beef Strips

Shrimp and Chinese Beer Fried Rice

White Chocolate-Dipped Lemon Fortune Cookies

COCONUT RUM AND INDO-ECLECTIC CUISINE FOR 6

*T*his menu is a blend of Malaysian, Thai, and Indian cuisines. An ingredient in many of these ethnic recipes is coconut milk. Malibu rum, a sweet and powerful coconut liqueur, is the perfect sophisticated accent for this food.

I was introduced to Malay cooking in Australia. One terrific dish was a simple chili-crusted shrimp reminiscent of a Chinese kung pao preparation without the sauce. Though Malay and Indian restaurants are few in Los Angeles, there seems to be a Thai cafe in every strip mall. There is even a Thai Elvis who performs in the food court of the Thai Town shopping plaza. He impersonates The King exactly, and then shyly speaks with a Thai accent between songs. Thai cuisine is very creative, full of zesty lime, salty peanuts, and cilantro in salads, soups, and entrées. Curry is a popular spice for Indian food, and coconut milk is used mostly in southern India.

Coconut Rum and Lime Shrimp Soup

Coconut Rum Chicken Curry

Coconut Rum Basmati Rice with Roasted Cashews

Coconut Rum Pudding on a Banana Leaf

FOOD AND DRINK PLANNER

ONE DAY BEFORE: Make Coconut Rum Pudding on a Banana Leaf. Make Coconut Rum and Lime Shrimp Soup.

PARTY DAY: Make Coconut Rum Chicken Curry. Make Coconut Rum Basmati Rice with Roasted Cashews.

COCKTAIL SUGGESTION: Malibu Hawaiians: Pour 1 ounce Malibu rum over ice in a tall glass. Fill glass with pineapple juice and float peach schnapps on top.

WINE SUGGESTION: 1998 Trefethen Vineyards Dry Riesling (see "The Wine List," page 23 for more information).

TIMESAVERS: Substitute steamed white rice for Coconut Rum Basmati Rice with Roasted Cashews. Substitute fresh pineapple chunks laced with Malibu rum for Coconut Rum Pudding on a Banana Leaf.

TABLE SETTING AND DECORATING IDEAS: Vibrant Orchid and Coconut Table

TABLE LINEN: Use Summer Brights suggested in "Color Families and Complementary Shades" (see page 6).

Floating Orchid Flower Bowl

Place 1 inch of clean black pebbles in the bottom of a 12-inch-diameter glass bubble bowl. Fill bowl halfway with water and float Dendrobium orchid blossoms in water. Place bowl in center of table and circle the bowl base with greenery and an orchid stem.

Tile Chopstick Holder

Place a 6-inch-square glazed tile in center of each guest's place at table and rest chopsticks on tile. Tile color should be compatible with cloth.

Paper Umbrella and Orchid Place Setting

Place a small paper umbrella, used for cocktail garnish, and a 4-inch Dendrobium orchid stem around each chopstick tile.

Coconut Candles

Remove milk from 2 or 3 coconuts. Saw coconuts in half and remove white meat. Place a votive candle in each half and arrange them around table. Make sure candle is securely upright and coconut shell is steady. Place a few lemon leaves and orchid blossoms sprinkled with water around coconuts on table. The coconut halves can be stored and reused.

Coconut Rum and Lime Shrimp Soup

This hot and sour soup is typical of Thai cuisine. Lemongrass is a wonderful ingredient used in many Asian recipes. It is a pale green stalk, resembling a reed, that is very tough. My Cambodian friend pulverizes lemongrass in a mortar and pestle for her recipes, but I prefer to use the fragrant green stalks to decorate this soup.

---

1 POUND MEDIUM (50-COUNT) SHRIMP, SHELLED AND DEVEINED, SHELLS RESERVED

10 CUPS WATER

2 TABLESPOONS OLIVE OIL

1 LARGE RED ONION, CUT INTO SLIVERS

2 CLOVES GARLIC, MINCED

1 RED BELL PEPPER, CUT IN 1-INCH SLIVERS

¼ CUP MALIBU RUM

1 LEMONGRASS STALK, CUT INTO 3-INCH PIECES

½ CUP FRESH LIME JUICE

1 SMALL HOT RED CHILE PEPPER

½ CUP COARSELY CHOPPED FRESH CILANTRO LEAVES

1 TABLESPOON SALT

6 CILANTRO SPRIGS

6 LIME SLICES

12 THIN PAPAYA SLICES

Bring the shrimp shells and water to a boil in a large stockpot over medium heat. Reduce heat to low and simmer for 20 minutes. Strain liquid into a large bowl and set aside.

Heat the oil in a large stockpot over medium-high heat. Add the onion, garlic, and bell pepper; cook, stirring occasionally, until vegetables are tender, about 10 minutes. Add the rum and cook for 1 minute. Add the reserved liquid from shells, lemongrass, lime juice, chile, chopped cilantro, and salt; bring to a boil. Reduce heat to medium-low and cook for 10 minutes more. Add shrimp and cook until shrimp is pink, about 2 minutes. Remove from heat. (To make ahead, cool and store, covered, in the refrigerator up to 2 days. Reheat before serving.)

Pour soup into individual bowls, making sure that shrimp are evenly distributed. Garnish each bowl with a cilantro sprig, a lime slice, and 2 papaya slices. Serve hot.

Coconut Rum Chicken Curry

MAKES 6 TO 8 SERVINGS

*A*t my wedding reception, coconut chicken curry was served in a huge brass cauldron. Our party was on the Santa Monica pier inside a funky wood and glass structure housing the carousel featured in the movie The Sting. A sun parlor was on every corner of the building, each filled with a glorious food station. The golden cauldron inside the solarium was the most dazzling display I've ever seen.

2 TABLESPOONS BUTTER

1 TABLESPOON PEANUT OIL

4 CLOVES GARLIC, MINCED

1 LARGE BROWN ONION, CUT INTO SLIVERS

1 RED BELL PEPPER, CUT INTO 1-INCH CHUNKS

1 TABLESPOON MINCED FRESH GINGER

3 TABLESPOONS YELLOW CURRY POWDER

1/4 CUP MALIBU RUM

2 1/2 CUPS CANNED COCONUT MILK

6 BONELESS, SKINLESS CHICKEN BREAST HALVES, CUT INTO NUGGETS

1 POUND POTATOES, PEELED AND CUT INTO 1-INCH CUBES

1 MILD GREEN CHILE PEPPER

1 HOT RED CHILE PEPPER

1/2 CUP CHOPPED FRESH CILANTRO

1 TEASPOON SUGAR

1 TEASPOON SALT

CONDIMENTS

1/2 CUP FINELY CHOPPED PEANUTS

1/2 CUP RAISINS

1/2 CUP FLAKED COCONUT

1 CUP MANGO OR PEACH CHUTNEY

Heat the butter and oil in a stockpot over medium-high heat. Add the garlic, onion, bell pepper, and ginger; cook, stirring occasionally, until onion is tender, about 10 minutes. Stir in the curry powder and cook for 1 minute. Add the rum, coconut milk, chicken, potatoes, whole chiles, cilantro, sugar, and salt. Cook, stirring frequently, until mixture boils. Reduce heat to medium-low and simmer until chicken is cooked and potatoes are tender, 25 to 30 minutes. Remove chiles before serving. (Curry can be made up to 1 day ahead. Reheat before serving.)

Pour chicken curry into a large soup tureen and serve hot. Place condiments in small bowls and set alongside curry.

Coconut Rum Basmati Rice with Roasted Cashews

MAKES 6 TO 8 SERVINGS

Sweet, creamy rice sprinkled with toasted cashews is an ideal side dish for spicy entrées. Raita, an Indian yogurt sauce, is often served with curry dishes as a condiment. It cools the palate and makes eating spicy foods more enjoyable. This rice, containing yogurt, Malibu rum, and cashews, is excellent with chicken and fish.

2 CUPS BASMATI RICE OR LONG-GRAIN RICE	1 TABLESPOON VEGETABLE OIL
3 TABLESPOONS BUTTER	1 STICK CINNAMON
1 CUP UNSALTED CASHEWS	¼ CUP MALIBU RUM
2 CLOVES GARLIC, MINCED	3 CUPS WATER
1 TABLESPOON MINCED FRESH GINGER	3 TABLESPOONS PLAIN YOGURT
	½ TEASPOON SALT

Place rice in a colander and rinse with cold water until water draining from rice runs clear. Set aside in colander for 30 minutes to allow rice to dry.

Meanwhile, heat 1 tablespoon of the butter in a large skillet over medium heat. Add the cashews and cook, stirring frequently, until lightly browned, 3 to 5 minutes. Remove from heat and set aside. Grind the garlic and ginger into a paste, using a mortar and pestle.

Heat remaining 2 tablespoons butter and the oil in another large skillet over medium heat. Add the garlic-ginger paste and cinnamon stick; cook for 2 minutes. Stir in the rum and water; bring to a boil. Stir in the rice and cook for 3 minutes. Reduce heat to low, cover, and simmer for 8 to 10 minutes. Stir rice and cook, covered, for 5 more minutes, until rice is tender. Add more water to rice if necessary. Remove from heat and stir in the cashews, yogurt, and salt. (Rice can be made 1 day ahead and stored in an airtight container in the refrigerator. Reheat before serving.) Spoon into a large bowl and serve warm.

Coconut Rum Banana Pudding on a Banana Leaf

MAKES 16 SQUARES

*N*othing tops off a luau like coconut pudding, except for the guy, dressed as a native warrior, spinning fire sticks. This treat is not the creamy dessert we know here in America, but more like a combination of pudding and Jell-o gelatin dessert. Setting the dessert on a banana leaf is very Malaysian.

¼ CUP SUGAR

½ CUP CORNSTARCH

2 CUPS MILK

½ CUP MALIBU RUM

½ CUP CRÈME DE BANANA

2 BANANA LEAVES

EXOTIC FLOWERS (OPTIONAL)

Add milk, rum, crème de banana, and sugar to a medium saucepan. Slowly sprinkle cornstarch over milk mixture, stirring to avoid lumps. Cook, stirring constantly, over low heat until mixture thickens and bubbles, 12 to 15 minutes. Remove from heat and pour into an 8-inch-square baking dish. Refrigerate until set, about 1 hour.

Wash banana leaves and cut crosswise into 3-inch long sections. Cut pudding into 2-inch squares and place each square on a banana leaf. Serve on individual plates or arrange on a platter with exotic flowers.

VARIATIONS

American-Style Coconut Banana Pudding

For a creamier dessert, reduce cornstarch to ¼ cup and cook as instructed. Spoon the cooked mixture into small serving bowls and refrigerate until set.

If banana leaves are not available, substitute clean, large lemon or grape leaves, using 2 per pudding square.

CHINESE POTABLES FOR 8

The beauty of Chinese food and menu planning is that it encourages flavor mixing. Think of the traditional Chinese restaurant with the large lazy Susan in the center of the table. The very nature of this serving device breaks the ice and sparks conversation. More restaurants seem to be following this trend of offering food family style. I love this, but these restaurants are always a little noisy, with diners acting as if they were in their own home.

The Basques also subscribe to this casual way of dining. My wedding rehearsal dinner was at a Basque restaurant, and the experience of guests passing food from one to the other was a wonderful way for all to get acquainted. Most enjoy this dining style, provided that everyone in the group has similar tastes. A table of finicky eaters can make for a challenging evening.

Orange Liqueur Pork Dumplings

Oyster Bourbon Beef Strips

Shrimp and Chinese Beer Fried Rice

White Chocolate–Dipped Lemon Fortune Cookies

FOOD AND DRINK PLANNER

ONE DAY BEFORE: Make White Chocolate–Dipped Lemon Fortune Cookies.

PARTY DAY: Make Orange Liqueur Pork Dumplings. Make Shrimp and Chinese Beer Fried Rice.

JUST BEFORE SERVING: Steam Orange Liqueur Pork Dumplings. Make Oyster Bourbon Beef Strips.

COCKTAIL SUGGESTION: Mai-Tais: Pour 1½ ounces rum, ¾ ounce Triple Sec, ¾ ounce crème de noyeaux, 2 ounces liquid sweet and sour mix, and a splash of grenadine over ice in a glass. Float ½ ounce dark rum on top.

WINE SUGGESTION: 1997 De Loach Vineyards Early Harvest Gewurztraminer (See "The Wine List," page 23 for more information)

TIMESAVERS: Substitute steamed white rice for Shrimp and Chinese Beer Fried Rice. Substitute purchased fortune cookies for the White Chocolate–Dipped Lemon Fortune Cookies; dip the cookies in the white chocolate.

MENU EXTRA: Serve steamed broccoli.

TABLE SETTING AND DECORATING IDEAS: Glamorous Chinese New Year's Table (see "Traditional Candle Sticks with Accents," page 4)

TABLE LINEN: Use bright red table linen.

Golden Wok Flower Centerpiece

Purchase an inexpensive wok along with the ring stand that the wok rests on. Spray-paint wok and ring metallic gold in a well-ventilated area. Allow paint to dry fully. Set floral foam in wok so foam fills bottom half and has a level surface. Add water to foam. Cover top of foam with green moss. Trim stems of three bird of paradise flowers to 1-foot lengths. Insert flowers in center of foam. Surround flowers with about 6-inch lengths of reed-type filler such as horsetail, which looks like thin green bamboo. Keep arrangement sparse and very simple. Scatter noisemakers and multicolored metallic confetti over table around wok ring base.

Chinese Character Under Gold Glass Place Mats

Purchase 1-foot-square glass pane from glazier or large hardware store for each place setting. Ask the store to buff the edges, making them safe and smooth. Wipe panes clean of dust. Using an indelible black felt-tip pen with a thick tip, write a Chinese character or letter in the center of each pane. For reference, go to your local library and check out a book on the Chinese language or go to a local Chinese restaurant and ask for help.

Purchase metallic gold acrylic paint. Using a 1-inch wide paintbrush, paint six haphazard strokes of gold over the Chinese character and on the pane. Strokes should be random, with patches of glass showing through. Allow paint to dry completely. Flip pane over. Brush ¼-inch strip of glue around the outer edge of pane and dust with multicolored metallic glitter. Allow glue to dry completely. Place pane, painted side down, at each person's place at the table as a place mat.

NOTE: The Chinese character will be backward as you look through the glass pane on the table. If you are a skilled artist, you can write the character backward; it will be correct when the pane is flipped. Otherwise, ask forgiveness if one of your guests happens to notice.

Elegant Velvet Bag as Chopstick Holders

Purchase enough 45-inch-wide black velvet fabric to make a 12 × 5-inch rectangle for each person. For eight people, you will need about ½ yard. Cut 8 (12 × 5-inch) rectangles from fabric. Fold rectangles in half crosswise, making a 6 × 5-inch rectangle with right sides of fabric facing each other. Sew a seam ½ inch from edge along each 6-inch side. Turn bags inside out so velvet is right side out. Roll fabric down two times from opening to make a rolled rim for tops of bags. Fill bags with ½ cup rock salt or uncooked rice and set a bag at each place. Sprinkle multicolored metallic confetti on top of salt. Insert chopsticks into salt so they stand upright or rest chopsticks across top surface. It may be necessary to roll rim further down or add more salt to bags in order to make a steady base to hold the chopsticks.

Braided Gold Cord Napkin Rings

Purchase 1 yard per person of thin gold cord from a sewing or craft store. Cut cord into 3 (1-foot) lengths. Align them and knot together 1 inch from one end. Braid the strands and tie a knot to secure braid 1 inch from other end. Fold napkins in half and roll lengthwise. Tie braid around middle of roll and place a napkin at each place at the table.

Orange Liqueur Pork Dumplings

*S*erve these dumplings with soy sauce or Ponzu Sauce (page 70). Few can resist this tasty Chinese finger food, also known as dim sum.

¼ CUP CORNSTARCH	2 TEASPOONS FRESHLY GRATED ORANGE ZEST
½ POUND GROUND LEAN PORK	
½ TEASPOON SALT	¼ CUP MINCED CANNED WATER CHESTNUTS
2½ TABLESPOONS SOY SAUCE	
2½ TABLESPOONS SESAME OIL	1 CUP CHOPPED GREEN CABBAGE
1 TABLESPOON GRAND MARNIER	½ (50-COUNT) PACKAGE WONTON WRAPPERS
¾ CUP MINCED GREEN ONIONS	
1 TABLESPOON MINCED FRESH GINGER	VEGETABLE OIL

Line 2 baking sheets with waxed paper and sprinkle the cornstarch over paper.

Combine the pork, salt, soy sauce, sesame oil, Grand Marnier, green onions, ginger, orange zest, water chestnuts, and cabbage in a large bowl. With clean hands, mix ingredients until fully combined.

Moisten edge on one side of a wonton wrapper with water. Place 1 heaping teaspoon of pork mixture in center of wonton. Fold the wonton in half and pinch together edges to seal. Place on prepared baking sheet and refrigerate, covered, until ready to cook or up to 1 hour. Repeat with remaining wontons and filling.

Place a wok on wok ring set over burner on stovetop. Add 3 inches water to wok bottom. Heavily oil the inside of each level of a bamboo steamer. Arrange dumplings in steamer so that they are not touching each other. Set bamboo steamer basket inside wok. Place lid on steamer and cook over medium-high heat for 15 to 20 minutes or until wonton wrappers have shrunk around pork and appear crinkled. Gently remove dumplings and serve hot with dipping sauces.

Oyster Bourbon Beef Strips

MAKES 8 SERVINGS

*O*yster sauce is no stranger to the Chinese kitchen. Its rich, smoky flavor can be used on beef straight out of the bottle, like steak sauce or Worcestershire sauce.

3½ POUNDS BEEF FLANK STEAK

1 CLOVE GARLIC, MINCED

⅔ CUP OYSTER SAUCE

1 CUP BEEF BROTH

2 TABLESPOONS BOURBON

2 TABLESPOONS PEANUT OIL

2 LARGE BROWN ONIONS, CUT INTO SLIVERS

1 POUND OYSTER MUSHROOMS, SLICED

Cut the steak crosswise into thin slices, about ⅛ inch thick, and place in a 13 × 9-inch pan. Whisk together the garlic, oyster sauce, broth, and bourbon in a small bowl. Pour mixture over beef. Cover and refrigerate for 1 hour, turning 4 times.

Heat the oil in a large skillet over medium-high heat. Add the onions and mushrooms and cook, stirring occasionally, for 5 minutes. Add the steak and marinade; cook, stirring occasionally, until beef reaches desired doneness. Cook about 5 minutes for rare meat and 8 to 10 minutes for well-done meat. (Cooked dish can be refrigerated up to 1 day. Reheat before serving.) Serve hot.

Shrimp and Chinese Beer Fried Rice

MAKES 6 TO 8 SERVINGS

Fried rice is a meal in itself, and this recipe yields a bundle. You will need a very large skillet or wok to prepare this dish. Stir the rice as little as possible to prevent it from becoming mushy.

3 CUPS LONG-GRAIN RICE	¾ CUP CHOPPED GREEN ONIONS
4½ CUPS WATER	8 OUNCES SLICED MUSHROOMS
1 (12-OUNCE) BOTTLE CHINESE BEER	⅓ CUP SOY SAUCE
2 TABLESPOONS PEANUT OIL	1 POUND MEDIUM SHRIMP, SHELLED, DEVEINED, AND CHOPPED
2 LARGE CARROTS, PEELED AND FINELY DICED	3 EGGS, LIGHTLY BEATEN

Place the rice in a colander and rinse with cold water until water draining from rice runs clear. Set aside in colander for 30 minutes to allow rice to dry.

Bring the water and beer to a boil in a large saucepan over medium-high heat. Stir in the rice, cover, and reduce heat to low. Cook until liquid is absorbed, 15 to 20 minutes. Remove from heat, keeping covered, and set aside to cool completely.

Heat the oil in a large skillet or wok over medium-high heat. Add the carrots, green onions, and mushrooms; cook, stirring occasionally, until vegetables are tender, 8 to 10 minutes. Mix in the cooked rice and soy sauce; cook for 5 minutes. Stir in the shrimp until evenly distributed. Quickly stir in the eggs and cook until eggs are set and shrimp is pink, 3 to 5 minutes. (Store, covered, in the refrigerator up to 2 days and reheat before serving.) Spoon into a large bowl and serve warm.

White Chocolate–Dipped Lemon Fortune Cookies

MAKES ABOUT 12 COOKIES

Take this opportunity to tell your guests how you really feel about them. Write humorous little ditties, personalized fortunes, or words of wisdom on small strips of paper and slide them into fortune cookies. If you can't say something nice about someone, don't invite them to this particular dinner party.

¼ CUP UNSALTED BUTTER, SOFTENED	1 TEASPOON FRESHLY GRATED LEMON ZEST
¼ CUP SUGAR	½ TEASPOON GROUND GINGER
1 EGG	WHITE CHOCOLATE GLAZE
1 EGG WHITE	
1 TABLESPOON VILLA MASSA LIMONI LIQUEUR	4 OUNCES GOOD-QUALITY WHITE CHOCOLATE, CHOPPED
⅓ CUP ALL-PURPOSE FLOUR	1 TEASPOON VEGETABLE OIL

Preheat oven to 400F (205C). Spray baking sheets with nonstick cooking spray. Place the butter and sugar in a mixing bowl and beat until creamy. Beat in the egg and egg white for 10 seconds. Add the liqueur and beat well. Beat the flour, zest, and ginger into mixture until blended.

Spoon level tablespoons of batter 3 inches apart on prepared baking sheet. Limit each baking sheet to 4 cookies. Spread batter into very thin 4-inch circles.

Bake for about 7 minutes, keeping a very watchful eye. When cookies have a brown ring around edges, remove from the oven. Immediately slide cookies off the baking sheet and place fortune paper strips in the center of warm cookies. Fold the cookies in half, and then bend them cookie fortune cookie style. If cookies are not folded immediately, edges will become too crisp and break when folded. Repeat process with remaining dough. Allow cookies to cool completely and harden.

To make White Chocolate Glaze: Melt the white chocolate and oil in top of a double boiler or in small saucepan over a larger pot of simmering water, stirring constantly. Dip cool fortune cookie tips into the chocolate and place on waxed paper until chocolate sets.

NOTES: The first time I made fortune cookies, I had a difficult time remembering exactly how they were folded. You may wish to use a purchased fortune cookie as an example.

Try to find paper for the fortunes that has a light laminated coating on one side; the cookie may leave an oily spot on regular paper.

Libatious Lunches

A LACED LUNCH FOR 4

Gourmet Turkey Bacon Burgers

Shoestring French Fries with Bloody Mary Ketchup

Sour Brussels Sprout Slaw

Apple Schnapps Sorbet

AN AFTERNOON OF ARCHITECTURAL SALADS FOR 6

Boxed Shrimp and Spinach Salad with a Mandarin Orange Dressing

Planet Mexico Salad with Lime Vinaigrette and Avocado Drizzle

California Cobb Circle with Smoky Tomato Vinaigrette

French Bread with Liqueur-Laced Butter

AFTERNOON TEA FOR 8

Hazelnut-Currant Scones

Whipped Café de Crème Fraîche

Cashew and Poppy Seed Chicken Salad in Cucumber Cups

Elegant BLT Bites

Raspberry Almond Tartlets

Chocolate Liqueur—Dipped Strawberries

A LACED LUNCH FOR 4

The Bloody Mary is my cocktail of choice, and this ketchup spiked with vodka does the drink absolute justice. The items on this light menu have a French café feel with the slaw-type salad and shoestring fries.

But the Apple Schnapps Sorbet epitomizes Los Angeles. Just about every party I attend these days serves a liquid incarnation made with Original Sour Apple Pucker Sweet & Sour schnapps in a martini glass. Neon green in color, with the tart taste of a Jolly Rancher candy, the cocktail is always the talk of the party.

Also hot on the event scene is the use of sod in floral displays and centerpieces. In the table setting idea for this menu, patches of sod are used as mini golf greens and a little croquet lawn. Between the sod and the schnapps, this will be an unforgettable lunch.

Gourmet Turkey Bacon Burgers

Shoestring French Fries with Bloody Mary Ketchup

Sour Brussels Sprout Slaw

Apple Schnapps Sorbet

FOOD AND DRINK PLANNER

ONE DAY BEFORE: Make Bloody Mary Ketchup. Make Apple Schnapps Sorbet.

PARTY DAY: Make Sour Brussels Sprout Slaw. Make Shoestring French Fries.

JUST BEFORE SERVING: Make Gourmet Turkey Bacon Burgers.

COCKTAIL SUGGESTION: Bloody Mary: Run a lemon wedge around rim of a tall glass. Dip the rim in a dish of celery salt. Add ice to glass. Pour 1 ounce vodka, ½ ounce lemon juice, 1 teaspoon Worcestershire sauce, and dash hot pepper sauce over ice. Fill glass with tomato juice and garnish with a leafy celery stalk.

WINE SUGGESTION: 1998 Cakebread Cellars Vin de Porche (see "The Wine List," page 23, for more information)

TIMESAVERS: Substitute pre-cut fries and prepared ketchup for Shoestring Fries with Bloody Mary Ketchup. Substitute prepared sorbet for Apple Schnapps Sorbet.

TABLE SETTING AND DECORATING IDEAS: The Lawn Sports Lunch (see ideas below)

TABLE LINEN: Use Summer Brights suggested in "Color Families and Complementary Shades" (see page 6).

Croquet and Daisies on Grass Centerpiece

Purchase a 1-foot-square piece of sod from a nursery. Lay a 1-foot-square sheet of plastic wrap in center of the table and place the sod on the plastic. Trim the plastic around the edges for a neater look. Stick two croquet wickets in sod and place one or two croquet balls on sod. Trim stems of daisies to 3 inches in length. Poke holes in sod, using a skewer. Lightly water holes and insert daisies.

Golf Ball on a Tee Place Cards

Purchase enough sod from a nursery to make a 4-inch sod circle for each person. Cut out sod circles, using scissors, and place circles on small saucers, bowls, or plates. Place saucers at each place at the table. Write names on golf balls, using a thin-tip liquid marker. Or use rub-on letters (from a stationery store). Stick a golf tee in center of sod circle and set golf ball on tee.

Gourmet Turkey Bacon Burgers

MAKES 4 SERVINGS

Though most burgers place the bacon slices on top, these gourmet patties contain crumbled bacon. My husband is a master meatball maker and uses the same basic formula for his burgers. This recipe is a variation of his, with all the goodies and a splash of white wine.

4 SLICES TURKEY BACON

1½ POUNDS GROUND TURKEY

2 CLOVES GARLIC, MINCED

1 EGG, LIGHTLY BEATEN

2 TEASPOONS DRY MUSTARD

3 TABLESPOONS WHITE WINE

3 TABLESPOONS WORCESTERSHIRE SAUCE

½ CUP FRESHLY GRATED PARMESAN CHEESE

½ CUP CHOPPED BROWN ONION

¼ TEASPOON RED PEPPER FLAKES

1 TEASPOON SALT

½ TEASPOON PEPPER

4 ONION HAMBURGER ROLLS

BLOODY MARY KETCHUP (PAGE 209) AND MUSTARD ON THE SIDE

Cook the bacon in a large skillet over medium-high heat until crisp, about 5 minutes. Remove bacon to paper towels to absorb excess fat. Crumble bacon into coarse bits. Pour off all but 1 tablespoon bacon fat from skillet.

Using clean hands, mix crumbled bacon, turkey, garlic, egg, dry mustard, wine, Worcestershire sauce, Parmesan cheese, onion, red pepper flakes, salt, and pepper in a large bowl until thoroughly combined. Form turkey mixture into 4 (1-inch-thick) patties.

Heat the skillet with bacon fat over medium-high heat. Place turkey patties in skillet and cook for 5 to 7 minutes on one side. Flip over and cook for another 5 to 7 minutes on other side for medium doneness. Remove from heat and serve on hamburger rolls with ketchup and mustard on the side.

Shoestring French Fries
with Bloody Mary Ketchup

MAKES 4 SERVINGS; 2 CUPS KETCHUP

Recently, a local television station started showing vintage commercial and program clips that I remember from my childhood. One report, titled "In the News Today," was a 5-minute piece on the history of ketchup. Ketchup (or catsup) originated in China as, I believe, a sauce for fish. Now one of America's favorite condiments has been spiked with vodka.

4 LARGE (ABOUT 2 POUNDS) YUKON GOLD POTATOES, WASHED

VEGETABLE OIL

SALT, SEASONED SALT, OR CELERY SALT

BLOODY MARY KETCHUP

⅓ CUP VODKA

2 CUPS TOMATO KETCHUP

3 TABLESPOONS WORCESTERSHIRE SAUCE

1 TABLESPOON FRESH LEMON JUICE

2 TEASPOONS CELERY SALT

1 TEASPOON PREPARED HORSERADISH

To make the Bloody Mary Ketchup: Combine the vodka, ketchup, Worcestershire sauce, lemon juice, celery salt, and horseradish in a medium saucepan. Bring to a boil over medium-high heat. Reduce heat and simmer for 20 minutes, stirring occasionally, until sauce thickens. Allow to cool to room temperature so flavors blend.

Cut the potatoes into thin matchsticks. Fill a large pot half full with oil and heat over medium-high heat to 350F (175C). Drop the potatoes, in small batches, into hot oil and fry until golden brown, 2 to 3 minutes. Remove with a wire wok basket or slotted spoon and place on paper towels to drain off excess oil. Season with salt and serve piping hot with Bloody Mary Ketchup.

Sour Brussels Sprout Slaw

MAKES 4 SERVINGS

Brussels sprouts always remind me of tiny cabbage heads. This side dish is a cross between coleslaw and sauerkraut, making it a zesty partner for burgers and fries.

4 TABLESPOONS OLIVE OIL

1 TABLESPOON BUTTER

1 CLOVE GARLIC, MINCED

1½ POUNDS BRUSSELS SPROUTS, TRIMMED AND SHREDDED

½ CUP WHITE WINE

3 TABLESPOONS GRAINY BROWN MUSTARD

2 TABLESPOONS LIGHT BROWN SUGAR

5 TABLESPOONS WHITE WINE VINEGAR

½ TEASPOON SALT

⅛ TEASPOON BLACK PEPPER

Heat 1 tablespoon of the oil, butter, and garlic in a large skillet over medium-high heat. Add the Brussels sprouts and wine; cook, stirring occasionally, until wilted, 5 minutes.

Whisk together the remaining oil, mustard, brown sugar, vinegar, salt, and pepper in a small bowl. Pour mixture over sprouts and toss until coated. Serve warm or at room temperature.

Apple Schnapps Sorbet

I used to work for a large catering company that always served sorbet between courses as a palate cleanser. At one very elegant party, a watermelon sorbet and a frozen tomato soup were both on the menu. Somehow, the two got mixed up. The guests' expressions were priceless. This refreshing sorbet is made without an ice cream maker because I've found most people do not own one. The apple schnapps tastes just like Jolly Rancher candy.

2 CUPS UNSWEETENED APPLESAUCE	3 TABLESPOONS CORN SYRUP
2 TABLESPOONS SUGAR	3 TABLESPOONS FRESH LEMON JUICE
3 TABLESPOONS ORIGINAL SOUR APPLE PUCKER SWEET & SOUR SCHNAPPS	

Place the applesauce, sugar, schnapps, corn syrup, and lemon juice in a medium saucepan. Cook, stirring occasionally, over low heat until sugar dissolves and mixture thickens slightly, about 10 minutes. Pour mixture into an 8-inch-square glass baking dish and freeze until almost solid.

Break frozen puree into small chunks and place in a food processor. Process until mixture is smooth. Spoon back into dish and freeze until just firm, at least 1 hour.

Using a small scoop, place sorbet into small bowls. Serve at once. Store covered in the freezer up to 1 week.

VARIATIONS

If Original Sour Apple Pucker Sweet & Sour schnapps is not available, substitute any green apple schnapps or, in a pinch, Midori melon liqueur.

Slice off the top of a Granny Smith apple, core it, and hollow the apple, creating a shell to hold the sorbet.

AN AFTERNOON OF ARCHITECTURAL
SALADS FOR 6

*B*ecause I have many friends who are architects, I thought a structurally challenging menu with a theme devoted to their careers would be great fun. Chefs and architects seem to have a lot in common. Both are creative people, designing with a variety of materials for an end result that must be successful in form and function. Granted, a fallen soufflé doesn't have quite the impact of a caved-in skyscraper, but a superb chocolate torte can rival an office building any day.

My friend Susan Budd, Ms. Ivy League architect, and her sweet husband, Bill, are master cooks and awesome designers. Her blueprints have been used as place mats for some of my outrageous table settings, and sparked the idea for the one below. Sue is always an inspiration, so I hope this upwardly mobile menu meets with her approval.

———

Boxed Shrimp and Spinach Salad with a Mandarin Orange Dressing

Planet Mexico Salad with Lime Vinaigrette and Avocado Drizzle

California Cobb Circle with Smoky Tomato Vinaigrette

French Bread with Liqueur-Laced Butter

———

FOOD AND DRINK PLANNER

ONE DAY BEFORE: Make tortilla shapes for Planet Mexico. Make Liqueur-Laced Butter.

PARTY DAY: Make Boxed Shrimp and Spinach Salad and Mandarin Orange Dressing. Make Lime Vinaigrette and Avocado Drizzle. Make Smoky Tomato Vinaigrette.

ONE HOUR BEFORE SERVING: Make California Cobb Circle. Prepare Planet Mexico Salad ingredients except lettuce.

JUST BEFORE SERVING: Assemble and dress salads according to instructions.

COCKTAIL SUGGESTION: Cosmopolitan: Pour 1 ounce vodka, 1 ounce Grand Marnier, ½ ounce cranberry juice, and a splash of lime juice into a cocktail shaker with ice. Shake and strain into a martini glass. Garnish with a lime twist.

WINE SUGGESTION: 1998 Husch Mendocino Sauvignon Blanc (see "The Wine List," page 23, for more information).

TIMESAVERS: Use bottled dressings with flavors similar to recipe dressings. Substitute prepared tortilla chips for tortilla spirals.

TABLE SETTING AND DECORATING IDEAS: The Architect's Table

TABLE LINEN: Use white or deep blue table linen.

Fun Blueprint Place Mats

Find an architectural blueprint drafted for your home, a friend's home, or from a textbook on architecture. In a pinch, call an architectural firm. Go to a copy center and copy blueprint on 11 × 17-inch paper, making one copy for each person.
Write names on blueprint place mats with colored pencils. Set a place mat at each person's place at the table. Place a glass full of colored pencils on the table so guests can draw on their place mats.

Cloth Tape Measure Napkin Ties

Cut several cloth tape measures into 1-foot lengths. Fold napkins in half and roll lengthwise. Wrap tape measure lengths around middle of rolls and tie them into bows.

Boxed Shrimp and Spinach Salad with Mandarin Orange Dressing

MAKES 6 TO 8 SALAD COURSE SERVINGS

*S*pinach can be very versatile, as this salad shows. The leaves are lightly wilted and then packed into a mold. A vibrant green box is the bed for ornately placed ingredients in this edible triumph.

½ POUND MEDIUM SHRIMP, SHELLED, DEVEINED, AND COOKED

1 RED BELL PEPPER, MINCED

1 CUP LIMA BEANS, COOKED

8 LARGE BUNCHES SPINACH, STEMS TRIMMED

MANDARIN ORANGE DRESSING

5 TABLESPOONS MANDARIN ORANGE JUICE

8 MANDARIN ORANGES, DIVIDED INTO SEGMENTS

3 TABLESPOONS SESAME OIL

2 TABLESPOONS RICE WINE VINEGAR

1 TEASPOON GRAND MARNIER

½ TEASPOON MINCED FRESH GINGER

Line bottom and sides of a 13 × 9-inch baking pan with long sheets of plastic wrap.

Place the shrimp flat and in a diagonal row on bottom of prepared pan, from corner to corner. Place a row of bell pepper on either side of shrimp. Place the lima beans on each side of bell pepper so lima beans fill remaining space on pan bottom and extend into corners. Set aside.

Place the spinach in a large bowl or stockpot. Pour boiling hot water over spinach and toss with metal tongs for 30 seconds. Drain the spinach completely in a colander and pat dry with paper towels. Carefully layer the spinach over ingredients in pan. Pack the spinach down and cover loosely with plastic wrap. Place another 13 × 9-inch baking pan on plastic wrap, covering spinach, and lightly weigh down with a heavy book. Refrigerate for 20 minutes.

To make the Mandarin Orange Dressing: Place the orange juice and oranges in a small bowl. Crush the oranges with the back of a spoon. Add the remaining ingredients to bowl and whisk until combined. Place in a small bowl or cruet.

Just before serving, remove top pan and plastic wrap cover from salad. Place a large, flat platter or nice rectangular wooden cutting board facedown on top of pan. (Rims can interfere with unmolding and cause the salad to lose its shape.) Gently turn pan over so salad rests on platter. Remove pan and plastic wrap. Reshape salad or replace ingredients if they have become disheveled during unmolding. Drizzle a little Mandarin Orange Dressing over top of salad and serve remaining dressing on the side. Serve cold.

Planet Mexico Salad with Lime Vinaigrette and Avocado Drizzle

MAKES 6 SALAD COURSE SERVINGS

A salad that looks like Saturn with a Mexicali flair! The culinary wizardry at the Los Angeles International Airport restaurant Encounter inspired me to create this salad. Flying into LAX, you will see the futuristic structure that houses this haven amid the terminals. Its interplanetary decor is just as fabulous as the food.

4 LARGE CORN TORTILLAS

VEGETABLE OIL

1 LARGE HEAD ROMAINE LETTUCE, FINELY CHOPPED

1/3 CUP COARSELY CHOPPED CILANTRO LEAVES

2 GREEN ONIONS, COARSELY CHOPPED

1 (15-OUNCE) CAN BLACK BEANS, DRAINED AND RINSED

1 (15-OUNCE) CAN WHOLE-KERNEL CORN, DRAINED

1 AVOCADO, DICED

1/2 CUP (2 OUNCES) SHREDDED CHEDDAR CHEESE

1/2 CUP (2 OUNCES) SHREDDED MONTEREY JACK CHEESE

LIME VINAIGRETTE
1 CLOVE GARLIC, MINCED

1/4 CUP FRESH LIME JUICE

1 TEASPOON TEQUILA

2 1/2 TABLESPOONS WHITE WINE VINEGAR

1/3 CUP OLIVE OIL

1 TABLESPOON MINCED FRESH CILANTRO

1/2 TEASPOON SALT

AVOCADO DRIZZLE
1/4 CUP MASHED AVOCADO

1/4 CUP OLIVE OIL

2 TABLESPOONS WATER

1 TABLESPOON FRESH LIME JUICE

1 TABLESPOON SOUR CREAM

1/2 TEASPOON SALT

Using clean kitchen scissors, cut each tortilla into a spiral, starting at outer edge. Cut 1/2 inch into tortilla, then turn scissors and continue cutting in a circle until you reach the tortilla center. Each tortilla should be a long 1/2-inch-wide strip that coils from outer edge to center.

Fill a large pot two-thirds full with oil and heat oil over medium-high heat to 350F (175C). As a precaution, wear an oven mitt while frying. Using long, metal tongs, hold the center end of tortilla strip, allowing rest of strip to dangle and spiral down. Gently immerse strip into oil, holding center end, so strip fries into a free-form shape. Fry until its crisp and holds its shape, 1 to 2 minutes. Place on paper towels to absorb excess oil and cool. Repeat process with remaining tortillas.

Combine the lettuce, cilantro, green onions, black beans, corn, avocado, and cheeses in a large bowl.

To make the Lime Vinaigrette: Whisk together all the ingredients in a small bowl until blended. Pour vinaigrette over salad and toss to combine.

Place salad on a large serving platter. Set tortilla shapes on top of salad.

To make the Avocado Drizzle: Place all the ingredients in a blender jar and puree until smooth. Lightly drizzle over tortilla shapes and salad. Serve immediately. Guests can break off sections of tortilla shapes for their salads as they serve themselves.

VARIATION

For individual salad servings, make a tortilla shape for each salad. Place salad in a mound on plate and set tortilla shape on salad.

California Cobb Circle with Smoky Tomato Vinaigrette

Gourmet bacon, smoked with woods such as apple or mesquite, is a trendy food fad. I've found that most people take pleasure in a woody flavor because it is reminiscent of barbecue, and everyone loves barbecue. Because the classic Cobb salad has many ingredients with a rustic edge, I've matched it with a smoke-infused vinaigrette.

1 HEAD ICEBERG LETTUCE, FINELY CHOPPED

½ CUP BLUE CHEESE, CRUMBLED

8 STRIPS BACON, DICED AND CRISP-COOKED

1 AVOCADO, DICED

3 BONELESS, SKINLESS CHICKEN BREAST HALVES, COOKED AND DICED

1 CUP SEEDED, DICED TOMATOES

3 HARD-COOKED EGGS, DICED

SMOKY TOMATO VINAIGRETTE

¼ CUP RED WINE VINEGAR

½ CUP OLIVE OIL

2 TABLESPOONS FRESH LEMON JUICE

1 TEASPOON SMIRNOFF'S CITRUS TWIST VODKA

½ CUP CANNED, PEELED TOMATOES, DICED

½ TEASPOON LIQUID SMOKE

¼ TEASPOON DRY MUSTARD

½ TEASPOON SALT

¼ TEASPOON PEPPER

Place the lettuce in an even layer over bottom of a 9-inch springform pan. Place blue cheese in a circle in center. Arrange the rest of the ingredients in concentric circles on top of lettuce, around the cheese, in the following order: bacon, avocado, chicken, tomatoes, and egg. Chill, uncovered, for 30 minutes.

To make the Smoky Tomato Vinaigrette: Whisk together all ingredients until combined. Place in a small bowl or cruet. (Store dressing in an airtight container up to 3 days. Bring to room temperature before serving.)

Place the springform pan on a large serving plate. Release latch on the side and carefully unmold salad. Serve dressing on the side.

French Bread with Liqueur-Laced Butters

MAKES 1 ½ CUPS

A light trace of liqueur enhances sweet cream butter for a charming spread. For a stunning presentation, emboss each round of butter, using a cookie stamp or a clean wax stamp.

1 ½ CUPS (3 STICKS) UNSALTED BUTTER, SOFTENED

1 TEASPOON GRAND MARNIER

1 TEASPOON FRESHLY GRATED ORANGE PEEL

1 TEASPOON ANISETTE

1 TEASPOON ANISE SEEDS

1 TEASPOON LAIRD'S APPLEJACK

1 TEASPOON MINCED DRIED APPLE

EDIBLE FLOWERS (OPTIONAL)

1 LOAF FRENCH BREAD, SLICED CROSSWISE

Place each stick of butter in a separate small bowl. Beat butter in each bowl until creamy. Add Grand Marnier and orange zest to one bowl and beat until blended. Add the anisette and anise seeds to another bowl and beat until blended. Add the applejack and dried apple to the last bowl and beat until blended.

With clean hands form each mixture into a small log, about 1 inch in diameter. Wrap each log tightly in plastic and refrigerate for 1 hour or until butter is firm.

Just before serving, cut a portion of each log crosswise into ¼-inch-thick rounds. Place a round of each butter on individual bread and butter plates and garnish with flower, if desired. Serve with slices of French bread. Wrap remaining butter logs in plastic and store in the refrigerator for up to 2 weeks.

AFTERNOON TEA FOR 8

What an elegant ritual afternoon tea is. Although I lived in London, I never attended tea at famed department store Harrods. But I have enjoyed teatime at the Bel Air Hotel, which was a delightful experience for a mere $16.00 per person. I highly recommend having tea there if you visit Los Angeles.

I've swapped the usual cucumber and butter sandwiches for savory BLT bites. The scones are standard fare, but the sophisticated version in this menu is enhanced with Franjelico. Even though this midafternoon meal is meant for relaxation, make the effort to create a special table. Or at least dress up the sugar cubes in dipped chocolate or with sprinkles, as suggested on page 228. The fancy cubes are a great conversation piece.

Hazelnut-Currant Scones

Whipped Café de Crème Fraîche

Cashew and Poppy Seed Chicken Salad in Cucumber Cups

Elegant BLT Bites

Raspberry Almond Tartlets

Chocolate Liqueur–Dipped Strawberries

FOOD AND DRINK PLANNER

ONE DAY BEFORE: Make Whipped Café de Crème Fraîche. Make Almond Tartlet shells. Make Hazelnut-Currant Scones.

PARTY DAY: Make Cashew and Poppy Seed Chicken Salad in Cucumber Cups. Make Elegant BLT Bites. Make Chocolate Liqueur–Dipped Strawberries. Assemble Raspberry Almond Tartlets.

COCKTAIL SUGGESTION: Fuzzy Navel: Pour 1 ounce peach schnapps over ice in a tall glass; fill with orange juice.

WINE SUGGESTION: 1991 Domaine Carneros Blanc de Blanc (see "The Wine List," page 23, for more information)

TIMESAVERS: Substitute prepared bakery tarts for Raspberry Almond Tarts.

TABLE SETTING AND DECORATING IDEAS: Eclectic Tea Set Table (see Traditional Candlesticks with Accents, page 4).

TABLE LINEN: Use Spring Pastels suggested in "Color Families and Complementary Shades" (see page 6).

Teapot Vase

Arrange beautiful flowers in a large, interesting teapot and place in the center of the table.

Tapers in Teacups

Use an assortment of old teacups. Cut green floral foam to fit snugly inside each cup. Cover top of foam with green moss. Cut slit in center of moss and insert a tall, tapered candle through slit down into foam. Make sure candle is well anchored. Sprinkle water on small flowers and place in moss at base of candle. Keep foam dry; wet foam may not fully support lit candle.

Edible Sugar Cup for Sugar Cubes

Use an 8-ounce teacup with smooth sides and level rim as a mold to make a sugar cup. Dilute a few drops of food coloring in 1 teaspoon water. Gradually mix into ¾ cup sugar until sugar is thoroughly moistened and color is even. Using your fingers, firmly pack enough of the sugar on inside surface of teacup to a thin, even (1-centimeter) thickness. Sugar should cover entire inner surface in an even layer up to rim of cup. Place a sheet of waxed paper on a flat surface in a cool dry place. Hold a small piece of cardboard over teacup opening and gently flip cup over. Set cardboard with upside-down teacup on waxed paper surface. After 5 minutes, gently tap cup on sides and lift off cup. Allow sugar to dry and harden for at least 4 hours.

Turn sugar cup right side up and place on a tea saucer. Decorate cup by piping royal icing in a lacy design around rim of cup. (See recipe below.) Fill sugar cup with decorated sugar cubes and place on the table. It is not recommended to make or use this on a hot or rainy day.

Personalized Sugar Cube Place Cards

Write letters of each person's initials on sugar cubes with royal icing. To make royal icing: Beat 1 egg white (see Note, below) on high speed in a medium bowl until soft peaks form. Gradually add 1¼ cups powdered sugar and beat until mixture is stiff. Divide mixture into small bowls and color mixture in each bowl with a different food coloring. Spoon each color into a pastry bag fitted with a writing tip and pipe letters on one side of each sugar cube. Decorate additional sugar cubes by piping flowers and designs on cube sides. Fill Edible Sugar Cup with decorated cubes and arrange lettered sugar cubes on a small saucer at each place setting.

NOTE: Raw eggs should not be consumed by children, pregnant women, the elderly, or anyone with serious health issues. Substitute powdered egg whites, such as Just Whites, if this concerns you.

Hazelnut-Currant Scones

Low-fat scones are a myth. Yes, they exist, but the imposters I've tried are more like a dinner roll than a true scone. The combination of real butter and cream makes this melt-in-your-mouth English baked good a must at teatime. Serve with Whipped Café de Crème Fraîche (page 224).

2 CUPS ALL-PURPOSE FLOUR

⅓ CUP PACKED LIGHT BROWN SUGAR

1 TABLESPOON BAKING POWDER

⅛ TEASPOON SALT

½ CUP UNSALTED BUTTER, CHILLED, COARSELY CHOPPED

½ CUP CHOPPED UNSALTED HAZELNUTS

½ CUP DRIED BLACK CURRANTS

3 TABLESPOONS FRANGELICO

1 EGG

1 EGG YOLK

⅔ CUP PLUS 2 TABLESPOONS HEAVY CREAM

Preheat oven to 425F (220C). Line a baking sheet with waxed paper and lightly spray paper with nonstick cooking spray. Combine the flour, brown sugar, baking powder, salt, and butter in a food processor and process until mixture resembles coarse crumbs. Pour into a large bowl and fold in hazelnuts and currants until distributed throughout mixture.

Whisk together 2 tablespoons of the Frangelico, egg, egg yolk, and ⅔ cup cream until blended. Stir egg mixture into flour mixture until dough just begins to hold together. With clean hands, form ¼ cup portions of dough into rough balls and place 3 inches apart on prepared sheet. Mix together remaining 1 tablespoon liqueur and 2 tablespoons cream until blended. Lightly brush surfaces of scones with liqueur-cream mixture.

Bake for 15 minutes or until puffed and golden brown. Remove from oven and cool on a wire rack. (To make ahead, store scones in an airtight container at room temperature for up to 1 day.)

Arrange warm or room-temperature scones in a cloth napkin–lined basket.

Whipped Café de Crème Fraîche

Some gourmet grocery stores sell prepared crème fraîche, but the homemade version of this French cream is superb, especially when laced with Kahlua. Serve alongside the Hazelnut-Currant Scones (page 223).

2 TABLESPOONS BUTTERMILK	2 TABLESPOONS KAHLUA
2 CUPS HEAVY CREAM	1 TABLESPOON SUGAR

Heat the cream in a small saucepan over low heat until cream reaches 85F (30C). Do not allow heat to rise above 100F (40C). Stir in the buttermilk with a wooden spoon until blended. Pour into a wide-mouthed jar, cover, and let stand at room temperature for 6 hours. Chill in the refrigerator for 24 hours.

Just before serving, transfer the crème fraîche to a metal bowl and whip until thickened. Stir in the Kahlua and sugar until blended. Place in a small bowl.

Cashew and Poppy Seed Chicken Salad in Cucumber Cups

MAKES ABOUT 28 PIECES

There is a health food restaurant in my neighborhood that makes a super chicken salad with cashews and serves it on a green salad. I like to smother the salad in their poppy seed dressing. This refreshing appetizer was inspired by that salad.

¾ CUP CHOPPED CASHEWS

1 TABLESPOON OLIVE OIL

3 SKINLESS, BONELESS CHICKEN BREAST HALVES

½ CUP MAYONNAISE

1 TEASPOON WHITE WINE VINEGAR

1 TEASPOON RASPBERRY LIQUEUR

½ CUP MINCED RED ONION

½ TABLESPOON POPPY SEEDS

¼ TEASPOON SALT

½ TEASPOON BLACK PEPPER

4 SEEDLESS ENGLISH CUCUMBERS, PEELED

Preheat oven to 450F (230C). Scatter the cashews on a baking sheet and bake until toasted, about 5 minutes. Cool completely.

Heat the oil in a large skillet over medium-high heat. Add chicken and cook for 6 to 8 minutes on one side. Turn chicken and cook on other side until chicken center is no longer pink, 6 to 8 minutes. Remove from heat and cool slightly. Chop chicken into fine bits and place in a medium bowl.

Stir mayonnaise into chicken until combined. Add the cashews, vinegar, liqueur, red onion, poppy seeds, salt, and pepper; mix well. Refrigerate, covered, until ready to serve (up to 2 days).

Cut cucumbers crosswise into 1-inch-thick rounds. Using a melon baller, scoop ¾ of the way down into the center of each cucumber round, creating a cup to hold the chicken salad. Fill each cucumber cup with chicken salad and serve cold.

Elegant BLT Bites

MAKES 24 PIECES

One of my and my husband's favorite meals is a French baguette slathered in Camembert and topped with smoked oysters. That particular pairing will seem eccentric to people, but the pairing of a smoky food like bacon with Camembert is wonderful. In this recipe the bacon is caramelized, which picks up the sweetness of the cheese and changes this common sandwich into an elegant teatime snack.

8 SLICES BACON

3 TABLESPOONS LIGHT BROWN SUGAR

3 TABLESPOONS APPLE BRANDY

6 THIN SLICES WHITE BREAD, CRUSTS REMOVED

6 OUNCES CAMEMBERT CHEESE, SOFTENED

1 BUNCH WATERCRESS, LARGE STEMS REMOVED

8 RED PEAR TOMATOES OR BABY TOMATOES, SLICED CROSSWISE

Cook the bacon in a large skillet over medium-high heat until crisp, turning occasionally. Remove with tongs and drain on paper towels. Cool bacon and chop into coarse bits. Pour bacon fat from skillet and wipe clean.

In same skillet, place the brown sugar and brandy; cook over medium heat for 30 seconds. Add the chopped bacon and cook, stirring occasionally, until bacon is coated, 1 minute. Remove from heat.

Preheat oven to 350F (175C). Cut each bread slice into 4 equal squares. Place bread on a baking sheet and bake about 5 minutes or until lightly toasted.

Spread a thin layer of Camembert on toast and top each with ½ teaspoon bacon. Arrange a leaf of watercress and a tomato slice on top. Serve at room temperature.

Raspberry Almond Tartlets

MAKES ABOUT 15 TARTS

A *light, fruit-filled tartlet is just right for an afternoon tea. These simple sweets are also great on a brunch table because they do not have a custard base (as many fruit tarts do).*

2 CUPS FRESH RED RASPBERRIES

2 TABLESPOONS AMARETTO

2 TEASPOONS FRESH LEMON JUICE

2 TEASPOONS FRESHLY GRATED LEMON ZEST

3 TABLESPOONS POWDERED SUGAR

ALMOND CRUST

1 CUP UNSALTED BLANCHED ALMONDS

⅓ CUP SUGAR

1½ CUPS ALL-PURPOSE FLOUR

½ CUP BUTTER, CHILLED, CUT INTO TABLESPOONS

1 EGG YOLK

2 TABLESPOONS AMARETTO

To make the Almond Crust: Combine the almonds and sugar in a food processor; process until almonds are finely ground. Add the flour and process until combined. Add the butter, egg yolk, and amaretto; process until mixture forms a ball. Wrap ball in plastic wrap and refrigerate for 1 hour.

Preheat oven to 350F (175C). Spray 32 (2-inch) tartlet shells with nonstick cooking spray and place shells on baking sheets. Roll out chilled dough on a heavily floured surface to ⅛-inch thickness. Cut out dough, using a 2-inch round cookie cutter. Place dough rounds into prepared shells and trim any excess edges. Place a few dry kidney beans or pie weights in center of each dough round to keep it from puffing up during baking. Bake for 12 to 15 minutes or until light brown. Remove from oven and cool thoroughly before removing tarts from shells.

Meanwhile, combine the raspberries, amaretto, lemon juice, and lemon zest in a medium bowl. Gently toss raspberries to coat with liquid.

Fill each tart with about 5 raspberries and sift powdered sugar over top. Serve cold or at room temperature. (Store in an airtight container in the refrigerator for up to 2 days.)

Sugar Cube Art

During 1996, my comedic gingerbread house-making video was offered on the back of C&H powdered sugar boxes. My favorite building material for cookie house chimneys is the sturdy little sugar cube! Further research, and hours spent thinking of sugar and candy, led me to these sweet teatime ideas. Cubes with chocolate are recommended for coffee, because their tastes are more compatible. Chocolate will cloud tea.

Chocolate-Covered Sugar Cubes

Melt 2 ounces semisweet chocolate, 2 teaspoons unsalted butter, and 1 teaspoon liqueur in top of a double boiler. Cool 8 minutes. Dip half of each sugar cube in chocolate. Place cube, chocolate side up, on waxed paper until chocolate sets. Excellent liqueur flavors for these cubes are crème de menthe, Grand Marnier, Chambord, Baileys Original Irish Cream, and Kahlua.

Deco Art Cubes

Purchase Deco Art edible cake decorations from grocery store (found in the decorations section of the baking aisle). Mix 2 tablespoons powdered sugar with ½ teaspoon water to make a paste. Stick Deco Art decorations to sides of sugar cubes with dabs of sugar paste. Set on waxed paper until paste dries, about 1 hour.

Confetti Cubes

Place colored candy sprinkles on a small plate. Make sugar paste according to directions under Deco Art Cubes (above). Smear a thin coat of sugar paste on all sides of each sugar cube and roll cubes in sprinkles. Set on waxed paper until sugar paste dries, about 1 hour.

Chocolate Chip Cubes

Make sugar paste according to directions under Deco Art Cubes (above). Stick chocolate chips or pastel candy chips to sides of sugar cubes with dabs of sugar paste. Set on waxed paper until paste dries, about 1 hour

Flowers and Letters on Cubes

See "Personalized Sugar Cube Place Cards," page 222.

Chocolate Liqueur—Dipped Strawberries

MAKES 24 STRAWBERRIES

Just prior to writing this recipe, I catered an event where the hostess requested chocolate-dipped strawberries. What tales this delicacy evokes! A few people told me of parties they had attended where chocolate-dipped strawberries were at the bar. The bartender would infuse the strawberry with liqueur, using a clean hypodermic needle. It's a novel concept that I've never tried. Nor do I suggest that you do—liqueur in the chocolate is potent enough.

8 OUNCES SEMISWEET CHOCOLATE, CHOPPED

1 TABLESPOON CANOLA OIL

1 TABLESPOON GODIVA CHOCOLATE LIQUEUR

2 DOZEN LARGE, FIRM STRAWBERRIES, RINSED AND PATTED DRY

Line a baking sheet with waxed paper.

Melt the chocolate and oil in top of double boiler or in small saucepan over a larger pot of simmering water, stirring constantly. Remove from heat and stir in liqueur until blended.

Thoroughly dry each strawberry, or chocolate will not adhere. Holding the stem, dip strawberry into chocolate until three-fourths coated. Place on waxed paper until chocolate sets.

Arrange strawberries on a doily-lined silver tray and serve at room temperature or chilled. (Store, uncovered, in the refrigerator for no more than 6 hours because they will begin to turn soggy.)

TIPS: Chocolate can present a challenge when melting it. If heated too long, it will turn into a hard mass. When melting chocolate, add oil to make a glaze. Melt in a double boiler, not in a microwave. Always work with chocolate at room temperature, unless otherwise specified in the recipe. Some chocolates are better for melting, and the label will indicate this. When working with white chocolate, always choose the best quality.

Themed Mixers

FRUTTI DEL MAR FOR 4

Artichoke and Crab Vichyssoise

Flaked Salmon in Fennel Slivers

Lobster Saffron Flan

Port Wine in Melon

YO-HO-HO AND A BOTTLE OF RUM! FOR 6

Shark Burgers with Zombie Salsa

Jamaican Rum Plantains

Red Beans and Rum Rice

Rum and Sweet Potato Cornbread

GIN! FOR 8

Martini Olive Tapenade

Coriander Gin Rickey Vinaigrette on Field Greens and Pear Tomatoes

Broiled Orange and Tarragon Trout

Orange and Walnut Gin Rolls

FRUTTI DEL MAR FOR 4

"*Fruit of the sea*" is the translation of this maritime menu title. I've never seen the blooming gardens on the ocean's floor, but my scuba-diving husband has spoken of their beauty time and again. He's rolled around with seals and, much to my terror, escaped the path of sharks. After his adventures we always grab a bite of seafood, and should an item that he's seen underwater turn up on the plate, I'll get the full description of how it exists in its natural habitat.

The plated presentation of the dishes on this menu will appear as a scene from the depths of the ocean with a seashell garland table design as its shore. The Lobster Saffron Flan, surrounded by the salmon, will be as picturesque and tranquil as sea anemones floating around aquatic flora.

———

Artichoke and Crab Vichyssoise

Flaked Salmon in Fennel Slivers

Lobster Saffron Flan

Port Wine in Melon

———

FOOD AND DRINK PLANNER

ONE DAY BEFORE: Make Artichoke and Crab Vichyssoise (do not add crab).

PARTY DAY: Make Lobster Saffron Flan.

JUST BEFORE SERVING: Make Flaked Salmon in Fennel Slivers. Add crab to vichyssoise. Pour Port into melon halves.

COCKTAIL SUGGESTION: Lemon Licorice Whip: Add 1 ounce vodka, 1 ounce anisette, 1 ounce Triple Sec, and 1 ounce lemon juice to ice in a cocktail shaker. Shake and strain into a martini glass. Garnish with a lemon twist.

WINE SUGGESTION: 1998 Robert Mondavi Fume Blanc (see "The Wine List," page 23, for more information)

TIMESAVER: Substitute a dressed green salad for Artichoke and Crab Vichyssoise.

TABLE SETTING AND DECORATING IDEAS: Under the Sea Table (see "Garland Design," page 4).

TABLE LINEN: Use Spring Pastels suggested in "Color Families and Complementary Shades" (see page 6).

Seashell Garland

Place cloth on table. Lay white shimmery fabric in a flowing, pooled fashion along the center of the table. Pour a 4-inch strip of clean sand along the center of the fabric. Scatter a variety of seashells, starfish, and sand dollars in sand.

Seashell and Pasta Shell Napkin Rings

Glue small seashells in a bunch on a manicotti shell. Slide manicotti shell over napkin.

Silver or Crystal Candlesticks or Candelabra

Place your candleholders in the center of table, worked into the garland design.

Shell Place Cards

Write guests' names on large, light-colored shells, using gold or silver ink, and place a shell at each person's place at the table.

Artichoke and Crab Vichyssoise

MAKES 4 SERVINGS

*O*nly *a few cold soups appeal to me: the classics vichyssoise and gazpacho. Artichokes brighten up this creamy potato and leek soup, and a zesty cluster of crabmeat makes this potage an excellent choice for a hot day.*

3 CUPS COARSELY CHOPPED, PEELED RUSSET POTATOES

1 (8½-OUNCE) CAN ARTICHOKE BOTTOMS, DRAINED AND CHOPPED

2 LEEKS, COARSELY CHOPPED AND RINSED

4½ CUPS CHICKEN BROTH

½ CUP WHITE WINE

1 CUP HALF-AND-HALF

2 TEASPOONS SALT

½ TEASPOON WHITE PEPPER

1 CUP COOKED CRABMEAT

4 TEASPOONS FRESH LEMON JUICE

4 THINLY SLICED LEMON ROUNDS

Combine the potatoes, artichokes, leeks, broth, and wine in a large saucepan over medium-high heat. Bring to a boil. Reduce heat to medium-low and simmer until potatoes are tender, 25 minutes.

Add the vegetables and liquid, in batches, to a blender jar and puree until smooth. Pour pureed mixture into a large bowl and stir in the half-and-half, salt, and pepper. Cool completely and refrigerate, covered, until ready to serve or up to 1 day.

Just before serving, ladle soup into individual bowls. Mound ¼ cup of the crabmeat in center of each bowl and sprinkle 1 teaspoon of the lemon juice over each crabmeat mound. Garnish with a lemon slice on the side of each crabmeat mound. Serve cold.

Flaked Salmon in Fennel Slivers

My husband concocted this dish. The sugar in the Sambuca liqueur coats the delicate flakes of salmon and translucent slivers of fennel. A gorgeous plate is presented when this lush orange-specked entrée is served with the bright-colored Lobster Saffron Flan (page 236).

1 TABLESPOON OLIVE OIL

2 LARGE FENNEL BULBS, CUT INTO THIN SLIVERS

2 POUNDS SALMON FILET, SKINNED AND BONED

½ CUP ROMANA SAMBUCA LIQUORE CLASSICO

½ TEASPOON SALT

½ TEASPOON WHITE PEPPER

Heat the oil in a large skillet over medium-high heat. Add the fennel and cook, stirring occasionally, until tender, about 10 minutes. Push the fennel aside in skillet and add the salmon and Sambuca; cook for 5 minutes. Turn the salmon over and as it cooks, separate into flakes, using a spatula. Cook until liquid reduces completely into a glaze and salmon edges are browned, about 5 minutes. Remove from heat and stir in the salt and pepper.

Place the salmon and fennel on individual plates and serve hot. If serving with Lobster Saffron Flan, place flans in center of plate and surround with salmon and fennel.

Lobster Saffron Flan

MAKES 8 FLANS

Although I advocate using fresh lobster meat for these delicate flans, the live lobster production from start to finish can be arduous. Many grocery stores' seafood sections sell frozen lobster tails that you boil in water, or even cooked lobster tails that simply require defrosting. (See Lobster Steamed in Vodka, page 316, for instructions on how to cook a live lobster.)

1 TABLESPOON BUTTER	1/8 TEASPOON SAFFRON THREADS
2 SHALLOTS, MINCED	1/2 TEASPOON SALT
1/2 CUP DRY VERMOUTH	1/8 TEASPOON WHITE PEPPER
1/3 CUP HEAVY CREAM	1 CUP COARSELY CHOPPED, COOKED LOBSTER MEAT
4 EGGS	

Preheat oven to 325F (165C). Line 8 cups of a muffin pan with foil baking cups. Spray cups with nonstick cooking spray.

Melt the butter in a small saucepan over medium-high heat. Add the shallots and cook for 2 minutes. Add the vermouth and cook until liquid reduces completely, 3 to 5 minutes.

Place cooked shallots and cream in a food processor and puree until smooth. Add the eggs, saffron, salt, and pepper; pulse until just combined. Pour mixture into prepared cups. Distribute lobster meat equally among the cups.

Fill a large baking pan halfway with warm water. Set the muffin pan in the pan of water and place in the oven. Bake 35 to 40 minutes or until a wooden pick inserted off-center in custard comes out clean. Remove from heat and cool 5 minutes.

Gently remove foil from each custard and place, right side up, on a serving platter.

Port Wine in Melon

MAKES 4 SERVINGS

*S*ucculent fruit drenched in Port is an ideal ending to the Frutti del Mar menu. Fresh melon filled with Port is a simple dessert reminiscent of Spain.

1 CUP PORT	4 TABLESPOONS WHOLE MINT LEAVES
2 HONEYDEW MELONS	

Cut melon in half crosswise and scoop out seeds. Place each melon half on a serving plate. Fill hollow center of each half with ¼ cup of the Port. Scatter mint leaves over each melon and serve.

YO-HO-HO AND A BOTTLE OF RUM! FOR 6

An adult take on the renowned theme park pirate ride, this lusty menu with its treasure chest buffet will ensure a rowdy event. Have guests dress up as pirates and maidens, or host a Peter Pan party for grown-ups in the backyard. You'll be amazed at how quickly your next-door neighbor reverts to his childhood as he becomes a feisty swashbuckler lancing the burgers with a barbecue fork.

Everyone loves a cocktail turned into a food item, such as the Zombie Salsa. A Polynesian restaurant favorite, the mere thought of sipping a Zombie drink puts one in a prankish mood. Find island-type vessels and platters for serving these dishes. A toy pirate ship might make the perfect container for cornbread, and a large, clean conch shell can be a unique salsa bowl.

―――――

Shark Burgers with Zombie Salsa

Jamaican Rum Plantains

Red Beans and Rum Rice

Rum and Sweet Potato Cornbread

―――――

FOOD AND DRINK PLANNER

ONE DAY BEFORE: Make Rum and Sweet Potato Cornbread. Soak red beans.

PARTY DAY: Make Zombie Salsa. Make Red Beans and Rum Rice.

JUST BEFORE SERVING: Make Shark Burgers. Make Jamaican Rum Plantains.

COCKTAIL SUGGESTION: Zombie: Pour 1 ounce dark Jamaican rum, 1 ounce light rum, ½ ounce apricot brandy, ½ ounce lime juice, and splash of grenadine over ice in a tall glass; fill glass with a mixture of half orange juice and half pineapple juice. Garnish with a skewered pineapple wedge and maraschino cherry.

WINE SUGGESTION: 1998 Cape Indaba Sauvignon Blanc (see "The Wine List," page 23 for more information)

TIMESAVERS: Substitute a package of Zatarain's Red Beans and Rice (follow package instructions) for Red Beans and Rum Rice. Substitute prepared salsa mixed with chopped papaya for Zombie Salsa.

TABLE SETTING AND DECORATING IDEAS: Pirate's Treasure in a Jungle Buffet (see "Practical Tips and Ideas for Food Stations," page 10)

TABLE LINEN: Use bright green or Kelly green table linen.

Treasure Chest Buffet

Place cloth on table that is against a wall. Set varying heights of risers, using large books and plastic milk crates, on back of tabletop along wall. Place another cloth of same color over risers, allowing cloth enough slack to lie flat on each riser. Fold under cloth ends on top of table. Place tropical green plants in pots with liners on risers. Insert tropical flowers such as birds of paradise in potted plant soil. Lightly water soil to keep flowers fresh. Wrap bright-colored accent cloth around pots to mask them. Cover remaining tabletop with large, clean palm fronds and tropical leaves.

Find a small trunk (about 12 × 18 × 8 inches) resembling a treasure chest at a toy store or antique store. If chest has undesirable design on outside, spray with gold or silver paint. Place chest in center of table and fill with crumpled newspaper. Cover newspaper with a long piece of gold lamé and allow fabric to extend over sides of chest onto table. Place costume jewelry and trinkets, such as rhinestones, faux gem earrings, pearl necklaces, and gold foil-covered chocolate coins, on fabric in chest. Place food platters on top of palm fronds on either side of treasure chest. Scatter jewelry and chocolate coins on table and around food platters (see "Personalized Party Favors," page 242).

Pirate's Personal Eye-Patch Napkin Ties

Use bright-colored cloth, inexpensive cotton scarves, or bandanas for napkins. Fold napkins in half and roll lengthwise. Purchase a black eye patch from a costume store for each guest plus the host. Write guests' names on eye patches in bright-colored fabric paint and allow to dry completely. Wrap eye patches around center of napkin. Do not cut string on patches, so guests may wear them. Set the napkins in a basket on buffet table.

Shark Burgers with Zombie Salsa

MAKES 6 SERVINGS; ABOUT 2 CUPS SALSA

A Zombie is one of those classic tropical drinks that is honored with its own ceremonial glass at Polynesian restaurants. I've had Zombies served in everything from a ceramic volcano to a porcelain Buddha with a hole in his belly for the straw! Serve any remaining salsa on the side in a hollowed coconut or rustic vessel.

2 POUNDS SHARK FILET, SKINNED, BONED, AND FINELY CHOPPED

¾ CUP SOURDOUGH BREAD CRUMBS

1 CLOVE GARLIC, MINCED

¼ CUP MINCED RED BELL PEPPER

1 EGG, LIGHTLY BEATEN

½ TEASPOON DRY MUSTARD

½ TEASPOON SALT

½ TEASPOON BLACK PEPPER

VEGETABLE OIL

6 HAMBURGER BUNS

ZOMBIE SALSA

1½ CUPS SEEDED, DICED ROMA TOMATOES

¾ CUP DICED PAPAYA

½ CUP DICED RED ONION

⅓ CUP FINELY CHOPPED FRESH CILANTRO LEAVES

1 TABLESPOON FRESHLY GRATED ORANGE ZEST

1 TABLESPOON FRESH LIME JUICE

1 TABLESPOON PINEAPPLE JUICE

1 TEASPOON JAMAICAN RUM

1 TABLESPOON APRICOT BRANDY

½ TEASPOON SALT

To make Zombie Salsa: Place all the ingredients in a bowl and stir to combine. Cover the salsa and let stand for 1 hour at room temperature before serving, so flavors can blend. (To make ahead, store in an airtight container in the refrigerator for up to 4 hours. Bring to room temperature before serving.)

Combine the shark, bread crumbs, garlic, bell pepper, egg, mustard, salt, and black pepper in a large bowl; mix with clean hands until thoroughly combined. Form 6 (½-inch-thick) patties from mixture.

Heat 1 tablespoon oil in a large skillet over medium heat. Add the patties and cook until bottoms are browned, 5 to 8 minutes. Turn and cook on other side until browned and patties are cooked through, 5 minutes. Remove from heat and top with Zombie Salsa. Serve hot on hamburger buns.

Jamaican Rum Plantains

MAKES 6 TO 8 SERVINGS

Bananas Foster is my favorite dessert, so this caramelized Jamaican rum plantain recipe is now my favorite side dish. We served this sweet and pungent vegetable at my sister-in-law's bridal shower. It's a family tradition to throw a honeymoon destination-themed shower for all brides-to-be, and this prenuptial party was set in a Jamaican paradise.

6 RIPE PLANTAINS (ABOUT 5 POUNDS), PEELED

½ CUP (1 STICK) UNSALTED BUTTER

½ CUP PACKED LIGHT BROWN SUGAR

½ CUP JAMAICAN RUM

Slice the plantains crosswise on the diagonal into ¼-inch-thick pieces.

Melt the butter in a skillet over medium-high heat and add the plantains. Cook, stirring occasionally, until plantains begin to brown, 8 to 10 minutes. Reduce heat to medium and stir in the sugar and rum. Cook, stirring constantly, until sugar dissolves, 1 minute more.

Remove from heat and place in a serving dish. Serve hot.

NOTE: Plantains are bananas with a tough, brownish-yellow outer skin when ripe. Very starchy, they must be cooked before eating.

Personalized Party Favors

Bridal couples always offer cocktail napkins or books of matches embossed with their names as tokens for their guests. Here is a list of companies that personalize unique items for parties and special events. I imagine that most have minimum order requirements and charge for shipping costs. Call or visit the web site and ask for details, and possibly a sample of their work. Or visit adspecialty.com, an Internet resource for the promotions industry, whose companies put corporate logos on everything from glassware to golf balls.

BATH, BODY, CANDLE PRODUCTS—*Kiss Me in the Garden (800) 547-7889; www.kissmeinthegarden.com*

CANDY BAR WRAPPERS—*Carson Enterprises (800) 995-2288; www.heresheis.com*

CHAMPAGNE AND WINE BOTTLE LABELS—*Vino Design (619) 273-5695; www.vinodesign.com*

CHOCOLATE COINS, GOLD FOIL-WRAPPED—*Chocolate Cheers (888) 324-3377; www.chocolatecheers.com*

CHOCOLATE MINTS AND STICKS—*Courtney Enterprises, Inc. (800) 323-0789*

EVERGREEN SEEDLINGS IN TUBES—*The Green World Project (800) 825-5122; www.greenworldproject.com*

FLOWER AND TREE SEED PACKETS—*Forever & Always Company, L.L.C. (800) 404-4025; www.foreverandalways.com*

GOLF TEES—*House of Tees (800) 832-5457*

PLAYING CARDS AND CASINO SUPPLIES—*Kardwell International (800) 233-0828 www.kardwell.com*

RICE ROSES—*Rice Roses (800) 240-9900*

SATIN RIBBONS AND BUBBLES—*Regal Ribbons (800) 844-0114; www.regalribbons.com*

WINE CORKS—*L'Affaire du Temps (408) 946-7758; www.laffairedutemps.com*

Red Beans and Rum Rice

MAKES 6 TO 8 SERVINGS

A staple of Jamaican cuisine, these little red beauties look spectacular in a sea of rice accented with ripe golden mango. Black beans are also terrific in this rum rice.

1 CUP DRIED RED BEANS

1 CUP LONG-GRAIN RICE

1¾ CUPS WATER

¼ CUP JAMAICAN RUM

½ CUP DICED MANGO

1 TEASPOON FRESH THYME

2 TABLESPOONS BUTTER

½ TEASPOON SALT

¼ TEASPOON BLACK PEPPER

Rinse the beans and place in a medium saucepan. Fill the pan with water until water line is 2 inches above the beans. Soak the beans overnight in water.

Bring the beans, in the soaking water, to a boil over medium heat. Cover and simmer until beans are tender, 1½ hours. Remove from heat and drain beans.

Place the rice in a colander and rinse with cold water until water draining from rice runs clear. Set aside in colander for 30 minutes to allow rice to dry.

Bring the water and rum to a boil in a medium saucepan over medium-high heat. Stir in the rice, mango, and thyme; cover, and reduce heat to low. Cook until liquid is absorbed and rice is tender, 15 to 20 minutes. Remove from heat and pour into a large bowl.

Add the beans, butter, salt, and pepper to rice and toss until combined. Serve hot.

Rum and Sweet Potato Cornbread

I used to eat cornbread every morning for breakfast. Just sweet enough to give you a little energy and hearty enough to start your day, this bread is made extra special by the addition of sweet potatoes.

---

1 CUP ALL-PURPOSE FLOUR

1 CUP YELLOW CORNMEAL

1/3 CUP SUGAR

1 TABLESPOON BAKING POWDER

1/2 TEASPOON GROUND CINNAMON

1/2 TEASPOON SALT

1 CUP BUTTERMILK

2 EGGS

1/4 CUP UNSALTED BUTTER, MELTED AND COOLED

2 TABLESPOONS JAMAICAN RUM

1 CUP FINELY SHREDDED SWEET POTATO

1/2 CUP COOKED, CANNED, OR FROZEN WHOLE-KERNEL CORN

Preheat oven to 350F (175C). Butter an 8-inch round cake pan.

Sift the flour, cornmeal, sugar, baking powder, cinnamon, and salt into a large bowl. In another bowl, whisk together the buttermilk, eggs, butter, and rum until blended. Add the egg mixture to the dry mixture and stir until just combined. Fold in the sweet potatoes and corn until evenly distributed throughout mixture. Pour batter into prepared dish.

Bake for 45 minutes or until a knife inserted in center comes out clean. Cut into wedges and serve warm.

GIN! FOR 8

*T*he "Rat Pack" is back in full swing with this martini-inspired menu and its record biz table design. I came up with a lot of the record label ideas listed below for a TV appearance on ABC's *Caryl & Marilyn* talk show. The "countdown" king Casey Kasem was also on the show with his wife, Jeanne, and the song-themed crafts seemed to fit. Whip up this menu for a dinner party of music aficionados. Of course you may take a few lumps for being a disco fan as guests read the labels on their drink coasters. And don't destroy any classic Beatles albums or your friends may never speak to you again.

Gin may seem like an offbeat ingredient to cook with, but it was a very trendy flavoring in the early 80s. Many five-star restaurants seasoned gamier dishes, such as duck and venison, with juniper berries, whose flavor is the essence of gin. Juniper berries are usually found in a dried form and may have to be ordered by your grocer.

Martini Olive Tapenade

Coriander Gin Rickey Vinaigrette on Field Greens and Pear Tomatoes

Broiled Orange and Tarragon Trout

Orange and Walnut Gin Rolls

FOOD AND DRINK PLANNER

ONE DAY BEFORE: Make Martini Olive Tapenade. Make Orange and Walnut Gin Rolls.

JUST BEFORE SERVING: Make Coriander Gin Rickey Vinaigrette on Field Greens and Pear Tomatoes. Make Broiled Orange and Tarragon Trout.

COCKTAIL SUGGESTION: Classic Martini: Add 2 ounces gin and ½ ounce dry vermouth to ice in a cocktail shaker. Shake and strain into martini glasses. Garnish with a skewered green olive.

WINE SUGGESTION: 1998 B. R. Cohn Carneros Chardonnay (see "The Wine List," page 23, for more information)

TIMESAVERS: Substitute prepared rolls from a bakery for Orange and Walnut Gin Rolls. Substitute prepared dressing for Coriander Gin Rickey Vinaigrette.

TABLE SETTING AND DECORATING IDEAS: A Swingin' Record Table

TABLE LINEN: Use Summer Brights suggested in "Color Families and Complementary Shade" (see page 6).

45 Record Flower Holder

Cut top flaps off an 8-inch-square cardboard box. Spray box with bright-colored enamel spray paint and allow to dry completely. Glue old 45 records on each side of box. Set box in center of table. Place medium-size vase or watertight coffee can inside box. Top rim of vase should be lower than top rim of box. Fill vase halfway with water and arrange flowers such as tulips or roses in vase. Add greenery to vase to fill in arrangement and mask top edge of box.

LP Record Base Plates

Set old clean LP records at each person's place, to use as base plates under dinner plates.

45 Record Napkin Rings

Slip napkin through center hole of a 45 record and set at each place at the table.

LP Record Label Drink Coasters or Candle Bases

Using scissors, cut into old LP records to outer edge of center labels. Cut out center labels and trim off any rough edges. Use as drink coasters during cocktail hour. Or place votive candle in label center and set on a small saucer to catch melted wax. Place candles around table.

Martini Olive Tapenade

MAKES 2 ½ CUPS

*A*bout 5 years ago, Los Angeles trattorias began serving complimentary tapenade, or minced olives, as an accompaniment for bread. This tapenade rendition mixes the briny green martini olives with the mellow black olives. This spread will be a real winner with the olive lovers in the crowd.

⅓ CUP OLIVE OIL

2 (8-OUNCE) CANS BUTTON MUSHROOMS

1 TEASPOON DRY MUSTARD

1 TABLESPOON MUSTARD SEEDS

½ TEASPOON CRUSHED RED PEPPER FLAKES

3 TABLESPOONS GIN

1 (6-OUNCE) CAN LARGE BLACK OLIVES, PITTED

1 CUP PIMIENTO-STUFFED GREEN OLIVES

½ TEASPOON SALT

½ TEASPOON BLACK PEPPER

2 FRENCH BAGUETTES, THINLY SLICED, OR CRACKERS

Cook the oil, mushrooms, dry mustard, mustard seeds, red pepper flakes, and gin in a small saucepan over medium heat for 10 minutes. Remove from heat and cool to room temperature.

Place the mushroom mixture and olives in a food processor; pulse until olives are finely minced. For a creamier texture, process mixture until smooth.

Spoon tapenade into a small bowl. (To make ahead, tapenade can be stored in an airtight container in the refrigerator for up to 3 days.) Serve with thin baguette slices or crackers in a basket.

VARIATION

For a tray passed hors d'oeuvre, spoon 1 teaspoon tapenade on each baguette slice and serve.

Coriander Gin Rickey Vinaigrette on Field Greens and Pear Tomatoes

MAKES 8 SERVINGS

The lime, sugar, and gin used in this recipe are also the ingredients for the tart Gin Rickey cocktail. Crushed coriander, an aromatic spice and perfect partner for the unique flavor of gin, finishes off this spiked vinaigrette

1 BUNCH ARUGULA, WASHED AND PATTED DRY

2 HEADS RADICCHIO, WASHED AND PATTED DRY

1 LARGE HEAD RED LEAF LETTUCE, WASHED AND PATTED DRY

1/2 CUP RED PEAR TOMATOES, STEMS REMOVED

1/2 CUP YELLOW PEAR TOMATOES, STEMS REMOVED

1 TABLESPOON WHOLE CORIANDER SEEDS, CRUSHED

1 1/2 TABLESPOONS BALSAMIC VINEGAR

2 TEASPOONS GIN

1/4 CUP FRESH LIME JUICE

2 TEASPOONS SUGAR

1/2 CUP OLIVE OIL

Tear stems off the arugula and place it in a large bowl. Tear the radicchio and red leaf lettuce into bite-size pieces and add to bowl. Cut the tomatoes in half lengthwise and add to bowl.

Whisk together the coriander seeds, vinegar, gin, lime juice, sugar, and oil in a small bowl until blended. Pour vinaigrette over greens and toss to coat. Serve in a large salad bowl or on individual plates.

NOTE: Pear tomatoes may be labeled as teardrop tomatoes. Substitute baby tomatoes or cherry tomatoes if pear tomatoes are not available.

Broiled Orange and Tarragon Trout

MAKES 8 SERVINGS

I have a secret passion for trout farms that my family and friends occasionally indulge. I love how they outfit you with a rod, reel, and tiny balls of process cheese, the standard farm bait. Then they point out the spot in the pond where the fish are really bitin'. My husband jokes that we could just open the car door and the trout would jump into the backseat. It's a lot of fun, without a lot of effort, and the fish are tasty.

1 CLOVE GARLIC, MINCED

½ CUP (1 STICK) BUTTER, MELTED AND COOLED

½ CUP FRESH ORANGE JUICE

1 TABLESPOON GIN

3 TABLESPOONS CHOPPED FRESH TARRAGON

½ TEASPOON SALT

¼ TEASPOON WHITE PEPPER

8 (8-OUNCE) TROUT FILETS, SCALED

8 ORANGE SLICES

Preheat broiler to high. Mix the garlic, butter, orange juice, gin, tarragon, salt, and pepper until combined.

Arrange trout filets, skin side down, on a rack in a broiler pan. Brush the trout with generous amount of the orange-butter mixture. Broil for 8 for 10 minutes or until trout changes from translucent to opaque in center.

Place trout on a large platter or individual plates and garnish with orange slices on top.

Orange and Walnut Gin Rolls

MAKES 16 ROLLS

These orange-enriched nutty rolls are made with a combination of rye flour and bread flour. Rye, also a standard liquor in bar wells, is rarely ordered these days except for the infrequent mixed drink of rye and ginger ale. Its earthy taste blends beautifully with the hint of gin in these dinner rolls.

¾ CUP FRESH ORANGE JUICE

¼ CUP GIN

1 TABLESPOON SUGAR

2 TEASPOONS ACTIVE DRY YEAST

¼ CUP OLIVE OIL

½ TEASPOON SALT

2 CUPS BREAD FLOUR

1 CUP RYE FLOUR

2 TABLESPOONS FRESHLY GRATED ORANGE ZEST

½ CUP CHOPPED WALNUTS

Heat the orange juice and gin in a small saucepan over medium-low heat until liquid is lukewarm, about 110F (45C).

Place the lukewarm juice and gin mixture, sugar, and yeast in a large bowl. Let stand until yeast is bubbly, about 10 minutes.

Whisk the oil and salt into the yeast mixture until blended. Stir in bread flour and rye flour. Mix with a bread hook or knead with clean hands until flour is incorporated. Turn out dough onto a floured surface and knead until it is smooth and elastic, but not sticky, about 10 minutes. Use more flour if necessary.

Oil a large, clean bowl and transfer dough into bowl. Cover bowl with plastic wrap and place in a warm, draft-free area. Let dough stand until it doubles in size, about 2 hours.

Line 2 baking sheets with waxed paper. Turn out dough onto floured surface and knead dough until deflated. Sprinkle walnuts and orange zest over dough. Knead until walnuts and zest are evenly distributed throughout dough. Cut dough into 16 equal pieces. Roll each piece with palms of your hands into a smooth ball. Place rolls 1 inch apart on prepared sheets. Cover loosely with waxed paper and let stand in a warm place until dough slightly rises again, about 1½ hours.

Preheat oven to 375F (190C). Using clean scissors, snip small X on the top of each roll. Bake 20 minutes or until light brown. Serve piping hot. (To make ahead, store baked rolls in an airtight container at room temperature up to 2 days. Reheat, wrapped in foil, in a 350F [175C] oven about 10 minutes.)

Intimate Encounters

APHRODISIAC ALERT FOR 2

Caviar Mousse on Brioche Toast

Red Passion Salad

Pasta with Sweet Red Pepper and Sherry Cream Sauce

Chocolate and Orange Liqueur Truffle Torte

INAMORATO FOR 2

Wild Mushroom Ragout

Prosciutto and Artichoke Tagliati on Chicken

Seared Vegetable Polenta Tart

Tangerino Ice Cream

MY BIRTHDAY MENU FOR 4

Salmon with Vodka Dill Sauce

Tomato and Feta Couscous Cakes

Roasted Asparagus Spears in a Mustard-Wine Vinaigrette

Irish Cream Bread Pudding with Saucy Crème Anglaise

APHRODISIAC ALERT FOR 2

*M*ake the most of Valentine's Day and serve this sensuous menu complete with its romantic table setting design. Valentine's Day has a history rooted in both religion and social tradition. What originally was the Roman fertility feast of Lupercalia, February 15 was moved to February 14 and commemorated the martyr St. Valentine around A.D. 270. On that day hearts and flowers were exchanged by lovers who were experiencing difficulties in their relationship. By the seventeenth century, England recognized the day as a time to acknowledge loved ones rather than to save a couple in turmoil. We Americans decided to join in the celebration in the 1700s by giving tokens of affection to friends and notes to lovers. Even though the stores offer everything from greeting cards to chocolate roses for this holiday, a gift from the kitchen will make a lasting impression on one's heart.

———

Caviar Mousse on Brioche Toast

Red Passion Salad

Pasta with Sweet Red Pepper and Sherry Cream Sauce

Chocolate and Orange Liqueur Truffle Torte

———

FOOD AND DRINK PLANNER

ONE DAY BEFORE: Make Brioche Toast. Make Chocolate and Orange Liqueur Truffle Torte.

PARTY DAY: Make Caviar Mousse.

JUST BEFORE SERVING: Pipe Caviar Mousse on Brioche Toast. Make Red Passion Salad. Make Pasta with Sweet Red Pepper and Sherry Cream Sauce.

COCKTAIL SUGGESTION: Passion Fruit Cocktail: Pour 2 ounces Alize passion fruit liqueur over ice in a tall glass; fill glass with mango juice and add a splash of grenadine on top.

WINE SUGGESTION: 1997 Cakebread Cellars Rubaiyat (see "The Wine List," page 23, for more information)

TIMESAVERS: Substitute prepared brioche from a bakery. Substitute prepared chocolate cake from a bakery for the Chocolate and Orange Liqueur Truffle Torte.

TABLE SETTING AND DECORATING IDEAS: Valentine Hearts and Flowers (see "Traditional Candle Sticks with Accents," page 4)

TABLE LINEN: Use red table linen.

Red Roses in a Valentine Hatbox

During the week before your event, cut out heart shapes and Valentine images, such as Cupid, from magazines or greeting cards. Using spray adhesive, glue images to the side of hatbox, overlapping images until entire outer surface of box is covered. Spray a clear acrylic spray, found at craft or hardware stores, over images in a well-ventilated area. Allow acrylic to dry completely. Place a glass or plastic container about the same size as the hatbox inside. If there is a space between container and hatbox, add moss to fill the space. Roses should extend just above hatbox rim in a tight cluster and cover entire top surface of foam, like a beautiful floral blanket.

Silver or Crystal Candlesticks

Place candlesticks on either side of Valentine Hatbox centerpiece.

Valentine Place Cards

Place a Valentine card at each person's place at the table.

Red Ribbon Napkin Ties

Tie a wide red cloth ribbon in a large bow around napkins and place at each place setting. If desired, affix a Cupid or heart trinket to bow.

Caviar Mousse on Brioche Toast

MAKES ABOUT 1 ¼ CUPS

This light mousse is actually a Greek specialty typically served with pita bread. A light brioche is substituted for the pita, refining this appetizer into a chic nibbler. Although black caviar or lumpfish roe is commonly found in stores, the color of this mousse is an odd gray when black roe is used. The taste is remarkable no matter what color you use but the dish is more visually pleasing when red roe is used.

¾ CUP COARSELY CHOPPED, PEELED RUSSET POTATOES

¼ CUP CHOPPED RED ONION

3 TABLESPOONS RED CAVIAR OR RED SALMON ROE, PLUS EXTRA FOR TOPPING (OPTIONAL)

⅔ CUP OLIVE OIL

1 TABLESPOON FRESH LEMON JUICE

1 TABLESPOON DRY VERMOUTH

5 (¼-INCH-THICK) SLICES BRIOCHE (PAGE 257)

Boil the potatoes, covered, in a small saucepan of water until tender, 10 minutes. Drain potatoes and pat dry. Cool completely.

Place the onion and caviar in a blender jar. With blender running, slowly add the olive oil in a steady stream through hole in blender lid. Process until mixture emulsifies to a mayonnaise consistency, 3 to 5 minutes. Transfer to a small bowl and set aside. Place the potatoes, lemon juice, and vermouth in blender and puree until smooth. Add caviar mixture to potatoes and whip until blended. Spoon into small bowl, cover, and refrigerate until ready to use. (To make ahead, store mousse in an airtight container in the refrigerator for up to 2 days.)

Preheat oven to 350F (175C). Cut brioche slices crosswise into thirds and place on a baking sheet. Bake for 5 minutes or until lightly toasted. Cool for 5 minutes. (To make ahead, store toasted brioche in an airtight container at room temperature for up to 1 week or freeze for up to 1 month.)

Using a star tip, pipe about 1 teaspoon mousse on each brioche square or spread mousse on square with knife. If desired, top with a light sprinkling of caviar. Serve cool.

Brioche

*B*rioche is a rich classic French yeast bread made with eggs and butter. Although usually baked in a special fluted mold, here it is baked in a regular loaf pan. Thinly sliced and cut into hors d'oeuvre-size portions, it makes the perfect base for spreads. Leftover brioche is great for bread pudding or for breakfast French toast.

¼ CUP LUKEWARM MILK, ABOUT 110F (45C)

1 TABLESPOON SUGAR

1 TEASPOON ACTIVE DRY YEAST

⅓ CUP UNSALTED BUTTER, SOFTENED

2 EGGS

2 CUPS BREAD FLOUR

½ TEASPOON SALT

Place the milk, sugar, and yeast in a small bowl. Let stand until yeast is bubbly, about 10 minutes.

Beat the butter in a large bowl until smooth. Add the eggs and beat until blended. Stir in the yeast mixture. Add the flour and salt. Mix with a bread hook or knead with clean hands until flour is incorporated and dough forms a soft ball. Knead until dough is smooth and elastic, but not sticky, about 5 minutes. Use more flour if necessary.

Butter a large bowl and transfer dough into bowl. Cover the bowl with plastic wrap and place in a warm, draft-free area. Let dough stand until it doubles in size, about 2 hours.

Turn dough over in bowl and lightly punch dough until deflated. Cover and refrigerate for about 2 hours or until dough doubles in size.

Butter a 9 × 5-inch loaf pan. On a lightly floured surface, with floured hands, form dough into a loaf and place in prepared pan. Let stand, uncovered, in a warm place until loaf doubles in size, about 2 hours.

Preheat oven to 375F (190C). Bake on middle rack of oven for 15 to 20 minutes or until golden brown. Cool in the pan on a wire rack for 5 minutes. Remove from pan and cool completely on wire rack. (Brioche can be stored in an airtight container at room temperature up to 3 days or frozen up to 1 month.)

Red Passion Salad

*T*his simple salad sums up a love affair: passion-inducing ingredients, each with its own preparation technique and little quirks, leading to a whimsical romantic interlude.

---

2 TABLESPOONS ALIZE PASSION FRUIT LIQUEUR

3 TABLESPOONS OLIVE OIL

1 TABLESPOON BALSAMIC VINEGAR

1/8 TEASPOON SALT

1/8 TEASPOON BLACK PEPPER

1 SMALL HEAD RED LEAF LETTUCE, WASHED AND PATTED DRY

2 HEARTS OF PALM STALKS (SEE NOTE BELOW)

1/4 RED ONION

3 TABLESPOONS COARSELY CHOPPED WALNUTS

2 TABLESPOONS POMEGRANATE SEEDS

Whisk together the liqueur, oil, vinegar, salt, and pepper in a small bowl.

Tear the lettuce into bite-size pieces and place in a large bowl. Cut the hearts of palm stalks into 1/2-inch slices and add to lettuce. Shave wafer-thin slices from the red onion, using a mandolin or the wide blade of a grater. Add the onion and walnuts to the lettuce mixture. Pour dressing over ingredients and toss to coat.

Divide salad between 2 serving plates. Sprinkle pomegranate seeds on top and serve.

NOTE: Hearts of palm are velvety white stalks, usually available canned and packed in brine. They can be found in the canned vegetable section of your grocery store, typically next to the artichokes.

Aphrodisiac Foods

An aphrodisiac is any food, drink, herb, or spice that puts you in the mood for love. When entertaining that special someone, heat things up with sensuous food and facts.

Oysters

Oysters are a classic aphrodisiac. They have a supple, feminine texture and a high zinc content, known to make a man very potent.

Pomegranate Seeds and Nuts

Cleopatra's secret aphrodisiac was the ruby red seeds of the pomegranate. Seeds, such as pumpkin and sunflower seeds, and nuts are known for their fertility-enhancing powers. Like the oyster, they are loaded with zinc. The Latin name of the walnut genus is *Juglans*, which loosely translates as "glans of Jupiter." In ancient Rome, wedding guests threw walnuts instead of rice, wishing the new couple a fruitful family life.

Ginger, Cloves, and Saffron

Certain compounds in these pungent spices are known to be aphrodisiacs when used orally and topically. Mixtures containing ginger and cloves apparently cure impotence. Saffron has a hormonelike effect, which is thought to be from crocin. This expensive spice owes its orange color to crocin which plays a key role in the reproductive process of algae.

Nutmeg

This Yuletide spice for eggnog has been called a "legal hallucinogen." Nutmeg is a seed from an evergreen tree, *Myristica fragrans*. Myristicin, a component of nutmeg, supposedly has a structure similar to mescaline. Mescaline is the mind-altering element of the peyote cactus. Large doses of nutmeg have severe side effects.

Chocolate

The gift of a heart-shaped box of chocolates is my favorite aphrodisiac. Chocolate contains phenylethylamine, a natural substance that allegedly produces the physical feeling of falling in love.

Wine

Sine Cerere et Libero friget Venus basically translates as "Without food and wine, Venus will freeze." Venus, being the goddess of love, warms her heart through her mouth with delicious edibles.

Pasta with Sweet Red Pepper and Sherry Cream Sauce

MAKES 2 TO 4 SERVINGS

My sweet husband, John Sparano, developed this recipe, and we enjoy it monthly. We're cream sauce fanatics, and this rich, sherried blend loaded with Italian sausage is marvelous. You can use any pasta you like with this sauce, but I don't recommend smaller shells or penne. Our rule of thumb is that the pasta has to be larger or longer than the ingredients in the sauce. If you really love pasta, cook the larger amount.

2 MEDIUM RED BELL PEPPERS	1 CUP CREAM SHERRY
3 TABLESPOONS OLIVE OIL	1½ CUPS HEAVY CREAM
1½ POUNDS ITALIAN SAUSAGE LINKS	½ TO 1 POUND FETTUCCINE
1 TABLESPOON BUTTER	1 TEASPOON SALT
1½ TABLESPOONS CHOPPED FRESH ROSEMARY	¾ CUP FRESHLY GRATED PARMESAN CHEESE, PLUS EXTRA FOR SERVING
2 CLOVES GARLIC, MINCED	

Preheat oven to 450F (230C). Place bell peppers in a baking pan and bake, turning occasionally, for 30 minutes or until peppers are roasted and skin is lightly blackened. Cool slightly. Remove stems and seeds from peppers and cut into slivers. If desired, peel away the blackened portions of skin (I prefer to leave them on).

Meanwhile, heat 1 tablespoon of the oil in a large skillet over medium-high heat. Add the sausage links, and cook, turning occasionally, until browned on all sides, about 15 minutes. Remove from heat and cool slightly. Cut crosswise, on the diagonal, into ½-inch-thick slices and set aside.

In the same skillet, heat the butter and 1 tablespoon of the olive oil with the sausage drippings over medium-high heat. Add the rosemary and garlic; cook 2 minutes. Add the sherry and cook until it reduces to half, about 3 minutes. Reduce heat to medium-low and stir in the cream. Add the sliced sausage and cook, stirring occasionally, until mixture thickens and sausage is no longer pink in center, 10 minutes.

Meanwhile, cook pasta according to package directions, adding 1 teaspoon salt and remaining 1 tablespoon olive oil to water used to cook pasta.

Add the bell peppers to the cream sauce and cook until they are heated, about 3 minutes. Remove from heat and stir in the Parmesan cheese.

Drain the pasta in colander and transfer to a large bowl. Pour sauce over pasta and toss to coat completely. To make ahead, store sauced pasta, covered, in the refrigerator for up to 2 days. Reheat before serving. Place pasta on individual dinner plates or bowls and serve hot with freshly grated Parmesan on the side.

Chocolate and Orange Liqueur Truffle Torte

MAKES 6 SERVINGS

*C*hocolate and Grand Marnier are absolutely sinful in this truffle torte. For lovers who hold off on dessert and spend the evening dancing, this cake is best savored at midnight, as a romantic nightcap.

---

3 OUNCES UNSWEETENED CHOCOLATE, COARSELY CHOPPED

1/3 CUP UNSALTED BUTTER, SOFTENED

1 CUP SUGAR

2 EGGS

1 EGG YOLK

1 CUP ALL-PURPOSE FLOUR

1/4 CUP UNSWEETENED COCOA POWDER

1 TEASPOON BAKING POWDER

1/2 TEASPOON BAKING SODA

1/8 TEASPOON SALT

1/3 CUP GRAND MARNIER

1/3 CUP WATER

GLAZE

5 OUNCES SEMISWEET CHOCOLATE

2 1/2 TABLESPOONS UNSALTED BUTTER

1 TABLESPOON GRAND MARNIER

1/4 TEASPOON FRESHLY GRATED ORANGE ZEST

Preheat oven to 325F (165C). Butter a 9-inch round cake pan and line bottom with waxed paper. Butter waxed paper and dust with flour until pan bottom and sides are coated. Shake out excess flour. Place on a baking sheet.

To make the cake: Melt chocolate in top of double boiler or in small saucepan over a larger pot of simmering water, stirring constantly. Remove from heat and cool 5 minutes. Beat the butter and sugar in a large bowl until creamy. Add the eggs and egg yolk, one at a time, beating after each addition to incorporate. Beat in the chocolate until combined.

Sift together the flour, cocoa powder, baking powder, baking soda, and salt. While beating on low speed, add half of the dry ingredients to the egg mixture and beat until mixed. Gradually add the Grand Marnier, beating on low speed until mixed. Add the remaining dry ingredients and gradually add the water, beating on low speed until just mixed. Pour batter into prepared pan.

Place baking sheet with pan on middle rack of oven. Bake 30 to 40 minutes or until a knife inserted in center comes out clean. Cool in pan on a wire rack for 15 minutes. Run a knife around edge of cake in pan and invert on wire rack to cool completely.

To make the glaze: Melt the chocolate, stirring constantly, in top of a double boiler over simmering water or in a small saucepan, over a larger pot of simmering water. Remove from heat; stir in butter and Grand Marnier. Cool for 10 minutes.

Invert cake onto serving platter. Pour the glaze over top of cake so it runs down sides. Sprinkle orange zest over top. Cut into wedges and serve at room temperature. (To make ahead, store glazed cake, covered, in the refrigerator for up to 1 week. Leftovers can be frozen for up to 1 month. Bring to room temperature or warm before serving.)

INAMORATO FOR 2

*L*ove is the most popular theme in literature and song, and *inamorato* is the male embodiment of the emotion. "A man in love" is the word's literal translation (*inamorata* is the feminine version). So is the way to a man's heart through his stomach? I have a female friend who jokes, "Sure, it's the way, if you punch some sense into him." Okay, so some guys need more than an award-winning lasagna.

Romance can certainly be conjured up by stimulating the senses with a CD of "Bolero" and a liquor-laden entree. But creating a mood is a whole other art form. For you men and women searching for the perfect atmosphere for *amore*, look no further. You can magically turn your living room into a moonlit terrace by following the table decorating ideas below. As an uplifting note for my lovelorn gal pal, the Twinkling Light Table for Two is not my invention, but that of the man who set it up in my living room one very memorable night.

———

Wild Mushroom Ragout

Prosciutto and Artichoke Tagliati on Chicken

Seared Vegetable Polenta Tart

Tangerino Ice Cream

———

FOOD AND DRINK PLANNER

ONE DAY BEFORE: Make Tangerino Ice Cream. Make Seared Vegetable Polenta.

PARTY DAY: Make Wild Mushroom Ragout.

JUST BEFORE SERVING: Make Prosciutto and Artichoke Tagliati on Chicken.

COCKTAIL SUGGESTION: Amaretto Iced Tea: Pour 2 ounces amaretto and ½ ounce lemon juice over ice in a tall glass; fill glass with cold tea and garnish with a lemon wedge.

WINE SUGGESTIONS: 1997 Teruzzi & Puthod Terre di Tufi (see "The Wine List," page 23 for more information)

TIMESAVER: Substitute Italian bread and butter and a green salad for Seared Vegetable Polenta Tart.

TABLE SETTING AND DECORATING IDEAS: Moonlit Piazza and Thou

TABLE LINEN: Use a white cloth.

Twinkling Light Table for Two

Set up a card table or 36-inch round table in an outdoor area, if the climate permits, near an electrical outlet. If outdoors is not an option, set the table up in the living room. Rent or purchase 4 (about 5-foot-high) potted ficus trees from a nursery. Plant rental is easy in Los Angeles and other cities where movies are made; many nurseries rent to commercial productions, charging 10 percent of the cost plus a refundable deposit. Make the same financial offer to your nursery to rent the plants. Set trees around the table about 5 feet from table edge. Place plastic wrap under pots if set indoors on a carpet or wood floor. Wrap white fabric around pots to mask. Drape strands of miniature white lights around trees and plug into electrical outlet. Make sure cords are safely placed to avoid tripping. If your table is set up outside near bushes or trees, wrap lights around these instead of potted ficus trees.

Floating Gardenias

Fill a 6-inch-diameter glass bubble bowl halfway with water. Float 2 gardenias in water. Do not touch gardenia petals or they will quickly turn brown.

Votive Candles

Place votive candles in glass holders around table.

Wild Mushroom Ragout

MAKES 2 SERVINGS

*R*agout is stew with a fancy name. Mushrooms of all shapes and sizes make this incredibly easy and hearty dish a real one-pot wonder. Gourmet mushrooms can be pricey, often $4.00 per ounce. Make this dish with a combination of less expensive mushrooms: 8 ounces fresh button or brown mushrooms and 2 ounces of porcini, chanterelles, morels, or portabellos.

---

10 OUNCES ASSORTED MUSHROOMS, SLICED

1 MEDIUM BROWN ONION, CUT INTO SLIVERS

1 CUP BEEF BROTH

¾ CUP MERLOT

2 TABLESPOONS CHOPPED FRESH ITALIAN PARSLEY

1 TEASPOON SALT

¼ TEASPOON BLACK PEPPER

SEARED VEGETABLE POLENTA TART (PAGE 268)

Heat the mushrooms, onion, broth, and wine in a large skillet over high heat. Cook, stirring occasionally, until liquid reduces to half and mushrooms are very tender, about 15 minutes. Remove from heat and stir in the parsley, salt and pepper. (To make ahead, store, covered, in the refrigerator for up to 1 day. Reheat before serving.)

Spoon mushroom ragout into a medium bowl or on top of a Seared Vegetable Polenta Tart wedge and serve hot.

NOTES: Gourmet mushrooms may be available only dried. Use fresh mushrooms for half of the required amount and dried mushrooms for the remainder if necessary. One ounce of dried mushrooms is equivalent to 4 ounces fresh mushrooms. Dried mushrooms should be washed under running water to remove any sand or dirt. Leave dried mushrooms whole, and slice fresh mushrooms. There is no need to soak the dried mushrooms prior to cooking; just add them to the skillet with the wine and broth.

Prosciutto and Artichoke Tagliati on Chicken

MAKES 2 TO 4 SERVINGS

*M*y dear friend Susan Budd heard I was writing this book and told me of a delicious dish her mother makes with prosciutto-wrapped chicken. Tagliati means "chopped" in Italian, and the ingredients topping the chicken are prepared in this manner. The powerful flavors of salty ham and zesty artichoke make a brilliant combination.

3 OUNCES THIN-SLICED PROSCIUTTO, FINELY CHOPPED

1 CUP CANNED ARTICHOKE HEARTS, DRAINED AND FINELY CHOPPED

2 CLOVES GARLIC, MINCED

½ CUP FRESHLY GRATED PARMESAN CHEESE

2 TABLESPOONS DRY VERMOUTH

2 TABLESPOONS FRESH LEMON JUICE

1 TABLESPOON OLIVE OIL

1½ TEASPOONS SALT

1½ TEASPOONS BLACK PEPPER

4 BONELESS, SKINLESS CHICKEN BREAST HALVES, FAT TRIMMED

Preheat oven to 325F (165C). Grease a baking sheet with olive oil.

Mix the prosciutto, artichoke hearts, garlic, Parmesan cheese, vermouth, lemon juice, oil, ½ teaspoon of the salt, and ¼ teaspoon of the pepper until combined.

Rub the remaining salt and pepper on chicken. Place chicken on prepared baking sheet. Spread prosciutto mixture in an even layer over top of chicken.

Bake for 30 minutes or until the chicken is no longer pink in the center. (To make ahead, store, covered, in the refrigerator up to 2 days.) Transfer to plates and serve hot.

Seared Vegetable Polenta Tart

The first time I made polenta was at a Fellini-themed birthday party for my Italian husband. Fellini, the famed surreallistic film director, had such vibrant imagery in his work that we strove to mimic the master with every element of the party. The food got rave reviews, but the high point of everyone's evening was riding in the rowboat masquerading as a gondola in the pool.

1 TABLESPOON OLIVE OIL	½ CUP FRESHLY GRATED PARMESAN CHEESE
1 CLOVE GARLIC, MINCED	
1 JAPANESE EGGPLANT, THINLY SLICED CROSSWISE	2 CUPS VEGETABLE BROTH
	3 TABLESPOONS DRY WHITE WINE
1 SMALL ZUCCHINI, THINLY SLICED CROSSWISE	¾ CUP YELLOW CORNMEAL
	1 TABLESPOON CHOPPED FRESH BASIL
¾ TEASPOON SALT	
½ CUP CHOPPED SUN-DRIED TOMATOES (DRY PACK)	½ TEASPOON BLACK PEPPER

Heat the oil in a large skillet over high heat. Add the garlic, eggplant, and zucchini; cook, stirring frequently, until vegetables are charred, about 8 minutes. Remove from heat and season with ¼ teaspoon of the salt.

Place the sun-dried tomatoes in a small pot of boiling water for 5 minutes to rehydrate. Reserve 2 tablespoons of the sun-dried tomatoes and 2 tablespoons of the Parmesan cheese; set aside.

Spray a 9-inch round removable-bottom tart pan with nonstick cooking spray.

Bring the broth and wine to a boil in a medium saucepan over medium heat. Slowly sprinkle the cornmeal into broth while quickly whisking mixture. Cook, whisking constantly to smooth out any lumps, until mixture begins to thicken, 3 minutes. Replace the whisk with a wooden spoon and cook, stirring constantly, until mixture thickens, about 1 minute. Spoon should stand up in mixture and polenta will come away from sides of pan. Remove from heat and stir in the rest of Parmesan cheese and sun-dried tomatoes, basil, eggplant, zucchini, pepper, and remaining ½ teaspoon salt until thoroughly combined.

Spoon the mixture in an even layer into prepared pan. Sprinkle reserved sun-dried tomatoes and Parmesan cheese over top. Cool completely. Cover in plastic wrap and refrigerate until firm or up to 3 days.

Just before serving, preheat the broiler. Remove polenta from tart pan. Cut out 2 wedges; refrigerate remaining polenta, covered, for up to 3 days. Broil the polenta wedges until the tops are crisp, about 3 minutes. Serve hot.

Tangerine Ice Cream

*H*ere's the way to make ice cream in your freezer. I have never gotten around to purchasing an ice cream maker because I rarely have ice cream, and it is reasonably easy to prepare without one. Ice cream is basically frozen custard, and this outstanding version is flavored with tangerine and Galliano liqueur.

¾ CUP HEAVY CREAM	PINCH OF SALT
½ CUP MILK	3 EGG YOLKS
⅓ CUP SUGAR	¼ CUP FRESH TANGERINE JUICE
1½ TEASPOONS FRESHLY GRATED TANGERINE ZEST	1 TABLESPOON GALLIANO LIQUEUR

Combine the cream, milk, sugar, zest, and salt in a heavy saucepan. Cook, stirring occasionally, over low heat until mixture just boils, about 8 minutes.

Meanwhile, whisk the egg yolks in a large bowl until thickened. Slowly pour the hot cream mixture into yolks while whisking vigorously.

Pour the mixture back into the pan and cook over low heat, whisking constantly, until mixture thickens slightly, 5 to 7 minutes. Do not allow mixture to boil or it will curdle.

Pour the mixture into a large clean bowl and stir in the tangerine juice and Galliano. Cool to room temperature, stirring occasionally. Pour the cooled mixture into an 8-inch square metal baking pan and freeze covered until firm, 2 to 3 hours.

Transfer the frozen mixture to a food processor and process until smooth. Return to baking pan and freeze until just firm, about 1 hour. Spoon mixture into an airtight container and store in freezer until ready to serve.

MY BIRTHDAY MENU FOR 4

My birthday, January 15, is observed as a federal holiday—for I share it with civil rights leader Martin Luther King, Jr. Coincidentally, in the year of my birth King received the Nobel Peace Prize for his nonviolent political and social activism. As a child I was always happy to have the day off from school, and as an adult I take pride in our common birthday for less selfish reasons.

Other happenings on my birthday include the first time a donkey, drawn by the famed cartoonist Thomas Nast, was used to represent the Democratic Party in an 1870 issue of *Harper's Weekly*. And in 1558 Elizabeth Tudor, daughter of hearty eater Henry VIII and Anne Boleyn, was crowned queen of England. So with January 15 noted for Kings, queens, and, a cartoon figure symbolizing a political party's "assets," my day is pretty full. This menu offers some of my favorite dishes with a musical table setting. I have a passion for playing the classics on the piano.

———

Salmon with Vodka Dill Sauce

Tomato and Feta Couscous Cakes

Roasted Asparagus Spears in Mustard-Wine Vinaigrette

Irish Cream Bread Pudding with a Saucy Crème Anglaise

———

FOOD AND DRINK PLANNER

ONE DAY BEFORE: Make Irish Cream Bread Pudding.

PARTY DAY: Make Saucy Crème Anglaise. Make Tomato and Feta Couscous Cakes.

JUST BEFORE SERVING: Make Roasted Asparagus Spears in Mustard-Wine Vinaigrette. Make Salmon with Vodka Dill Sauce.

JUST BEFORE DESSERT: Reheat Irish Cream Bread Pudding.

COCKTAIL SUGGESTION: Melon Ball: Pour 1 ounce vodka and 1 ounce Midori melon liqueur over ice in a short glass; fill glass with orange juice.

WINE SUGGESTION: 1997 Cakebread Cellars Chardonnay (see "The Wine List," page 23 for more information)

TIMESAVER: Substitute rice or instant couscous for Tomato and Feta Couscous Cakes.

TABLE SETTING AND DECORATING IDEAS: Music Makes the Heart Grow Fonder

TABLE LINEN: Use white table linen.

Calla Lilies in a Violin Case

Buy or rent a violin case from a musical instrument store. Place the open violin case in center of the table. Drape a piece of plush fabric, such as red velvet, inside the case, allowing the fabric to spill over case sides onto table. Trim stems of 5 white calla lilies so entire flowers are approximately the length of the violin case. Lay the flowers in violin case so blooms rest on the rim at wide end of case. To keep the flowers fresh, insert the stems into individual floral tubes. Without water, the flowers will probably last 3 hours.

Sheet Music Place Settings

Purchase printed sheet music for songs that relate to your guests. For example, the perfect music for me would be "I Dream of Jeannie." Set sheet music at each place setting and have guests find where they are sitting by reading the sheet music. Or purchase blank pages of sheet music, on which music staff lines are preceded by treble and bass clefs. Using black ink or a calligraphy pen, write song titles at top of page and lyrics between staff lines. Write musical notes on the staff lines. Use printed sheet music for a reference.

Musical Ornament Napkin Ties

Find musical instrument ornaments at a craft, music, or Christmas store. Feed a thin white cloth ribbon through ornament loophole and tie ribbon in a bow around the napkin.

Salmon with Vodka Dill Sauce

MAKES 4 SERVINGS

Vodka Jeanne Sauce is the official name of this sauce in our home. I credit my husband John with this recipe. Overflowing with capers, dill, and a healthy dose of vodka, this silky masterpiece is my first choice for special occasions like my birthday.

1 TABLESPOON OLIVE OIL	1 CUP HEAVY CREAM
1 TABLESPOON BUTTER	1/4 TEASPOON SALT
1 CLOVE GARLIC, MINCED	1/8 TEASPOON WHITE PEPPER
1 CUP STOLICHNAYA VODKA	4 (8-OUNCE) SALMON FILETS, BONED
3 TABLESPOONS CHOPPED FRESH DILL	3 TABLESPOONS CAPERS
	4 SPRIGS FRESH DILL

Heat the oil, butter, and garlic in large skillet over medium-high heat. Add the vodka and chopped dill; cook until vodka reduces to one-third, 3 to 5 minutes. Reduce heat to medium-low and stir in the cream, salt, and pepper.

Add the salmon to pan, skin side down, along with the capers, and cook for 5 minutes. Turn salmon over and cook until it begins to flake, 8 to 10 minutes.

Place salmon on individual plates and spoon sauce over top. Garnish with fresh dill sprigs.

Tomato and Feta Couscous Cakes

MAKES ABOUT 18 CAKES

Couscous is made from moistened semolina, which is rolled into tiny balls and dried. Instant couscous is perhaps the easiest and quickest side dish to prepare, because it is combined with boiling-hot water or chicken stock and ready to eat in 5 minutes. My sister is the couscous queen! Laura is creative and eclectic so this recipe is dedicated to her.

1¾ CUPS CHICKEN BROTH

¼ CUP DRY VERMOUTH

1 (10-OUNCE) BOX INSTANT COUSCOUS

1 CLOVE GARLIC, MINCED

3 ROMA TOMATOES, SEEDED AND DICED

½ CUP FRESHLY GRATED PARMESAN CHEESE

½ CUP CRUMBLED FETA CHEESE

2 TABLESPOONS FINELY CHOPPED BASIL LEAVES

¼ TEASPOON SALT

¼ TEASPOON BLACK PEPPER

2 TABLESPOONS OLIVE OIL

Bring the chicken broth and vermouth to a boil in a medium saucepan over medium-high heat. Turn off heat and stir in the couscous. Cover and let stand 5 minutes. Fluff couscous with a spoon and stir in the remaining ingredients, except olive oil, until combined.

Preheat broiler. Using 2 tablespoons of the couscous mixture, form ½-inch-thick, 2-inch-diameter cakes. Place cakes on a baking sheet and lightly brush tops of cakes with olive oil. Broil cakes 3 to 5 minutes or until lightly browned.

Place cakes on individual plates and serve hot.

Roasted Asparagus Spears in Mustard-Wine Vinaigrette

MAKES 4 TO 6 SERVINGS

In 1991, I was on the staffing team for the Governor's Ball for the Academy Awards. I'll never forget when a very famous award-winning star picked up a spear of asparagus with his fingers and ate the stalk. Fortunately, the event slipped by the tabloids, but it was a topic for an advice columnist. Apparently, etiquette allows one to eat asparagus with one's fingers whether one is The Graduate *from upper society or not.*

---

2 POUNDS ASPARAGUS SPEARS	3 TABLESPOONS FRESH LEMON JUICE
¼ CUP WHITE WINE	½ TEASPOON SALT
½ CUP OLIVE OIL	¼ TEASPOON BLACK PEPPER
2 TABLESPOONS WHITE WINE VINEGAR	¼ CUP MINCED LEEK
3 TABLESPOONS DIJON MUSTARD	

Preheat oven to 450F (205C). Trim about ½ inch off bottom of asparagus and place in a 13 × 9-inch baking dish.

Whisk together the wine, oil, vinegar, mustard, lemon juice, salt, pepper, and leek in a small bowl. Pour mixture over asparagus spears and turn spears to coat.

Bake for 10 minutes or until spears are roasted. Remove from oven and arrange on a platter. Pour remaining vinaigrette from pan over asparagus and serve hot or at room temperature.

Irish Cream Bread Pudding with a Saucy Crème Anglaise

MAKES 4 TO 6 SERVINGS

Doughnuts, croissants, muffins—I've seen all of these baked goods in various chefs' prized bread pudding recipes. I fell in love with the classic rendition of this dessert smothered in crème anglaise. The Irish touch is a loving tribute to my mother and our saucy heritage.

3 (½- TO 1-INCH-THICK) SLICES DAY-OLD FRENCH BREAD, CRUSTS LEFT ON

1 CUP MILK

3 EGGS

¼ CUP PLUS 1 TABLESPOON SUGAR

⅓ CUP BAILEYS ORIGINAL IRISH CREAM

¼ TEASPOON FRESHLY GRATED NUTMEG

¼ TEASPOON GROUND CINNAMON

¼ CUP DARK RAISINS

¼ CUP GOLDEN RAISINS

CRÈME ANGLAISE

4 EGG YOLKS

⅓ CUP SUGAR

1 CUP MILK

1 TABLESPOON BAILEYS ORIGINAL IRISH CREAM

Preheat oven to 325F (165C). Butter an 8-inch square baking dish. Cut bread into 1-inch cubes.

Heat the milk in a small saucepan over medium-low heat until just boiling.

Beat the eggs and the ¼ cup sugar in a medium bowl until thick and pale yellow. Slowly add hot milk while beating until combined. Beat in the Baileys, nutmeg, and cinnamon until blended. Fold in the bread cubes and raisins; toss until ingredients are coated. Pour into prepared pan and sprinkle the remaining 1 tablespoon sugar over the top.

Bake for 45 minutes until top is golden brown and custard is set.

Meanwhile, to make the Crème Anglaise: Beat the egg yolks and sugar in a medium bowl until thick and pale yellow. Heat the milk in a small saucepan over medium-low heat until just boiling. Slowly pour milk into egg mixture while beating until blended.

Return the mixture to saucepan over low heat and cook, stirring constantly with a wooden spoon, until mixture thickens and coats back of spoon. Mixture must not come to a boil at any point. Remove from heat and pour the mixture through a strainer into a medium bowl and stir in the Baileys. Cool completely.

Remove pudding from oven and cool 5 minutes. Cut into 3-inch squares. Place squares on individual plates and pour a generous helping of Crème Anglaise over the top. Serve warm. Store pudding and Crème Anglaise, covered, in the refrigerator for up to 2 days.

California-Infused Cuisine

CALIFORNIA-ASIAN FOR 2

Crab Cakes with Lime Ginger Sauce

Black Sesame Seed-Coated Tuna with Asian Cilantro Pesto

Beer Batter Tempura Asparagus with Mirin Sauce

Vegetarian Teriyaki Temaki Wraps

CALIFORNIA-FRENCH FOR 4

Brandied Pecan and Pear Salad with Gorgonzola Vinaigrette

Pistachio-Crusted Swordfish with Kir Royale Sauces

Whipped Saffron Potatoes

Crème de Menthe Brûlée with Wild Berries

CALIFORNIA-ITALIAN FOR 4

Chardonnay Risotto Primavera

Rosemary- and Garlic-Marinated Mushrooms and Olives

White Wine Cheese Twists

Ice Cream Cassata with Chocolate Rum Sauce

CALIFORNIA-ASIAN FOR 2

*W*hat is nice about infused cuisine is that you can blend the best parts of both cultures into one dynamic dish. I think the very nature of California cuisine is a mixture of many types of food, often ethnic specific with an inventive twist. Fruit is added to Latin salsas, or nuts give an Italian pasta dish a crunchy new dimension. Food is prepared with fresh, healthy ingredients, so an entrée that is traditionally accompanied by a cream sauce may have it replaced by a vegetable-based sauce.

While this blending can seem offbeat, the talented chef will consider the common ingredients of the regions he or she is bringing together. It seems that many of the cuisines that are combined with California are from similar climates or geographical locations. This menu tends toward the marriage of Japan and California, the most obvious shared ingredients of both food styles being fresh fish and oranges.

Crab Cakes with Lime Ginger Sauce

Black Sesame Seed–Coated Tuna with Asian Cilantro Pesto

Beer Batter Tempura Asparagus with Mirin Sauce

Vegetarian Teriyaki Temaki Wraps

FOOD AND DRINK PLANNER

PARTY DAY: Prepare Crab Cakes with Lime Ginger Sauce. Make Asian Cilantro Pesto. Make Beer Batter Tempura Asparagus. Make Mirin Sauce.

JUST BEFORE SERVING: Fry Crab Cakes. Make Sesame Seed–Coated Tuna. Make Vegetarian Teriyaki Temaki Wraps.

COCKTAIL SUGGESTION: Kamikaze: Pour 1 ounce vodka, 1 ounce Triple Sec, and 1 ounce Rose's lime juice over ice in a cocktail shaker. Shake and strain into a short glass.

WINE SUGGESTION: Ozeki Karatamba sake (see "The Wine List," page 23, for more information)

TIMESAVER: Substitute purchased cucumber sushi roll for Vegetarian Teriyaki Temaki Wraps.

TABLE SETTING AND DECORATING IDEAS: Japanese Bonsai Table (see "Traditional Candle Sticks with Accents," page 4)

TABLE LINEN: Use Summer Brights suggested in "Color Families and Complementary Shades" (see page 6).

Bonsai Tree Centerpiece

Purchase a 1-foot high bonsai tree from a nursery, garden center, or home improvement center. Set tree in a rectangular ceramic planter and cover top of tree soil with green moss. Place a few small black rocks around moss. Often bonsai are sold in planters and decorated with similar items. A small evergreen tree would be a good substitute for the bonsai tree.

Orange Slice Rice Candle Holders

Slice an orange crosswise into ¼-inch-thick rounds. Press 2 rounds flat against the inside of a wide-mouth, 3-inch tall glass. Keep rounds pressed against glass as you fill glass halfway with wild rice or red or black rice. Fill to the rim with white rice. Place a tall taper candle down in the center of the rice. Place candles around table.

Japanese Fan Place Settings

Open a fan and set at each person's place at the table.

Crab Cakes with Lime Ginger Sauce

MAKES 2 TO 4 SERVINGS

Having grown up in Maryland, my good buddy Darby is a crab cake fiend. The process of cooking the crab and picking the meat out of the shell proves to be a bit lengthy for dear Darby when she gets a craving. So this recipe, approved by her, tastes great with canned crab, and the Lime Ginger Sauce gives the cakes that extra gusto.

---

2 (6-OUNCE) CANS CRABMEAT, DRAINED

1 TABLESPOON MINCED RED ONION

1 TABLESPOON FINELY CHOPPED FRESH CILANTRO

1 TEASPOON SESAME SEEDS

2 TEASPOONS GRAND MARNIER

1 EGG WHITE, LIGHTLY BEATEN

½ CUP SOURDOUGH BREAD CRUMBS

½ TEASPOON SALT

¼ TEASPOON BLACK PEPPER

BUTTER

OLIVE OIL

LIME GINGER SAUCE

3 TABLESPOONS OLIVE OIL

1 TABLESPOON PURE SESAME OIL

2 TABLESPOONS FRESH LIME JUICE

2 TEASPOONS TRIPLE SEC

2 TEASPOONS RICE VINEGAR

1 TEASPOON MINCED FRESH GINGER

Mix

the crab, onion, cilantro, sesame seeds, Grand Marnier, egg white, bread crumbs, salt, and pepper in a large bowl until thoroughly combined. Form mixture into ½-inch-thick patties, about 2 inches in diameter.

Preheat oven to 200F (95C). Line a baking sheet with waxed paper.

Heat 1 tablespoon butter and 1 teaspoon olive oil in a large skillet over medium heat. Add 6 to 8 crab cakes and cook until golden brown on bottom, 3 to 5 minutes. Carefully flip crab cakes over with a spatula and cook until golden brown on other side, about 1 minute. Transfer to paper towels to drain. Place on prepared baking sheet and keep warm in oven. Repeat process, using 1 tablespoon butter and 1 teaspoon oil for each batch.

To make the Lime Ginger Sauce: Whisk together all the ingredients in a small bowl until combined. Divide crab cakes among individual plates and top with sauce. Serve warm with extra sauce on the side.

Black Sesame Seed–Coated Tuna with Asian Cilantro Pesto

MAKES 2 SERVINGS

Tuna is prepared extremely rare in many restaurants these days. Mostly I order my tuna seared to a plum color inside, but I always consider where I'm dining. If the restaurant has a great reputation for quality of ingredients and cleanliness my concerns about food quality subside. If you plan on eating tuna on the rare side, tell the salesperson where you are buying the fish, and order the highest quality (sushi grade).

¼ CUP BLACK SESAME SEEDS

¼ CUP WHITE SESAME SEEDS

¾ TEASPOON SALT

½ TEASPOON BLACK PEPPER

2 (8-OUNCE) TUNA STEAKS

1 TABLESPOON OLIVE OIL

ASIAN CILANTRO PESTO

¼ CUP OLIVE OIL

2 TABLESPOONS PURE SESAME OIL

6 TABLESPOONS FRESH ORANGE JUICE

2 TABLESPOONS FRESH LIME JUICE

1 TABLESPOON TRIPLE SEC

1 CUP SHELLED PUMPKIN SEEDS (4 OUNCES)

1 CUP FRESH CILANTRO LEAVES

4 TEASPOONS SOY SAUCE

To make the Asian Cilantro Pesto: Place the olive oil, sesame oil, orange juice, lime juice, Triple Sec, pumpkin seeds, cilantro, and soy sauce in a blender jar. Blend mixture until seeds and cilantro are just minced, 3 to 5 seconds. Set aside.

Toss together the sesame seeds, salt, and pepper; place on a dinner plate. Lightly moisten the tuna with water and press into the sesame mixture. Turn the tuna to coat both sides with seeds.

Heat the oil in a large skillet over medium-high heat. Add the coated tuna and cook for 2 minutes. Turn tuna over and cook until it reaches desired doneness, about 5 minutes more.

Place tuna on individual plates and drizzle Asian Cilantro Pesto on top. Serve immediately with extra sauce on the side.

Beer Batter Tempura Asparagus with Mirin Sauce

MAKES 2 TO 4 SERVINGS

*M*irin is a sweet rice wine used in Japanese cooking. My friends over at Miya Sushi in Valley Village, California, have graciously shared some of their culinary secrets with me. This Mirin Sauce, based on a Miya version, is the traditional warm tempura sauce served with sushi.

1 POUND ASPARAGUS	2 TABLESPOONS MINCED CARROT
½ CUP CORNSTARCH	VEGETABLE OIL
1 CUP ALL-PURPOSE FLOUR	
1 EGG, LIGHTLY BEATEN	MIRIN SAUCE
½ CUP ICE WATER	1 CUP WATER
½ CUP COLD BEER	½ CUP SOY SAUCE
2 TABLESPOONS MINCED CHIVES	½ CUP MIRIN WINE

Trim about 1 inch off bottoms of the asparagus.

Sift the cornstarch and flour into a large bowl. Stir in the egg, water, and beer; mix until batter is just combined and a little lumpy. Stir in chives and carrot.

Fill a wok or large pot halfway with oil and heat over medium-high heat to 350F (175C). Dip asparagus in batter and then drop into hot oil. Fry until golden brown, 2 to 3 minutes. Remove with a wire wok basket or slotted spoon and place on paper towels to drain.

Meanwhile, to make the Mirin Sauce: Combine the water, soy sauce, and mirin in a small saucepan over medium heat and bring to a boil. Remove from heat and pour into small bowls for dipping. Arrange tempura on a platter and serve with warm sauce.

Vegetarian Teriyaki Temaki Wraps

MAKES 2 TO 4 SERVINGS

*W*ith the growing popularity of the wrap sandwich, I'm surprised that temaki, its Japanese version, hasn't hit the masses. Much healthier than an ice cream cone, this toasted seaweed cone is a fun way to get one's veggies.

---

3 TABLESPOONS SESAME OIL

½ TEASPOON MINCED GARLIC

1 MEDIUM CARROT, PEELED AND SHREDDED

½ CUP FRESH GREEN PEAS

½ CUP SLICED FRESH MUSHROOMS

½ CUP BEAN SPROUTS

3 TABLESPOONS SOY SAUCE

3 TABLESPOONS CREAM SHERRY

1 TEASPOON FRESH LEMON JUICE

3 TEASPOONS LIGHT BROWN SUGAR

½ TEASPOON MINCED FRESH GINGER

3 SEAWEED SHEETS (NORI)

½ RECIPE SUSHI RICE (PAGE 69)

2 TABLESPOONS TOASTED SESAME SEEDS

Heat the sesame oil and garlic in a wok or large skillet over medium-high heat. Add the carrot, peas, mushrooms, and bean sprouts; cook, stirring occasionally, for 5 minutes. Whisk together the soy sauce, sherry, lemon juice, brown sugar, and ginger until combined. Stir the soy sauce mixture into vegetables and cook until liquid reduces completely, 3 to 5 minutes.

Cut the seaweed sheets in half crosswise. Toast the sheets by carefully holding sheet, shiny side down, over an open flame for 5 seconds, or place in your toaster oven on a light setting. Place seaweed sheet, shiny side down, on a clean, flat surface, with long side lying left to right.

Place ⅓ cup of the rice on the left side of sheet, leaving a 1-inch margin along left and bottom edges. Form rice into a square and place ⅓ of the vegetables over the rice. Sprinkle 1 teaspoon sesame seeds over the vegetables. Fold bottom left corner over the vegetables and continue rolling seaweed, left to right, into a cone. Moisten right edge of seaweed with water and press against cone to secure roll. Lay temaki wraps on their side on a platter or on individual plates and serve immediately.

Sushi School

The artistry of sushi reaches far beyond a slice of raw fish on rice. You can enjoy this Japanese delicacy cooked, as is the crabmeat in California rolls, and in a variety of different styles.

Futo-Maki
Probably the most popular form of sushi in the USA, where ingredients are rolled up in rice with an outer sheet of nori (seaweed) and cut crosswise into bite-size pieces.

Gunkan
A strip of seaweed is wrapped around a small rice bar, forming a little seaweed cylinder. The rice bar fills the bottom half of the seaweed cylinder and is topped with creamy ingredients like scallop salad or salmon roe.

Hoso-Maki
Same as Futo-Maki, but with one ingredient, wrapped in a smaller rice roll.

Nigiri-Zushi
Oblong rice bars with a light spread of wasabi and a rectangular piece of fish on top.

Chirashi-Zushi or Maze-Zushi
A bowl of sushi rice with chopped vegetables and/or fish on top or mixed throughout the rice.

Temaki
A seaweed cone, similar to an ice cream cone, filled with ingredients.

CALIFORNIA-FRENCH FOR 4

"*R*estaurant speak" is my term for a basic vocabulary of foreign food words to help me avoid ordering gizzards (as I did on my honeymoon in France). Fear not, nothing on this menu would cause you to leap off the Eiffel Tower or spend a lot of francs at dinner and leave the table starving.

For those who've yet to visit France, an explanation of the table setting theme may be in order. The Hall of Mirrors is a famed room in the palace of Versailles on the outskirts of Paris. This hall was the concept of Louis XIV, who commissioned it to be built so he could walk through the hall with a complete view of his fabulous self. I thought the idea might blend well with a Los Angeles–infused French menu because we Angelenos are sometimes accused of being a tad narcissistic.

———

Brandied Pecan and Pear Salad with Gorgonzola Vinaigrette

Pistachio-Crusted Swordfish with Kir Royale Sauces

Whipped Saffron Potatoes

Crème de Menthe Brûlée with Wild Berries

———

FOOD AND DRINK PLANNER

ONE DAY BEFORE: Make Brandied Pecans.

PARTY DAY: Make Whipped Saffron Potatoes. Make Crème de Menthe Brûlée with Wild Berries.

JUST BEFORE SERVING: Make Pistachio-Crusted Swordfish with Kir Royale Sauces. Finish and assemble Brandied Pecan and Pear Salad with Gorgonzola Vinaigrette.

COCKTAIL SUGGESTION: Chambord Coolers: Pour 2 ounces Chambord and ½ ounce lemon juice over ice in a tall glass; fill glass with club soda.

WINE SUGGESTION: 1997 Grgich Hills Cellars Chardonnay (see "The Wine List," page 23 for more information).

TIMESAVER: Substitute vanilla ice cream and berries for Crème de Menthe Brûlée with Wild Berries

TABLE SETTING AND DECORATING IDEAS: Louis XIV's L.A. Hall of Mirrors

TABLE LINEN: Use Summer Brights suggested in "Color Families and Complementary Shades" (see page 6).

Mosaic Mirror and Tile Pot

WEAR PROTECTIVE GLOVES AND GOGGLES WHEN BREAKING MIRRORS AND WHILE MAKING THIS VASE. This is a great way to recycle a broken mirror (or purchase 3 large mirror tiles). You'll also need 10 complementary colored glazed tiles or pieces of glass, a skip trowel (a trowel with a small serrated edge), a small bag of black, thin-set mortar, and an 8-inch terra-cotta pot.

Wearing gloves and goggles, wrap an old towel around each mirror tile and hit tile with a hammer. Carefully remove broken mirror pieces from towel and wipe them clean. Break larger ceramic tiles or glass in the same fashion and wipe them. You can also use blue and green glass from designer water bottles, but make sure the pieces are flat.

Cover work surface with plastic sheeting. Mix the mortar with water according to manufacturer's package instructions and check instructions for setting time. Mortar should be the consistency of brownie batter. Wipe the outside of the terra cotta pot clean of dirt. Using the skip trowel, spread a ¼-inch-thick layer of mortar over entire outer surface of pot. Make grooves in mortar, using edge of skip trowel. Decoratively adhere mirror pieces to mortar and fill in spaces with ceramic or glass pieces, creating a mosaic design. Press pieces down into mortar so sharp edges are inset in mortar and pieces are flush with mortar surface. Rearrange pieces if necessary. Allow the mortar to set fully. Wipe off any excess mortar with a damp sponge.

Set a flowering plant such as California poppies in pot and place on a terra-cotta pot liner in the center of the table.

Mirror Tile Place Mats

Purchase a 12-inch-square mirror tile with safe, smooth edges from a tile or hardware store for each person. Wipe tiles clean, and set one at each place setting.

Hand Mirror and Faux Poppy Place Cards

Purchase a small hand mirror for each guest plus the host. Glue silk poppies to back of mirror, to cover it completely. Write each name on a cloth ribbon and tie in a bow around the mirror handle. Place a mirror at each place setting.

Brandied Pecan and Pear Salad with Gorgonzola Vinaigrette

MAKES 4 SERVINGS

*B*randied nuts with a sugary crust are a delicious accent in this exquisite salad. Many restaurants top their greens with caramelized nuts. The nuts are often left whole, but I prefer a sprinkling of sweet pecans rather than chunks of candy in my salad.

---

2 TABLESPOONS BUTTER

½ CUP CHOPPED PECANS

¼ CUP PACKED LIGHT BROWN SUGAR

1 TABLESPOON SPICED BRANDY

¼ CUP OLIVE OIL

2 TABLESPOONS BALSAMIC VINEGAR

3 TABLESPOONS APPLE JUICE

½ TEASPOON SALT

¼ TEASPOON BLACK PEPPER

½ CUP CRUMBLED GORGONZOLA CHEESE

1 HEAD BUTTER LETTUCE, TORN INTO BITE-SIZED PIECES

1 MEDIUM BARTLETT PEAR, PEELED, CORED, AND CUT INTO PAPER-THIN SLIVERS

Melt the butter in a small saucepan over medium-high heat. Add the pecans, brown sugar, and brandy; cook, stirring constantly, until pecans are toasted and sugar dissolves into a coating on nuts, about 1 minute. Remove from heat and scatter nuts on a waxed paper-lined baking sheet.

Whisk together the olive oil, balsamic vinegar, apple juice, salt, and pepper. Stir in the Gorgonzola cheese until combined.

Place the lettuce on 4 individual salad plates. Toss brandied pecans over lettuce. Arrange the pear slices in a star pattern on each serving. Pour the vinaigrette over top of each. Serve immediately.

Pistachio-Crusted Swordfish with Kir Royale Sauces

MAKES 4 SERVINGS

I served this fussy dish at my younger brother Daniel's 30th birthday party. Because some guests prefer less sauce than I do, I dress the entrée with a modest amount and serve extra sauce on the side.

CRÈME DE CASSIS
SAUCE

½ CUP CHAMPAGNE

½ CUP CRÈME DE CASSIS

CHAMPAGNE SAUCE

2 TABLESPOONS OLIVE OIL

1 TABLESPOON BUTTER

2 SHALLOTS, MINCED

1 CUP DRY CHAMPAGNE

1¾ CUPS HEAVY CREAM

3 SPRIGS FRESH THYME

½ TEASPOON SALT

¼ TEASPOON WHITE PEPPER

PISTACHIO-CRUSTED
SWORDFISH

1 CUP ALL-PURPOSE FLOUR

2 CUPS GROUND PISTACHIO NUTS

½ TEASPOON SALT

¼ TEASPOON BLACK PEPPER

4 (6-OUNCE) SWORDFISH STEAKS,
ABOUT ¾ INCHES THICK

2 EGG WHITES, LIGHTLY BEATEN

2 TABLESPOONS OLIVE OIL

To make Crème de Cassis Sauce: Bring the Champagne and crème de cassis to a boil in a small saucepan over medium-high heat. Boil until mixture foams and reduces into a thin syrup, 5 to 7 minutes. Remove from heat, cover, and set aside.

To make the Champagne Sauce: Heat the oil and butter in a large skillet over high heat. Add the shallots and cook for 1 minute. Add the Champagne and cook until liquid reduces to one-fourth, about 5 minutes. Reduce heat to medium and stir in the cream. Add the thyme sprigs and cook, stirring constantly, until mixture thickens, about 5 minutes. Remove from heat and discard thyme. Stir in the salt and pepper; cover skillet to keep warm while cooking swordfish.

To make the Pistachio-Crusted Swordfish: Add 1 tablespoon of the flour to the pistachio nuts and mix until combined. Place nut mixture on a dinner plate. Mix the salt and pepper with remaining flour and place on another dinner plate. Place the egg whites in a small bowl. Dip the swordfish in the flour, coating both sides. Brush egg white on one side of fish. Press egg white side of fish into pistachio nuts until coated. Place fish, nut side up, on a waxed paper-lined plate and refrigerate for at least ½ hour.

Heat the oil in a large skillet over medium heat. Add the swordfish, nut side down, to skillet and cook until nuts are lightly browned, 3 to 5 minutes. Turn the swordfish and cook on other side until fish changes from translucent to opaque in center, 5 minutes.

To serve: Spoon 3 tablespoons of Champagne Sauce in a pool on a dinner plate. Lightly swirl 1 tablespoon Crème de Cassis Sauce through Champagne Sauce pool. Place swordfish in center of pool and drizzle a small amount of both sauces over top. Serve warm. Pour rest of the sauces into separate bowls and serve on the side.

N O T E : If Crème de Cassis Sauce becomes too thick before using, reheat on low until mixture thins.

Whipped Saffron Potatoes

MAKES 4 TO 6 SERVINGS

S affron-hued potatoes whipped into a sensational side dish can accompany almost any fine entrée. The saffron threads are well worth the steep price as their unique flavor is irreplaceable.

4 YUKON GOLD POTATOES (ABOUT 2 POUNDS), PEELED AND CUT INTO 1-INCH CHUNKS	½ CUP HEAVY CREAM
1¾ TEASPOONS SALT	¼ TEASPOON SAFFRON THREADS, CRUSHED
2 TABLESPOONS BUTTER	⅛ TEASPOON WHITE PEPPER
2 TABLESPOONS DRY VERMOUTH	2 TEASPOONS MINCED CHIVES

Place the potatoes, 1 teaspoon of the salt, and enough water to cover in a stockpot. Bring to a boil over medium-high heat and cook until potatoes are tender, about 20 minutes. Drain potatoes in a colander. Turn potatoes out onto paper towels and pat completely dry.

Transfer the potatoes to a large bowl and mash until smooth and free of lumps. Add the butter to the potatoes and beat until blended, 1 minute. Beat in the vermouth and cream until potatoes are creamy and whipped. Add the saffron, remaining ¾ teaspoon salt, and pepper; beat until blended. Spoon into a large bowl or onto individual plates. Garnish with minced chives and serve hot.

Crème de Menthe Brûlée with Wild Berries

Crème brûlée has received a lot of media attention within the last few years for different chefs' avant-garde methods of caramelizing the sugar on top. Many chefs use a small blowtorch or butane-flamed device that they hold over the top of the custard until the sugar caramelizes. A preheated broiler works just as well, but certainly lacks the showmanship.

---

2 CUPS HEAVY CREAM

4 EGG YOLKS

¼ CUP SUGAR

4 TEASPOONS WHITE CRÈME DE MENTHE

4 TEASPOONS LIGHT BROWN SUGAR

2 CUPS MIXED BLACKBERRIES, RASPBERRIES, AND BLUEBERRIES

4 MINT SPRIGS

Preheat oven to 325F (165C). Heat the cream in a medium saucepan over medium-low heat until just boiling. Remove from heat.

Beat the egg yolks and sugar in a medium bowl until thick and pale yellow. Slowly add the cream while beating, until just combined. Pour the mixture through a strainer into a clean bowl. Stir in the crème de menthe until blended.

Pour the mixture into 4 (6-ounce) custard cups or ovenproof porcelain ramekins. Place the cups in a large pan and fill pan with enough hot water to reach halfway up sides of the cups.

Bake for 35 to 45 minutes or until custard sets. Remove cups from water and cool completely. Refrigerate, uncovered, for 1 hour.

Preheat broiler. Gently pat the tops of custard dry with paper towels. Sprinkle 1 teaspoon of the brown sugar evenly over top of each custard. Broil for 1 to 2 minutes or until sugar caramelizes. Watch custard carefully, to avoid burning the sugar. Remove from heat and cool for 5 minutes.

Place each cup on a dinner plate. Scatter mixed berries around cup and place a few berries on top of caramelized sugar. Garnish with a mint sprig and serve immediately.

CALIFORNIA-ITALIAN FOR 4

California and Italy have similar climates and sophisticated wine cultures. There could not be a more suitable theme for this menu than the Wine Tasting Bar for bringing these two worlds together. I suggest that you host a varietal tasting, comparing and tasting the same grape variety from different regions, such as Merlot from Chile, California, and Australia. Select a grape variety compatible with the dinner menu and schedule the tasting before you dine. Or have guests bring a bottle of their favorite wine from the same grape variety and share notes as you share a glass.

————

Chardonnay Risotto Primavera

Rosemary- and Garlic-Marinated Mushrooms and Olives

White Wine Cheese Twists

Ice Cream Cassata with Chocolate Rum Sauce

————

FOOD AND DRINK PLANNER

ONE DAY BEFORE: Make Rosemary- and Garlic-Marinated Mushrooms and Olives. Make Ice Cream Cassata and Chocolate Rum Sauce.

PARTY DAY: Make Chardonnay Risotto Primavera. Make White Wine Cheese Twists.

COCKTAIL SUGGESTION: none

WINE SUGGESTION: Wine Tasting Bar (see below)

TIMESAVERS: Substitute marinated mushrooms and olives from an Italian delicatessen for Rosemary- and Garlic-Marinated Mushrooms and Olives. Substitute prepared Italian rum cake from bakery for Ice Cream Cassata.

TABLE SETTING AND DECORATING IDEAS: Mama's Italian Kitchen and Wine Cellar.

Varietal Wine Tasting Bar

Choose about 6 bottles of wine, all from the same grape variety, and educate yourself about the characteristics of each. Store the wine properly prior to your event: dry whites chilled at 50F (10C) and reds at 60F (15C). You may wish to cover the labels so the tasters are sampling "blind" and are not influenced by the names of the wineries.

A white tablecloth is suggested for tastings because it will not influence the wine's color. Pour 2 ounces from the same wine bottle into each taster's glass. Read "Wine Tasting 101" (page 30) and have guests go through the steps of swirling, smelling, and sipping the wine. Some wines may be obvious, and guests will quickly point out the individual flavors and aromas. Other wines will be subtler and you may have to describe their nuances. Offer plain crackers or bread and water for cleansing palates between wines. Have a spittoon nearby for obvious reasons.

Mama's Italian Table

Contrast the formal atmosphere of the wine-tasting bar with a comfortable Italian table setup for dinner. Use a red-and-white checked tablecloth. Place decorative and food items in the center of the table, such as a canning jar with the Rosemary- and Garlic-Marinated Mushrooms and Olives, a designer cruet of seasoned olive oil, and the White Wine Cheese Twists in an empty olive oil can. Using a can opener, remove the top of a 1-gallon, rectangular olive oil can and wipe the inside clean of excess oil. Make sure that the top rim is safe and free of jagged edges by folding a wide cloth ribbon over the rim all around the can. Fasten the ribbon to both the inside and the outside of the can with glue or tape.

Wine Cork Place Cards

Save the wine corks from bottles of white wine (red wine corks are often stained). Using a hot glue gun, fasten tiny trinkets, such as silk flowers, ribbon, beads, or Italian coins, to the top end of the cork. Set a cork at each person's place at the table or place corks in a basket set in the table's center.

Artichoke Votive Candles

Slice off the bottom stems of fresh artichokes. Trim the bottoms as necessary so the artichokes stand level with the pointed ends of the leaves upright. Place a votive candle in its glass holder and insert the glass into the center of the artichoke leaves. Do not set the candle directly into the artichoke; the flame may ignite the leaves. Set the artichoke candles in small bowls and arrange around the table.

Chardonnay Risotto Primavera

MAKES 4 TO 6 SERVINGS

*M*ost Americans, if they order traditional risotto in a restaurant, would think the rice slightly underdone. I prefer rice on the tender side, and leave the crispier rice to breakfast cereal. For a moist risotto, add more broth or wine until the desired texture is achieved.

2 TABLESPOONS OLIVE OIL

2 TABLESPOONS BUTTER

2 CLOVES GARLIC, MINCED

1 LARGE BROWN ONION, MINCED

1 CUP DICED CARROT

2 CUPS ARBORIO RICE OR LONG-GRAIN RICE

1 CUP COARSELY CHOPPED BROCCOLI FLORETS

6 CUPS VEGETABLE OR CHICKEN BROTH

1 CUP CHARDONNAY

1 CUP FRESH OR FROZEN GREEN PEAS

1 CUP FRESHLY GRATED PARMESAN CHEESE

Heat the oil and butter in a large skillet over medium-high heat. Add the garlic, onion, and carrot; cook, stirring occasionally, until tender, 8 to 10 minutes. Add the rice and cook, stirring constantly, until rice is translucent, 3 to 5 minutes.

Add the broccoli and stir in the broth, 1 cup at a time. Cook, stirring constantly, until each cup of broth is fully absorbed before adding the next cup. Add the wine and peas; cook, stirring constantly, until liquid is fully absorbed. If rice is not tender, stir in more broth until it reaches desired consistency. Total cooking time is about 30 minutes. Remove the skillet from heat, and stir in the Parmesan cheese, and serve.

Rosemary- and Garlic-Marinated Mushrooms and Olives

MAKES ABOUT 4 CUPS

*B*ecause this menu is full of strong flavors, an uncomplicated yet hearty side dish is a welcome addition. There are large chunks of garlic in the marinade that may be consumed, but only in small amounts. Too much garlic can make one ill.

---

1 CUP OLIVE OIL

1/2 CUP CHIANTI

1/2 CUP RED WINE VINEGAR

3 TABLESPOONS COARSELY CHOPPED FRESH ROSEMARY

16 CLOVES GARLIC, HALVED LENGTHWISE

1 TEASPOON SALT

1/2 TEASPOON BLACK PEPPER

1 POUND FRESH BUTTON MUSHROOMS, TRIMMED

2 (6-OUNCE) CANS PITTED BLACK OLIVES, DRAINED

Whisk together the oil, Chianti, vinegar, rosemary, garlic, salt, and pepper until combined.

Place the mushrooms and olives in a large, clean screw-top jar or plastic container with an airtight lid. Pour marinade over mushrooms and olives. Seal the container. Shake jar to combine and coat ingredients. Refrigerate for 2 days, shaking jar occasionally.

To serve, bring ingredients to room temperature. Pour into a serving bowl or place on relish trays. Store, covered, in the refrigerator for up to 1 week.

White Wine Cheese Twists

MAKES 9 STRIPS

As I was making this treat, I noticed that the puff pastry package had a similar recipe that involved a lot more rolling, cutting, and filling. It looked delicious, but the ease of merely cutting and sprinkling, as in this recipe, appeals to me, especially when making enough for a large party.

½ (17.3-OUNCE) PACKAGE FROZEN PUFF PASTRY

3 TABLESPOONS WHITE WINE

3 TABLESPOONS OLIVE OIL

1 TEASPOON FINELY MINCED FRESH ROSEMARY

½ TEASPOON SALT

½ TEASPOON BLACK PEPPER

¼ CUP FRESHLY GRATED PARMESAN CHEESE

Thaw the puff pastry in its package for 15 minutes at room temperature. Preheat oven to 400F (205C). Line a baking sheet with waxed paper.

Whisk together the wine, olive oil, rosemary, salt, and pepper. Unfold the puff pastry sheet on a flat surface. Cut 1-inch strips, widthwise. Brush strips with wine mixture. Twist strips several times like a corkscrew and lay on prepared baking sheet. Sprinkle strips with cheese.

Bake for 15 to 18 minutes or until puffed and golden brown. Cool for 5 minutes and gently peel away from waxed paper. Arrange in a napkin-lined basket and set on the table.

Ice Cream Cassata with Chocolate Rum Sauce

MAKES 10 TO 12 SERVINGS

I enjoyed cassata, a traditional Italian dessert, for the first time in the San Fernando Valley of southern California. This dessert is shaped like a block with layers of pound cake, sweetened ricotta cheese, and candied fruit. The Neapolitan cassata contains ice cream and many other sweet little tidbits, which I've altered and boosted with a generous dose of rum. The Chocolate Rum Sauce is not as sweet as most, which makes it a perfect complement to this dessert.

1 CUP (2 STICKS) UNSALTED BUTTER, SOFTENED

1¼ CUPS SUGAR

4 EGGS

3 TABLESPOONS PLUS 2 TEASPOONS RUM

½ CUP HEAVY CREAM

2 CUPS ALL-PURPOSE FLOUR

1 TEASPOON BAKING POWDER

¼ TEASPOON SALT

1½ PINTS YOUR FAVORITE ICE CREAM, SLIGHTLY SOFTENED

¼ CUP CHOPPED ALMONDS

CHOCOLATE RUM SAUCE

½ CUP WATER

½ CUP RUM

2 TABLESPOONS CORN SYRUP

1 (12-OUNCE) PACKAGE SEMISWEET CHOCOLATE CHIPS

2 TABLESPOONS UNSALTED BUTTER

Preheat oven to 325F (165C). Butter a 9 × 5-inch loaf pan and dust pan lightly with flour. Shake out excess flour.

Beat the butter and sugar in a large bowl until fluffy. Add the eggs, one at a time, beating after each addition to incorporate. Add the 3 tablespoons rum and cream; beat well. Sift together the flour, baking powder, and salt; beat into egg mixture until blended. Pour into prepared pan and smooth the top.

Bake for about 70 minutes or until golden brown. Cool in pan on a wire rack for 15 minutes. Run a knife along edge of cake to loosen from pan and invert onto wire rack. Cool completely.

Trim sides and bottom crust off cake. Slice cake horizontally into 3 even layers. Place bottom layer on a large sheet of plastic wrap. Sprinkle 1 teaspoon rum over cake. Spread half of the softened ice cream evenly over bottom cake layer. Place the middle cake layer on ice cream and sprinkle the remaining 1 teaspoon of the rum over cake. Spread remaining half of the ice cream evenly over middle cake layer. Place top cake layer on ice cream and wrap cassata tightly in plastic wrap. Even up the block shape and place back into loaf pan. Freeze for 2 hours or until solid.

Just before serving, make the Chocolate Rum Sauce: Heat the water, rum, and corn syrup in a medium saucepan over medium-high heat just until boiling. Reduce heat to low and stir in the chocolate and butter until smooth. Remove from heat.

Unwrap the cassata and place on a large serving platter. Pour a generous amount of sauce over top so it runs down the sides. Sprinkle the almonds over the top. Pour the remaining sauce into a bowl or spouted vessel and serve on the side. Cut the cassata crosswise per each person's request and top with extra sauce.

Store, wrapped in plastic, in the freezer for up to 2 weeks. Store sauce, covered, in the refrigerator up to 1 week.

VARIATION

Cappuccino Cassata

Substitute Kahlua for the rum. Use coffee-flavored ice cream.

Outdoor Elegance

A PARISIAN SIDEWALK CAFÉ FOR 4

Bistro Carrot Ribbon Salad

Beaujolais Bouillabaisse

Pepper Vodka Rouille with Toasted Gruyère Croustade

Anise Almond Madeleines

MOSCOW MEETS THE NEW ENGLAND SHORE FOR 8

Oyster Shooters

Vodka Corn on the Cob

Vodka Seafood Chowder

Lobster Steamed in Vodka

Cranberry Vodka Crumble Bars

A HOPPIN' AMERICAN BARBECUE FOR 20

Baby Back Ribs with Beer Barbecue Sauce

German Beer Potato Salad

Raspberry Beer Coleslaw

Cinnamon Schnapps Chocolate Brownies

A PARISIAN SIDEWALK CAFÉ FOR 4

The last time I was in Paris, artists lined the sidewalks, capturing famous landmarks and quaint French scenes on canvas. Conversing with the local artists was romantic but somewhat daunting because my French is not very good. The imagination fills in bits of dialogue when language skills fall short. You could be bargaining with a Parisian artist for his "still life," and he could be telling you that your socks don't match.

There is definite style to the food of a French café. It is uncomplicated yet flavorful, with a delightful presentation. The salad on this menu consists only of carrots in an orange liqueur vinaigrette, the carrots artfully prepared as ribbons. Most bistros offer a bouillabaisse or fish soup with croutons floating on top. The main allure of the Paris café is dining outside, watching ancient streets animated by modern life.

———

Bistro Carrot Ribbon Salad

Beaujolais Bouillabaisse

Pepper Vodka Rouille with Toasted Gruyère Croustade

Anise Almond Madeleines

———

FOOD AND DRINK PLANNER

ONE DAY BEFORE: Make Pepper Vodka Rouille with Toasted Gruyère Croustade. Make Anise Almond Madeleines.

PARTY DAY: Make Bistro Carrot Ribbon Salad. Make Beaujolais Bouillabaisse.

COCKTAIL SUGGESTION: John's Vodka Martini: Pour 2 ounces Stolichnaya vodka and ½ ounce dry vermouth over ice in a cocktail shaker. Shake and strain into a martini glass. Garnish with 1 large caperberry or 6 small capers.

WINE SUGGESTION: 1998 Louis Jadot Beaujolais Villages (see "The Wine List," 23, for more information)

TIMESAVER: Substitute butter cookies from a bakery for the Anise Almond Madeleines.

TABLE SETTING AND DECORATING IDEAS: Struggling Artist's Masterpiece Table

TABLE LINEN: Use Summer Brights suggested in "Color Families and Complementary Shades" (see page 6.)

Faux Flower Palette Centerpiece

Purchase an artist's palette, preferably in the classic kidney shape, and a couple of thin paintbrushes from an art supply store. Purchase 6 bright-colored silk flowers from a craft store. Cut stems off flowers and glue flower heads to palette. Place palette in center of table with paintbrushes alongside.

Masterpiece Place Mats

Purchase inexpensive small posters. Laminate with plastic sheeting. You may also be able to copy photos of art on 11 × 17-inch paper. Check copyright for usage. Set a place mat at each place setting.

Paint Pot Floating Flowers

Fill baby food or other small glass jars with water and add different food coloring to each jar. Cut stems of flowers such as daisies or tulips to 2-inch lengths. Place a flower in each jar and set around table.

Beret Place Cards

Purchase a felt beret, found at costume stores, for each person. Using bright colored fabric paint, write each guest's name on front of a beret. Allow paint to dry completely. Place a beret at each place setting.

Bistro Carrot Ribbon Salad

A simple vegetable salad such as this is an ideal accompaniment to a menu full of diverse flavors.

4 LARGE CARROTS, PEELED

1 TABLESPOON MINCED CHIVES

1 TABLESPOON TRIPLE SEC

1 TABLESPOON WHITE WINE VINEGAR

2 TABLESPOONS FRESH ORANGE JUICE

¼ CUP OLIVE OIL

¼ TEASPOON SALT

⅛ TEASPOON WHITE PEPPER

Draw vegetable peeler lengthwise down each carrot to create long carrot ribbons.

Whisk together the chives, Triple Sec, vinegar, orange juice, olive oil, salt, and pepper until combined. Place carrots in a large bowl, add vinaigrette, and toss until carrot ribbons are dressed.

Pile the carrot ribbons on individual salad plates and serve.

Beaujolais Bouillabaisse

MAKES 4 TO 6 SERVINGS

Bouillabaisse sounds much grander than its origin as a fisherman's soup. Use a medley of white fish of different textures, such as a glossy sole with a firmer halibut and a touch of sea bass. The idea is to combine bits and pieces from the catch of the day into a glorious soup. So buy whatever fish are on sale and make a feast!

2 TABLESPOONS OLIVE OIL

1 CLOVE GARLIC, MINCED

1 MEDIUM ONION, COARSELY CHOPPED

1 LEEK, COARSELY CHOPPED

1 SPRIG FRESH THYME

1 SPRIG PARSLEY

1 BAY LEAF

1/2 TEASPOON SAFFRON THREADS, CRUSHED

1 CUP CANNED, PEELED, DICED TOMATOES AND JUICE

1 1/2 POUNDS WHITE FISH FILETS, BONED, SKINNED, AND CUT INTO 1-INCH CUBES

6 CUPS WATER

1 CUP BEAUJOLAIS

2 TEASPOONS SALT

1/2 TEASPOON BLACK PEPPER

Heat the oil in a large pot over medium-high heat. Add the garlic, onion, leek, thyme, parsley, bay leaf, and saffron; cook, stirring occasionally, until onion is tender, about 10 minutes.

Stir in the tomatoes and cook for 2 minutes. Reduce heat to medium-low and add the fish, water, and wine. Cook, covered, until the fish is done, about 20 minutes. Stir in the salt and pepper; cook 2 minutes more. Remove from heat and discard bay leaf, parsley, and thyme.

Pour into a soup tureen and serve hot with Pepper Vodka Rouille and Toasted Gruyère Croustades. Or float croustades on soup in individual bowls with a dab of rouille on top.

Pepper Vodka Rouille with Toasted Gruyère Croustade

Rouille is a spicy mayonnaise spread on croustades and served with fish soup or bouill-abaisse. Pepper vodka gives this traditional garnish a fiery new edge.

1 MEDIUM RUSSET POTATO, PEELED AND CUT IN 1-INCH CHUNKS	1 TEASPOON ABSOLUT PEPPAR VODKA
4 CLOVES GARLIC, PEELED	¼ TEASPOON SAFFRON THREADS, CRUSHED
2 EGG YOLKS, PREFERABLY PASTEURIZED (SEE NOTE, PAGE 54)	¾ TEASPOON SALT
3 TABLESPOONS CHOPPED RED BELL PEPPER	1 FRENCH BAGUETTE
	OLIVE OIL
1 CUP OLIVE OIL	¾ CUP SHREDDED GRUYÈRE CHEESE

Place the potato in a medium saucepan and cover with water. Bring to a boil over medium-high heat and cook until potato is tender, about 10 minutes. Drain and let cool to room temperature.

Place the garlic in a blender jar and blend until minced. Add the potato, egg yolks, and bell pepper to jar and puree until mixture is smooth, about 1 minute. With blender running, slowly add the olive oil in a steady stream through hole in lid. Puree until the mixture emulsifies to a mayonnaise consistency, 3 to 5 minutes. Add the vodka, saffron, and salt; puree until just blended. Spoon into a dish and serve as a spread for croustade. Store in an airtight container in the refrigerator for up to 1 day.

To make Toasted Gruyère Croustade: Preheat oven to 400F (205C). Cut French baguette crosswise into ½-inch-thick slices and lay flat on a baking sheet. Lightly drizzle olive oil over bread and scatter cheese on each slice. Bake for 8–10 minutes until bread is toasted and cheese is melted. Arrange in a lined basket and serve with rouille.

Anise Almond Madeleines

Traditionally, madeleines are baked in a special pan that has molded cups in the form of a seashell. The batter is poured into the mold and baked in a similar fashion to a cupcake or muffin. This classic French sponge cookie is a perfect ending for a menu with diverse tastes such as this one.

¾ CUP GRANULATED SUGAR

4 EGGS

½ CUP UNSALTED BUTTER, MELTED AND COOLED

2 TABLESPOONS ANISETTE

1 TABLESPOON ORANGE ZEST

1¼ CUPS ALL-PURPOSE FLOUR

¾ CUP GROUND ALMONDS

½ CUP POWDERED SUGAR

Preheat oven to 350F (175C). Butter a pan of 3-inch madeline molds. Beat sugar and eggs in a medium bowl until thick and pale yellow. Add butter, anisette, zest, and flour to egg mixture; beat until combined. Gently fold in almonds until distributed evenly throughout mixture.

Spoon 1 tablespoon of batter into each cup of prepared pan. Bake for 12 to 15 minutes or until a wooden pick inserted into a cookie comes out clean. Remove from mold. Repeat with remaining batter. Dust madeleines with powdered sugar. Store in an air-tight container at room temperature up to 2 days.

MOSCOW MEETS THE NEW ENGLAND SHORE
FOR 8

*L*iving in Connecticut during high school, I experienced the splendor of autumn in New England. I still have dear friends living in a quaint pocket of the East Coast who've offered a standing invitation during lobster season or when I need to escape my 90 mph L.A. lifestyle. The onset of fall always reminds me of the beauties of the East, and the West Coast's warm winters remind me of why I left.

Being a weather wimp, one January day spent near the Atlantic feels like a year in Moscow to me. This fun beach-themed menu is ideal for an adventurous end-of-summer party or a birthday party with a scavenger hunt centered on the guest of honor is a hoot. If the birthday girl has a thing for the color red, have players collect 10 red items found along the shoreline or perhaps borrowed from fellow beach-combers.

———

Oyster Shooters

Vodka Corn on the Cob

Vodka Seafood Chowder

Lobster Steamed in Vodka

Cranberry Vodka Crumble Bars

———

FOOD AND DRINK PLANNER

ONE DAY BEFORE: Make Cranberry Vodka Crumble Bars. Make Vodka Seafood Chowder.

DURING PARTY: Make Oyster Shooters. Make Vodka Corn on the Cob. Make Lobster Steamed in Vodka. Reheat Vodka Seafood Chowder.

COCKTAIL SUGGESTION: Vodka Bar (see below)

WINE SUGGESTION: 1997 Ashley Nicole Chardonnay (see "The Wine List," page 23, for more information)

TIMESAVERS: Substitute cookies or pie from a bakery for Cranberry Vodka Crumble Bars.

TABLE SETTING AND DECORATING IDEAS: World Explorer's Beach Party and Scavenger Hunt

NOTE: States have laws about parties on a public beach. Find out the laws in your city and state; most beaches allow barbecues or bonfires only in designated areas.

TABLE LINEN: Use paper napkins and no table linen.

Global Vodka Bar

Fill an aluminum tub with ice cubes or crushed ice. Set a variety of flavors and brands of vodka in center of ice. Set shot glasses in ice around inside rim of tub. Let guests serve themselves.

World Map Lap Tables for Beach Dining

Obtain a selection of inexpensive maps of foreign countries from a travel agency or tourist bureau. Cut a 12-inch wide plank of wood into 20-inch lengths, 1 (20 × 12-inch) plank for each person. Sand the rough edges of planks until smooth. Cut the maps into 20 × 12-inch rectangles and glue to planks. Apply a hard shellac over maps according to manufacturer's instructions. Allow to dry completely. Set planks, napkin rolls, and plates on a table near the grill. Use the planks as lap tables, or place them directly on the beach blanket or sand as a flat surface to dine upon.

Knotty Fishing Net Carryall Bag for Scavenger Hunt

Purchase a large fishing net from a sporting goods store. Cut net into 2-foot-diameter circles. Weave a strong cloth ribbon or cotton rope through the holes around entire edge of square. Hold ends of ribbon together and slide net edges down ribbon. Edges of the net circle will gather and form a bag opening, with ribbon as the bag's drawstring. Divide guests into teams of 5 and give each team a bag. Fill bags with 12-ounce bottles of water, sunscreen, plastic shovel, small shopping bag, and scavenger hunt list.

Compasses Around Napkins and Plastic Silverware

Purchase inexpensive plastic compasses from a sporting goods store or buy toy compasses from a toy or party store. Roll sets of a plastic fork, spoon, and knife in large paper napkins. Affix a ribbon to each compass and tie in a bow around a napkin roll. Place napkins in a large basket next to plates on food table.

Map Rocks for Beach Blanket

Use decorative map rocks to hold down the corners of a beach blanket. Find a variety of rocks about the size of a softball. Clean and dry rocks. Cut out shapes of countries from the same maps used for the lap tables (see above). Glue shapes to rocks and coat with hard shellac just as you did the lap tables. Allow to dry completely. Place a beach blanket on sand and set a rock on each corner.

Scavenger Hunt

Make a list of beach items for guests to collect and place the list in the Knotty Fishing Net Carryall Bag. Also place a small shopping bag in the net bag; some of the smaller items may slip through the holes. Give guests a time limit and reward the team that returns with the most items on the list.

Oyster Shooters

MAKES 16 SHOOTERS

I used to sing with a band in Westwood at a popular University of California hangout that was called Yesterdays. At breaks, we'd down a few oyster shooters and get just the kick we needed to perform until 2 A.M. Shucking oysters is an arduous and dangerous task. Make sure you have the proper shucking knife and a thick towel or special oyster glove. Hold the oyster in the towel and stick the knife in the shell opening near the tough, fleshy piece that connects the upper and lower shells.

---

16 RAW OYSTERS, SHUCKED AND RINSED

⅓ CUP VODKA

⅓ CUP FRESH LEMON JUICE

⅓ CUP PURCHASED COCKTAIL SAUCE

¼ CUP PREPARED HORSERADISH

Slide 1 oyster into each of 16 shot glasses. To each glass add, in this order, 1 teaspoon each of the vodka, lemon juice, and cocktail sauce. Top with a dash of horseradish.

Serve immediately, while still cold. Enjoy just as you would a shot of liquor—in one quick gulp.

NOTE: For an outdoor party, keep oysters on ice and covered.

Vodka Seafood Chowder

MAKES 8 SERVINGS

A chowder medley is always a winner. This recipe requires a lot of work in the fish preparation. Save yourself some time and ask the clerk behind the fresh seafood counter if he will bone and skin your fish and cut it into cubes. Promise some Vodka Seafood Chowder for their effort!

1/4 CUP BUTTER

1 LARGE ONION, COARSELY CHOPPED

2 CLOVES GARLIC, MINCED

1/4 CUP VODKA

1 TABLESPOON MINCED FRESH THYME

1 TABLESPOON MINCED FRESH OREGANO

2 BAY LEAVES

4 RUSSET POTATOES, PEELED AND CUT INTO 1/2-INCH CUBES

2 CUPS HEAVY CREAM

6 CUPS MILK

1/2 POUND HALIBUT FILET, BONED, SKINNED, AND CUT INTO 1-INCH CUBES

1/2 POUND SWORDFISH, BONED, SKINNED, AND CUT INTO 1-INCH CUBES

2 (10-OUNCE) CANS BABY CLAMS AND JUICE

2 TEASPOONS SALT

1/2 TEASPOON WHITE PEPPER

Melt the butter in a large stockpot over medium-high heat. Add the onion, garlic, vodka, thyme, oregano, and bay leaves. Cook, stirring occasionally, until onion is tender, about 5 minutes.

Reduce heat to medium-low and add the potatoes, cream, milk, halibut, swordfish, and clams with juice. Cook, uncovered, stirring occasionally, until fish is cooked and potatoes are tender, 30 to 40 minutes. Stir in the salt and pepper. (To make ahead, store, covered, in the refrigerator for up to 2 days. Reheat before serving.)

Pour the chowder into a soup tureen or individual bowls and serve hot.

NOTE: For an outdoor party, place the covered pot of prepared chowder on a hot grill and reheat, stirring occasionally, until warm. Place ladle next to pot and let guests serve themselves.

Vodka Corn on the Cob

MAKES 12 PIECES

When mixing this potent glaze, it may seem like the liquor bottle accidentally spilled on the corn. Never fear, as the corn cooks, the vodka mellows into a light coating with just a trace of orange.

½ CUP (1 STICK) BUTTER, MELTED

¼ CUP STOLICHNAYA ORHANJ VODKA

¼ CUP PACKED LIGHT BROWN SUGAR

12 EARS OF CORN, SHUCKED

Preheat grill. Stir together the butter, vodka, and brown sugar in a small bowl until sugar dissolves. Brush the butter mixture on corn and wrap each ear in foil. Place corn on grill. Cook over medium coals for 30 minutes, turning occasionally.

Unwrap corn and arrange on a large platter or let guests serve themselves, using metal tongs, right from the grill.

Lobster Steamed in Vodka

I have the great fortune of having friends with fabulous homes right on the coast of Maine. On one of my sojourns at "Camp Bartlett," my title for their compound, we had the complete lobster adventure. We selected our lobsters fresh from the sea and steamed them New England style in a pot of seaweed and ocean water. I added a splash of vodka and a new tradition was born.

---

8 LIVE LOBSTERS

STOLICHNAYA LIMONNAYA VODKA

SALT

DRAWN BUTTER

2 CUPS (4 STICKS) UNSALTED
BUTTER

1 CLOVE GARLIC, MINCED

1 TABLESPOON FRESH LEMON JUICE
OR TO TASTE

Place about 4 inches water, ¼ cup vodka, and 1 tablespoon salt in a stockpot and bring to a boil over medium-high heat. Place as many of the lobsters as will easily fit into the pot. Steam, covered, for 20 minutes or until lobsters turns bright red. Repeat with remaining lobsters, ¼ cup vodka, 1 tablespoon salt and another 4 inches of water.

Meanwhile, to make the Drawn Butter: Melt the butter in a saucepan over low heat until butter separates. Skim off any foam and pour the clear liquid into another saucepan. Discard the white solids. Add the garlic and heat until fragrant. Stir in lemon juice to taste.

Serve the lobsters with the butter.

VARIATION

Seaside Lobster Vodka

Line the bottom of a large pot with fresh seaweed. Add about 4 inches ocean water and ¼ cup vodka to pot; bring to a boil over medium-high heat. Steam lobsters as directed above.

How to Eat Lobster

Eating one's first lobster can be an intimidating and messy task. Here's a step-by-step lesson on picking lobster meat out of its shell. Most enjoy lobster meat dipped in a small bowl of drawn butter, which is sometimes seasoned with crushed garlic or lemon juice.

1. Tie a plastic bib around your neck. Arm yourself with a nutcracker, seafood fork, and sharp knife.

2. Break off the lobster's tail from the main body. Turn the tail over to expose the underside. Cut the soft transparent shell down the middle and remove the meat with seafood fork.

3. Break off the lobster's claws. Crack claws, using the nutcracker. Remove the meat with the seafood fork.

4. Break off the small legs on the side of the lobster. Bite down on a leg and pull it through your teeth, stripping the meat from inside.

Cranberry Vodka Crumble Bars

MAKES 16 BAR COOKIES

*C*ranberries are the quintessential New England fruit. These tart rubies are spiked with cranberry vodka and then layered in a crumbly brown sugar dough. Bar cookies are my choice for outdoor events because these finger sweets are more elegant than a regular cookie and easier than pie or cake.

---

2 CUPS ALL-PURPOSE FLOUR

⅓ CUP SUGAR

½ CUP (1 STICK) UNSALTED BUTTER, CHILLED AND CUT INTO PIECES

⅛ TEASPOON SALT

1 EGG

1 TABLESPOON FINLANDIA CRANBERRY VODKA

CRANBERRY CRUMB TOPPING

1 (12-OUNCE) PACKAGE FRESH OR FROZEN CRANBERRIES

½ CUP SUGAR

3 TABLESPOONS FINLANDIA CRANBERRY VODKA

3 TABLESPOONS GRAND MARNIER

2 TEASPOONS FRESHLY GRATED ORANGE ZEST

⅓ CUP UNSALTED BUTTER, SOFTENED

½ CUP PACKED LIGHT BROWN SUGAR

⅔ CUP ALL-PURPOSE FLOUR

Preheat oven to 400F (205C). Lightly spray an 8-inch square baking pan with nonstick cooking spray.

Combine the flour, sugar, butter, and salt in a food processor and process until mixture resembles coarse meal. Add the egg and vodka; pulse until dough just begins to hold together. Pat an even layer of dough in bottom of prepared pan. Bake for 10 to 12 minutes or until edges are lightly browned. Remove from heat and cool to room temperature.

To make Cranberry Crumb Topping: Place the cranberries, sugar, vodka, Grand Marnier, and orange zest in a medium saucepan over medium heat. Cook, stirring frequently, until cranberries pop and mixture thickens, 8 to 10 minutes. Remove from heat. In another bowl, mix together the butter, brown sugar, and flour until just combined and crumbly.

Pour an even layer of cranberry mixture over cookie surface in pan. Crumble the brown sugar mixture over the cranberry mixture. Return pan to oven and bake for 25 minutes or until top is golden brown. Cool to room temperature. Cut into 2-inch squares. Store in an airtight container at room temperature.

A HOPPIN' AMERICAN BARBECUE FOR 20

*A*lthough I'm more of a wine drinker, nothing says barbecue like a cold beer. Within the last 10 years, microbreweries have taken the country by storm, supplying quality, handcrafted beer at surprisingly low prices. Entire books have been devoted to cooking with beer, which may seem like an odd ingredient. But the hops and grains that go into the brew are very compatible with hearty dishes, zesty sauces, and earthy baked goods.

I've discovered many foods containing beer in my travels in Latin countries. Mexican beer has a certain bite that makes it a perfect match for spicy food. With the variety of beer available today, one could season just about every dish with a splash of ale or a stein of stout. Experiment cooking with your favorite brand of beer and give an old dish a hoppin' new kick.

Baby Back Ribs with Beer Barbecue Sauce

German Beer Potato Salad

Raspberry Beer Coleslaw

Cinnamon Schnapps Chocolate Brownies

FOOD AND DRINK PLANNER

ONE DAY BEFORE: Make Beer Barbecue Sauce. Make German Beer Potato Salad. Make Cinnamon Schnapps Chocolate Brownies.

PARTY DAY: Make Raspberry Beer Coleslaw, Precook ribs.

JUST BEFORE SERVING: Barbecue ribs.

COCKTAIL SUGGESTION: None

BEER SUGGESTIONS: Offer regular and light, American and imports, such as Sam Adams, Bud Light, Heineken, and Amstel Light.

TIMESAVERS: Substitute purchased potato salad for German Beer Potato Salad. Substitute purchased coleslaw for Raspberry Beer Coleslaw.

MENU EXTRAS: Corn on the cob and baked beans.

TABLE SETTING AND DECORATING IDEAS: Rustic Western Barbecue

TABLE LINEN: Don't use a cloth if meal is served outside on a wood table, or choose red or Western theme table linen.

Belted Grassy Vase of Wildflowers

Use an inexpensive glass vase with a slight hourglass shape. Measure height and circumference of vase. Purchase a piece of grass sod from a nursery that is large enough to wrap around vase once and will cover vase completely. (Sod with a mesh backing is better for this.) Find an old, casual brown belt with a western or rustic buckle. Lay sod, dirt side up, on flat surface and lay vase on its side in center of sod. Wrap sod around vase until sod edges meet; trim off any overlapping sod for a neat seam. Wrap belt around middle of sod on vase until belt buckle can fasten at tightest belt hole. Wrap green floral or thin wire around top and bottom of vase over sod to secure sod edges for a cleaner look. Fluff sod to cover wire. Fill vase with water and wildflowers; set on table. If necessary, place vase on a plate or cloth base (dirt may leave a ring).

Denim Place Mats

Purchase denim at a fabric store. Cut 17 × 13-inch rectangles from denim and use as place mats, making 1 per person. Sew or glue decorative trim or ribbon around edge of rectangles as a finishing touch or leave as is for a rustic look.

Sheriff Star Pin Place Cards on Bandanna Napkins

Purchase tin sheriff star pins at a toy store. Write the names of guests across stars, using a thin, felt-tip pen with black indelible ink. Fold bandannas anyway you like and pin stars in center. Place on dinner plates or on place mats.

Baby Back Ribs with Beer Barbecue Sauce

Recently, I appeared on a male-oriented television talk show. My segment theme was "Cooking with Beer." There I was in the studio with four guys and a bevy of beautiful models on a fake patio. This tangy barbecue sauce got the guys' eyes on the grill and off the women.

---

20 POUNDS BABY BACK PORK LOIN SPARERIBS

GUINNESS STOUT

WATER

BEER BARBECUE SAUCE

2 CUPS GUINNESS STOUT

6 TABLESPOONS PACKED LIGHT BROWN SUGAR

2 TEASPOONS SALT

2 TEASPOONS BLACK PEPPER

2 TABLESPOONS CHILI POWDER

2 CLOVES GARLIC, MINCED

½ CUP WORCESTERSHIRE SAUCE

4 CUPS KETCHUP

2 TEASPOONS LIQUID SMOKE

Place the ribs in a large stockpot. Add 1 part Guinness to 2 parts water until the ribs are covered. Parboil ribs by bringing the liquid to a boil over high heat. Then reduce heat to low, cover, and simmer for 1 hour. Remove ribs from pot and discard the liquid.

Meanwhile, to make the barbecue sauce: Combine all the ingredients in a large pot. Bring to a boil over medium-high heat. Reduce heat and simmer, stirring occasionally, until sauce thickens, about 20 minutes. Cool to room temperature for flavors to blend.

Heat a gas barbecue according to manufacturer's instructions for low heat or follow instructions on charcoal bag for low coals. Set the grill rack about 6 inches above coals and place the parboiled ribs on grill. Brush sauce over ribs and grill, turning ribs over and basting with sauce every 10 minutes, until tender and browned, about 20 minutes. Ribs will be done when the meat separates from the bone about ½ inch on the ends and the rib backing often cracks.

Place racks on a serving platter or cut ribs in between bones for individual portions.

Folklore Food

These legendary booze foods are just right for picnics and barbecues.

Vodka Watermelon

Bore a hole halfway into a watermelon. Pour 1 cup vodka in the hole. Cover the hole and chill the melon overnight. Cut melon in half lengthwise and, using a melon baller, scoop out flesh into bite-size balls. Place balls in melon half and serve.

Jell-o Shooters

Boil 1 cup water. Dissolve 1 (3-ounce) package any flavor Jell-o gelatin dessert in boiling water. Stir in 1 cup chilled vodka. Pour into 1-ounce plastic cups and chill until firm, 4 to 6 hours. Place cups in a bowl of ice to keep them cold when served outdoors. Plastic cups can be found at most party or restaurant supply stores.

Drunken Chicken

Thaw 1 (5-pound) whole chicken. Discard the neck and gizzards. Rinse the chicken and rub salt and pepper on inside cavity and outer skin. Wash 1 (12-ounce) can beer. Pop open beer can and, keeping can upright, slide it (unopened end first) into the body cavity of the chicken.

Place the chicken, with the open end of the can upright, on an outdoor grill 6 inches above low coals. Cover the grill with a lid or loosely tent the chicken with foil. Cook for 3 to 4 hours, keeping a watchful eye because chicken drippings can cause flare-ups. Use oven mitts to carefully remove HOT can from inside chicken. Carve chicken, and serve. WARNING: DO NOT USE A GLASS BEER BOTTLE WITH THIS TECHNIQUE. GLASS WILL SHATTER WHEN HEATED.

German Beer Potato Salad

I discovered this German potato salad in a quaint Bavarian-theme village while shopping for a cuckoo clock for my husband. Unlike the classic creamy salad, this version has a zesty oil-vinegar-beer base and is best served warm. This recipe is for my beer-loving bro, Bob.

8 POUNDS RED POTATOES, SCRUBBED AND CUT INTO 1½-INCH CUBES

½ CUP HEINEKEN BEER

1 CUP OLIVE OIL

¾ CUP RED WINE VINEGAR

3 TABLESPOONS GRAINY BROWN MUSTARD

½ CUP MINCED GREEN ONIONS

½ CUP CHOPPED FRESH DILL

1 TEASPOON SALT

½ TEASPOON BLACK PEPPER

Place the potatoes in large pot; cover with water and 1 tablespoon salt. Bring to a boil over medium-high heat and cook until tender, about 20 minutes.

Meanwhile, whisk together the beer, oil, vinegar, mustard, green onions, dill, salt, and pepper until combined.

Drain the potatoes and place in a large bowl. Pour the beer mixture over hot potatoes and toss until potatoes are completely coated. Serve warm.

Raspberry Beer Coleslaw

MAKES 20 SERVINGS

*T*rader Joe's is a terrific store that sells lesser-known brands of quality food and beverage at discount prices. Their products are labeled with intricate sketches of Old World seaports and rustic scenes. Originally a West Coast store, this creative outlet is now nationwide. I purchased the raspberry beer for this recipe, there, but I believe larger brewers are now making fruit-flavored beer that may be available in your local grocery store.

---

1 LARGE HEAD RED CABBAGE, SHREDDED

1 LARGE HEAD GREEN CABBAGE, SHREDDED

1 CUP SHREDDED JICAMA

1 CUP SHREDDED CARROT

1 CUP ROASTED PEANUTS

½ CUP RASPBERRY-FLAVORED BEER

¼ CUP RASPBERRY VINEGAR

1 CUP VEGETABLE OIL

1 CUP MAYONNAISE

¼ CUP SUGAR

2 TABLESPOONS POPPY SEEDS

¾ TEASPOON SALT

Combine the cabbages, jicama, carrots, and peanuts in a large bowl. Whisk together the beer, vinegar, oil, mayonnaise, sugar, poppy seeds, and salt in a medium bowl until blended. Pour the dressing over the cabbage mixture and toss to combine. Refrigerate until ready to serve.

NOTES: Unless you own a very large bowl, it may be necessary to divide the cabbage, jicama, and peanuts equally between 2 large bowls and toss each with half of the dressing mixture.

Jicama is a vegetable with a crisp, white interior, similar in taste and texture to an apple, and a rough brown skin. Peel off the skin before shredding.

If raspberry beer is not available, substitute any fruit-flavored beer or light ale.

Cinnamon Schnapps Chocolate Brownies

MAKES ABOUT 25 SQUARES

*G*oldschlager cinnamon schnapps has glistening 24-carat golden flakes floating in the liqueur. Cake decorators often use gold flakes and dust to accent their creations, but only 24-carat and a very small amount.

¾ CUP SEMISWEET CHOCOLATE CHIPS

½ CUP UNSALTED BUTTER, SOFTENED

1 CUP SUGAR

2 EGGS

⅓ CUP GOLDSCHLAGER CINNAMON SCHNAPPS LIQUEUR

½ CUP ALL-PURPOSE FLOUR

½ CUP UNSWEETENED COCOA POWDER

Preheat oven to 325F (165C). Lightly spray an 8-inch square baking pan with nonstick cooking spray.

Place chocolate chips in top of a double boiler over simmering water and stir until melted. Cool for 5 minutes. Beat the cooled chocolate and butter in a medium bowl until combined. Beat in the sugar until smooth. Add the eggs and liqueur; mix well. Gently fold in the flour and cocoa powder until just combined. Pour mixture into prepared baking pan.

Bake for 20 minutes or until a knife inserted into center comes out clean. Cool in pan to room temperature. When chocolate sets, cut into 1½-inch squares. Store in an airtight container at room temperature.

Sophisticated Sweets

COCKTAIL CAKES AND DESSERTS

Irish Whiskey Fruitcake

White Russian Flan Fudge Cake

Brandy Alexander Soufflé

Apple Rum Raisin Pie Crisp

French Connection Roulade

Screwdriver Bundt Cake

CHEERS TO THE CHEESECAKE!

Black Russian Brownie Swirl Cheesecake

Manhattan Sour Cherry Cheesecake

Irish Cream Chocolate Chip Cheesecake

Fancy Lemon Curd White Chocolate Cheesecake

Toasted Almond Caramel Cheesecake

Easy Chocolate Cheesecake

WINE SUGGESTION FOR DESSERTS: NV Leustau Amontillado Bodega Vieja, (see "The Wine List," page 23, for more information)

COCKTAIL CAKES AND DESSERTS

A dessert party can be a wonderful nightcap after an evening of Christmas carol-
ing or an alternative to an open house buffet. There are a number of elegant
buffet setups in this book that would work beautifully for a dessert-only event. But in
place of the standard "Table Setting and Decorating Ideas" listed under each menu in
the preceding chapters, I've shared some "Presentation Ideas for Giving Cakes as
Gifts" in addition to menus featuring my favorite dessert combinations. A cocktail
cake will be twice as sweet when given to your friends and family in a creative package. Always include a note or label stating that alcohol is one of the ingredients.

MY FAVORITE INDULGENCES

T hese sweet favorites have garnered rave reviews time and again. When all these
treats are served on a luxurious dessert station, you have created the ultimate
indulgence.

———

Irish Cream Bread Pudding with a Saucy Crème Anglaise (page 276)

Toasted Almond Caramel Cheesecake (page 351)

Screwdriver Bundt Cake (page 338)

Kentucky Derby Pie (page 46)

Irish Cream Chocolate Chip Cheesecake (page 347)

———

WARM WEATHER COMFORT DESSERTS

P erfect for an open house or after a community function, this menu of spirited,
fruity desserts is sure to warm souls and satisfy every palate.

———

Chocolate Amaretto Biscotti and Pear Brandy Betty (page 149)

Peach Brandy Cobbler (page 142)

Cranberry Vodka Crumble Bars (page 318)

Apple Rum Raisin Crisp Pie (page 335)

Irish Whiskey Fruit Cake (page 331)

———

AN EXTRAVAGANT À LA MODE BAR

*T*his dessert bar transforms the simple brownie à la mode into a delicious, decadent affair. Offer guests a variety of ice creams to top off a chocolate torte slice or a spiked cookie.

———

Black Russian Brownie Swirl Cheesecake (page 343)

Chocolate and Orange Liqueur Truffle Torte (page 262)

Scotch Chocolate Chip Cookies (page 136)

French Connection Roulade (page 336)

———

PRESENTATION IDEAS FOR GIVING
CAKES AS GIFTS

Cocktail Cake in Bakeware

Bake a cake in a designer baking pan, holiday-themed mold, or a Bundt pan. Cool baked product completely and wipe outside of bakeware clean. Wrap a large sheet of cellophane around bakeware. Gather cellophane in a bunch at top center of cake with cellophane ends standing straight up. Tie a bright ribbon in a bow around bunch. Affix label to ribbon listing name of cake and spirit that was used to flavor it. Or use a blow-dryer to heat the decorative label from a bottle of spirits and gently peel off the label. Adhere label to cellophane with spray adhesive or clear tape.

Elegant Cake Gift Baskets

Here are some ideas for cake gift baskets in a variety of price ranges. Obviously the basket must be large enough to hold a cake and other goodies. I've found a wicker or rattan laundry basket works great. Place the cake on a gift dish or cake platter and wrap tightly with plastic wrap. Always pad the bottom of the basket with tissue or shredded paper. Wrap the entire basket securely in cellophane and attach a big bow in front.

Tea or Coffee Cake Basket

A collection of items around $35.00, including the cocktail cake, *Sophisticated Entertaining* cookbook, a small decorative gift bottle containing the spirit that was used in the cake, teacups or coffee mugs, a teapot, or coffee accessories, a package of gourmet coffee or herbal tea, flowers, fruit.

Gourmet Cake Basket

A collection of items around $50.00, including the cocktail cake, *Sophisticated Entertaining* cookbook, a small decorative gift bottle containing the spirit that was used in the cake, hand-crafted apron, jars of gourmet spices, gift certificate to a gourmet cooking store, flowers, fruit, chocolates.

Cocktail Cake Basket

A collection of items around $50.00, including the cocktail cake, *Sophisticated Entertaining* cookbook, an assortment of mini liquor bottles, cocktail glassware, bar supplies, chocolate-dipped strawberries, flowers, fruit, chocolates.

Cocktail Cake Wrapped in a Liqueur-Soaked Cloth in Tin

Cut a 1½-foot square of clean cheesecloth or muslin. Immerse cloth in a bowl of the spirit that was used in the cake. Remove the cloth and wring lightly. Use a dense cake without frosting for this presentation, such as a pound cake, Bundt cake, fruitcake, or nut bread. Place the cake upside down in center of cloth and wrap cloth around cake. Place cake right side up in a large holiday theme tin with cloth edges tucked neatly under cake. Tin should have an airtight lid and a shape similar to the cake. Place lid on tin and allow the cake to sit for a couple of days at room temperature for a truly potent gift. Wrap a ribbon around the tin and tie into a bow. Affix a label to ribbon listing cake name and spirited ingredient used as its flavoring.

Irish Whiskey Fruitcake

MAKES ABOUT 15 SERVINGS

*M*y mother receives an Irish whiskey cake every Christmas. The cake is wrapped in a whiskey-soaked cloth and packed in a round tin. Intrigued by this sophisticated gift, I pried off the lid and got a tad tipsy from the fumes.

½ CUP (1 STICK) UNSALTED BUTTER, SOFTENED

1 CUP PACKED LIGHT BROWN SUGAR

3 EGGS

½ CUP JAMESON'S IRISH WHISKEY, PLUS EXTRA FOR SOAKING

¼ CUP FRESH ORANGE JUICE

1 TEASPOON FRESHLY GRATED ORANGE ZEST

1 TEASPOON FRESHLY GRATED LEMON ZEST

2 CUPS ALL-PURPOSE FLOUR

1 TEASPOON BAKING SODA

1 TEASPOON GROUND CINNAMON

2 TABLESPOONS FINELY MINCED CRYSTALLIZED GINGER

¼ CUP FINELY MINCED DRIED APRICOTS

¼ CUP FINELY MINCED PITTED DATES

½ CUP DRIED BLACK CURRANTS

½ CUP GOLDEN RAISINS

1 CUP COARSELY CHOPPED PECANS

Preheat oven to 275F (135C). Grease a 12-cup Bundt pan with vegetable shortening.

Beat the butter and sugar until fluffy. Beat in the eggs, one at a time, until incorporated. Add the whiskey, orange juice, and zests; beat well.

Sift together the dry ingredients and toss with the dried fruit and nuts until coated. Stir fruit mixture into butter mixture and stir until completely blended. Pour into prepared pan.

Bake for 1 hour or until a knife inserted into cake comes out clean. Cool in pan for 15 minutes and invert cake on a wire rack to cool completely.

Cut a 2-foot square of clean cheesecloth or muslin. Place the cake in center of cloth and sprinkle cake with 2 to 4 tablespoons whiskey. Wrap cloth around the cake, then wrap cake and cloth in foil. Store at room temperature for up to 1 week. Unwrap and cut cake into slices to serve.

White Russian Flan Fudge Cake

The White Russian was my signature cocktail when I lived in New York. At 19, I worked in a disco right off Central Park. Each night after work I'd enjoy this liquid dessert on the rocks.

This complicated cake makes a dazzling and fudgy finale to a fine meal.

CARAMEL

1/3 CUP SUGAR

2 TABLESPOONS WATER

1 TEASPOON KAHLUA

FUDGE CAKE

2 OUNCES UNSWEETENED CHOCOLATE

1/2 CUP PLUS 2 TABLESPOONS SUGAR

2 TABLESPOONS WATER

2 1/2 TABLESPOONS BUTTER

1 EGG

1 TEASPOON STOLICHNAYA KAFYA VODKA

1/2 CUP ALL-PURPOSE FLOUR

1/2 TEASPOON BAKING SODA

1/8 TEASPOON SALT

1/4 CUP MILK

COFFEE FLAN

2 EGGS

1/4 CUP SUGAR

1/2 CUP HEAVY CREAM

1 TEASPOON INSTANT COFFEE GRANULES

1 TABLESPOON KAHLUA

To make the Caramel: Combine the sugar, water, and Kahlua in a small saucepan. Bring to a boil over high heat and boil without stirring until mixture turns golden brown, 3 to 5 minutes. Watch carefully to avoid burning. Remove from heat and pour hot caramel into a 9-inch round cake pan. Tilt pan to coat bottom with caramel. Set aside.

Preheat oven to 325F (165C).

To make the cake: Melt the chocolate, the 2 tablespoons sugar, and water in top of a double boiler over simmering water. Stir until blended. Remove from heat and cool 5 minutes. Beat the butter and remaining 1/2 cup sugar in a medium bowl until fluffy. Add the chocolate mixture, egg, and vodka; beat until smooth. Sift together the dry ingredients. Beat the dry ingredients alternately with the milk into mixture until combined. Set aside.

To make the Coffee Flan: Beat the eggs and sugar until thick and pale yellow. Add the cream and beat until blended. Dissolve the coffee granules in the Kahlua and stir into cream mixture until thoroughly combined.

To assemble: Pour flan mixture into caramel-lined pan. Gently spoon fudge cake batter over top of flan.

Place cake pan in a larger pan. Pour enough hot water in larger pan to reach halfway up sides of cake pan. Bake for 50 minutes or until cake is done. Cool completely.

Run a knife along the edge of cake to loosen from pan. Invert cake onto a flat serving platter; wipe off excess caramel and liquid around base of cake with a paper towel. Chill, uncovered, for at least 1 hour. Serve cold. Store covered in the refrigerator for up to 2 days.

Brandy Alexander Soufflé

When I think of soufflés an odd analogy comes to mind: rock climbing. Sugar is often sprinkled on the bottom and up the sides of soufflé dishes. The theory is that the soufflé needs something to grab onto as it rises in the oven and climbs the side of the dish. A rock climber's challenge is much greater when climbing the sheer face of a mountainside, than a rocky face.

3 TABLESPOONS UNSALTED BUTTER	4 EGG YOLKS
¼ CUP ALL-PURPOSE FLOUR	6 EGG WHITES
1 CUP MILK	POWDERED SUGAR
½ CUP GRANULATED SUGAR	SWEETENED WHIPPED CREAM,
2 TABLESPOONS BRANDY	CHOCOLATE OR FRUIT SAUCE, OR
2 TABLESPOONS CRÈME DE CACAO	SAUCY CRÈME ANGLAISE (PAGE 276), TO SERVE

Preheat oven to 375F (190C). Butter 1½-quart soufflé dish. Sprinkle sugar over bottom and sides of dish. Turn dish over and shake out excess sugar.

Melt the butter in a medium saucepan over medium-low heat. Add the flour and cook, whisking constantly, for 2 minutes. Add the milk and cook, whisking constantly, until mixture thickens. Remove from heat and beat in ¼ cup of the sugar, brandy, and crème de cacao. Beat in the egg yolks until blended.

Using clean beaters, beat 3 of the egg whites on high speed in a large bowl until foamy. Gradually beat in 2 tablespoons of the sugar until frothy. Add the 3 remaining egg whites and remaining 2 tablespoons sugar; beat until stiff peaks form. Eggs should appear shiny and not dry. Gently fold egg whites into egg yolk mixture. Spoon batter into prepared dish.

Bake for 30 to 35 minutes or until center is puffed and golden brown. Remove from oven and lightly sift powdered sugar over top. Immediately place soufflé dish on a heatproof base plate and bring to the table. Puncture top and spoon soufflé onto individual plates. Serve hot with whipped cream or sauce.

Apple Rum Raisin Pie Crisp

MAKES 12 SERVINGS

A streusel topping of brown sugar and oatmeal tops this towering lusty fusion of a pie and a crisp. The combination of rum and raisins is irresistible to my father, especially in ice cream. This special dessert is made, with love, for his sweet tooth and kind heart.

OATMEAL CRUST AND STREUSEL TOPPING

½ CUP (1 STICK) UNSALTED BUTTER, SOFTENED

1 CUP SUGAR

1 EGG

2 TABLESPOONS LAIRD'S APPLEJACK

2½ CUPS REGULAR ROLLED OATS

1 CUP ALL-PURPOSE FLOUR

1 TEASPOON BAKING POWDER

1 TEASPOON GROUND CINNAMON

APPLE RUM RAISIN FILLING

2 TABLESPOONS UNSALTED BUTTER

¾ CUP DARK RUM

1 TEASPOON FRESH LEMON JUICE

½ CUP PACKED LIGHT BROWN SUGAR

¼ CUP ALL-PURPOSE FLOUR

1 TEASPOON FRESHLY GRATED NUTMEG

1 TEASPOON GROUND CINNAMON

8 GRANNY SMITH APPLES, PEELED AND CUT INTO THICK SLIVERS

1 CUP RAISINS

½ CUP SLIVERED ALMONDS

Butter a 9-inch pie pan. To make Oatmeal Crust and Streusel Topping: Beat the butter and sugar in a large bowl until creamy. Add the egg and applejack; beat until fluffy. Toss together the oats, flour, baking powder, and cinnamon; beat into mixture until thoroughly combined. Reserve ½ cup oatmeal mixture for topping. Press remaining mixture on bottom and up sides of pie pan. Refrigerate, uncovered, for 1 hour.

Preheat oven to 350F (175C). Meanwhile, to make the Apple Rum Raisin Filling: Melt the butter in a large saucepan over medium heat. Stir in the rum, lemon juice, sugar, flour, nutmeg, and cinnamon until smooth. Add the apples, raisins, and almonds; cook, stirring occasionally, until apples are tender, about 15 minutes.

Remove from heat and pour apple mixture over chilled oatmeal crust in pie pan. Pack remaining oatmeal mixture in dollops around rim of crust and over top of apples. Bake for 25 to 30 minutes or until filling is bubbly and streusel topping is golden brown.

Cool for 5 minutes and cut into wedges. Serve hot.

French Connection Roulade

MAKES 10 SERVINGS

The combination of a laced cake and chocolate ganache filling makes this rolled dessert one of the most traditional in the book. Ganache desserts have received much fanfare on the restaurant circuit in the last few years. Most know ganache as a chocolate cream frosting for cakes. I've seen it as a solo dessert in little pots and as frozen chocolate slices.

COGNAC SPONGE CAKE	CHOCOLATE AMARETTO GANACHE
4 EGGS, SEPARATED	1⅓ CUPS HEAVY WHIPPING CREAM
1 CUP GRANULATED SUGAR	1½ CUPS SEMISWEET CHOCOLATE CHIPS
2 TABLESPOONS BUTTER, MELTED AND COOLED	3 TABLESPOONS AMARETTO
2 TABLESPOONS COGNAC	FOR ASSEMBLY
1 CUP CAKE FLOUR	1 TABLESPOON AMARETTO
1 TEASPOON BAKING POWDER	1 CUP SLIVERED ALMONDS
⅛ TEASPOON SALT	¼ CUP UNSWEETENED COCOA POWDER
POWDERED SUGAR	¼ CUP POWDERED SUGAR

Center a rack in the oven and preheat oven to 350F (175C). Butter a 15 × 10-inch jelly roll pan and line pan with waxed paper. Butter and flour waxed paper, shaking off excess flour.

To make the cake: Beat the egg yolks and ½ cup of the granulated sugar in a medium bowl until pale yellow. Add the butter and cognac; beat until blended. In another large bowl, using clean beaters, beat the egg whites on high speed until soft peaks form. Gradually add remaining ½ cup granulated sugar and beat until stiff peaks form. Fold yolk mixture into egg whites. Sift together dry ingredients and gently fold into mixture.

Pour batter into prepared jelly roll pan and smooth top with a rubber spatula. Bake for 12 minutes or until center springs back to the touch. Remove from oven and cool 5 minutes on a wire rack.

Lay a clean kitchen towel on a flat surface and dust lightly with powdered sugar. Trim ¼ inch off all sides off cake, using a sharp knife. Lift waxed paper under cake away from pan and invert cake onto towel. Peel waxed paper away from cake. Starting at a 10-inch end, roll up cake, jelly roll style, in towel. Place roll on a wire rack and cool completely. Wrap cake roll and towel in plastic wrap and refrigerate until ready to use or up to 2 days.

To make Chocolate Amaretto Ganache: Bring the cream to a boil in a small saucepan over medium heat. Place the chocolate chips in a medium bowl and pour hot cream over chocolate, stirring until completely smooth. Stir in the Amaretto until blended. Cool to room temperature; cover and refrigerate until ready to use or up to 2 days.

When ready to use, remove chocolate ganache from refrigerator and beat until mixture thickens to consistency of frosting.

To assemble roulade: Bring cake to room temperature to avoid its cracking when unrolled. Carefully unroll cake on a flat surface. Brush cake surface with Amaretto. Spread ganache in an even layer on cake and sprinkle ¾ cup almonds over ganache. Reroll cake and place, seam side down, on a serving platter. Cover with plastic wrap and refrigerate for 3 hours or until ganache is firm.

Mix cocoa powder and powdered sugar until combined. Dust roulade with cocoa-sugar mixture and a light sprinkling of almonds just before serving. Slice crosswise at the dinner table to serve.

Screwdriver Bundt Cake

A moist Bundt cake with one of America's best-loved cocktails, the screwdriver, this is a real winner! I like to apply a double coating of glaze to this cake because it looks better and gives it an extra punch. This cake would be appropriate following lunch or on a brunch buffet.

1 CUP UNSALTED BUTTER, MELTED AND COOLED

2 CUPS SUGAR

5 EGGS

1 TABLESPOON STOLICHNAYA OHRANJ VODKA

1 CUP MILK

1/2 CUP FRESH ORANGE JUICE

2 TABLESPOONS FRESHLY GRATED ORANGE ZEST

3 1/4 CUPS ALL-PURPOSE FLOUR

1/2 TEASPOON SALT

1/2 TEASPOON BAKING SODA

1 TABLESPOON BAKING POWDER

SCREWDRIVER GLAZE

1 1/4 CUPS POWDERED SUGAR

2 TABLESPOONS STOLICHNAYA OHRANJ VODKA

2 TABLESPOONS FRESH ORANGE JUICE

1 TABLESPOON FRESHLY GRATED ORANGE ZEST

Preheat oven to 350F (170C). Butter a 12-cup Bundt pan.

Beat the butter and sugar in a large bowl until combined. Add the eggs, vodka, milk, orange juice, and zest; beat until smooth. Sift together the dry ingredients and beat into orange mixture until blended. Pour into prepared pan.

Bake for 45 to 50 minutes or until a knife inserted comes out clean. Cool in pan for 5 minutes, then invert cake on a wire rack. Cool completely.

Meanwhile, to make the Screwdriver Glaze: Mix the powdered sugar, vodka, orange juice, and orange zest until smooth. Place cake on to serving platter and drizzle half of the glaze over the top and down the sides of the cake. Allow glaze to set for 10 minutes, then drizzle remaining glaze over cake. Store, covered, at room temperature for up to 1 week.

Cut the cake into slices to serve.

VARIATION

If Stolichnaya Ohranj vodka is not available, substitute regular vodka.

CHEERS TO THE CHEESECAKE!

The cheesecake is so celebrated that many restaurants have built their reputation upon a successful secret recipe for this luscious, velvety dessert. One reason for its popularity is that this cake can easily be flavored with generous amounts of liqueurs and spirits. Too much liquid in most flour-and-egg-based cakes will inhibit the cake's rising. A cheese-based cake can handle a lot of liquid, making it the ultimate sophisticated dessert.

Cheesecake is easy to make adequately, but difficult to make superbly. Some of the many versions include New York cheesecake, which adds cream or sour cream to the mix; Chicago style, with fruit on the bottom; and Italian cheese pie, which uses ricotta cheese. These distinctive styles have merged throughout the years, with the cake's appeal determined by individual flavor and texture rather than regional characteristics.

———

Black Russian Brownie Swirl Cheesecake

Manhattan Sour Cherry Cheesecake

Irish Cream Chocolate Chip Cheesecake

Fancy Lemon Curd White Chocolate Cheesecake

Toasted Almond Caramel Cheesecake

Easy Chocolate Cheesecake

———

DESSERT WINE SUGGESTION: 1997 Clos du Bois Late Harvest Semillon (see "The Wine List," page 23 for more information)

GENERAL NOTES ON CHEESECAKE

- Place cheesecake pan on a baking sheet on the middle rack of the oven to ensure that cake cooks evenly.

- A pan of water on the oven's lower rack will prevent the cake top from cracking.

- Bake cheesecake for the instructed time or until it puffs up and a knife inserted off-center comes out clean. Cheesecake center will firm up and sink slightly as cake cools.

- After cooling, release the latch that holds the side of the pan onto the bottom, and remove the side. Because cheesecake is fragile, it is usually left on the pan bottom and placed on a plate for serving.

Easy Chocolate Cheesecake

MAKES 12 SERVINGS

This easy cheesecake can be made with any kind of cookie dough crust. Try different combinations, such as a chocolaty cheese filling over a white chocolate chip cookie crust or any new variety that's on the market.

See "General Notes on Cheesecake," page 339.

---

1 (18-OUNCE) PACKAGE REFRIGERATED CHOCOLATE COOKIE DOUGH

2 (8-OUNCE) PACKAGES CREAM CHEESE, SOFTENED

½ CUP SUGAR

2 EGGS

½ CUP PLUS 2 TABLESPOONS CANNED CHOCOLATE FROSTING

3 TABLESPOONS GODIVA CHOCOLATE LIQUEUR

¾ CUP COOL WHIP TOPPING

Preheat oven to 350F (175C). Press the cookie dough in an even layer over the bottom of a 10-inch springform pan. Set pan on a baking sheet.

Beat the cream cheese and sugar in a large bowl until fluffy. Add the eggs, the ½ cup frosting, and liqueur; beat until creamy. Pour the batter into springform pan over cookie dough.

Place baking sheet with pan on middle rack of oven. Bake 1 hour or until cheesecake puffs up and a knife inserted off-center comes out clean. Cheesecake center will continue to cook and become firm once cake is removed from oven. Cake will sink slightly as it cools. Place baking sheet with pan on a wire rack and cool cake to room temperature.

Run a knife around edge of cake to loosen from pan. Release latch and remove pan collar. Spread an even layer of Cool Whip on top of cooled cake. Using a knife tip, swirl remaining 2 tablespoons frosting throughout Cool Whip, creating a marbled appearance. Place cheesecake on a large plate and chill, uncovered, for 1 hour. Cut into wedges and serve cold. Store covered in the refrigerator for up to 1 week.

Transform your personal photo into an edible image as a cake topping. At the web site www.sugarcraft.com, they can print your photo on an edible frosting sheet for about $7.00 plus shipping and handling. Visit the web site for more information.

Black Russian Brownie Swirl Cheesecake

MAKES 12 SERVINGS

*B*lack Russian cocktails are without a doubt the most appealing in a baked good. Countless friends and consumers who purchased my first book, *The Sophisticated Cookie*, made the Black Russian Espresso Cookies before any other. This chocolate, chewy marble cheesecake with its brownie crust is loaded with that luscious coffee liqueur from south of the border, Kahlua!

See "General Notes on Cheesecake," page 339.

BROWNIE BATTER AND CRUST (PAGE 326, CINNAMON SCHNAPPS CHOCOLATE BROWNIES)	2 EGGS
	½ CUP SWEETENED CONDENSED MILK
2 (8-OUNCE) PACKAGES CREAM CHEESE, SOFTENED	⅓ CUP KAHLUA
¼ CUP SUGAR	

Preheat oven to 325F (165C). Butter a 10-inch springform pan and set pan on a baking sheet.

Prepare the brownie batter according to instructions, substituting 3 tablespoons Stolichnaya Kafya vodka and 3 tablespoons Kahlua for the ⅓ cup Goldschlager cinnamon schnapps liqueur. Cover and refrigerate until ready to use.

Beat the cream cheese and sugar in a large bowl until fluffy. Add the eggs, one at a time, beating to incorporate. Add the sweetened condensed milk and Kahlua; beat until creamy and blended.

Pour half of the brownie batter in prepared pan, for cheesecake crust. Pour the cheesecake batter over brownie batter. Dollop remaining brownie batter around top surface of cheescake batter. Using a spoon, swirl brownie batter into cheesecake batter. Do not swirl into batter for crust.

Place baking sheet with pan on it on middle rack of oven. Bake 1 hour and 15 minutes or until cheesecake puffs up and a knife inserted off-center comes out clean. Cheesecake center will firm up and sink slightly as cake cools. Place baking sheet with pan on wire rack; cool cake completely. Run a knife around edge of cake to loosen from pan;

release latch and remove pan collar. Place cheesecake on a large dish and chill, uncovered, for at least 2 hours. Cut into wedges and serve cold. Store, covered in plastic wrap, in the refrigerator for up to 1 week.

VARIATIONS

If Stolichnaya Kafya vodka is not available, substitute regular vodka.

Brownie Tower Cheesecake

Bake Black Russian Brownie Swirl Cheesecake as directed and bake a separate pan of your favorite brownies. Cut the brownies into 1-inch squares. Pile the squares in a pyramid on top of cheesecake, using prepared fudge sauce to stick brownies together. Chill and allow fudge sauce to set. Cut, if you dare, wedges of any size, and serve.

Manhattan Sour Cherry Cheesecake

MAKES 12 SERVINGS

The urban flavors of this ultra rich cheesecake remind me of my maternal grandmother. She loved Manhattan cocktails and lived in the Bronx all her life. Our only family recipe is for her cream cheese pressed cookies. My mother made the cookies every Christmas until she realized that I could bake and, thankfully, passed the baton.

See "General Notes on Cheesecake," page 339.

---

2 CUPS GRAHAM CRACKER CRUMBS

½ CUP (1 STICK) UNSALTED BUTTER, MELTED

1 CUP PLUS 1 TABLESPOON SUGAR

2 (8-OUNCE) PACKAGES CREAM CHEESE, SOFTENED

3 EGGS

1½ CUPS SOUR CREAM

3 TABLESPOONS BOURBON

1 TEASPOON SWEET VERMOUTH

CHERRY BOURBON SAUCE

2 (14.5-OUNCE) CANS RED TART PIE CHERRIES, DRAINED

⅓ CUP SUGAR

½ TABLESPOON BOURBON

2 TABLESPOONS FRESH LEMON JUICE

Mix the graham cracker crumbs, butter, and ¼ cup of the sugar. Pat mixture on bottom and up sides of buttered 10-inch springform pan. Freeze, covered, 30 minutes.

Preheat oven to 350F (175C). Set the springform pan containing crust on a baking sheet.

Beat the cream cheese and ¾ cup of the sugar in a large bowl until fluffy. Add the eggs, one at a time, beating until incorporated. Beat in 1 cup of the sour cream, bourbon, and sweet vermouth until thoroughly blended. Pour batter into prepared pan over crust.

Place baking sheet with pan on middle rack of oven. Bake 1 hour and 15 minutes or until cheesecake puffs up and knife inserted off-center comes out clean. Cheesecake center will continue to cook and become firm once cake is removed from oven; cake will sink slightly as it cools. Place baking sheet with pan on a wire rack. Cool cake to room temperature.

Mix remaining ½ cup sour cream and 1 tablespoon sugar until blended.

Run a knife around edge of cake to loosen from pan. Release latch and remove pan collar. Spread an even layer of sour cream mixture over top of cheesecake. Place cheesecake on a large plate, and chill, covered, for at least 2 hours.

To make Cherry Bourbon Sauce: Combine the cherries, sugar, bourbon, and lemon juice in a medium saucepan. Cook, stirring occasionally, over medium heat until mixture thickens, 8 to 10 minutes. Cool completely. Spread cooled sauce in an even layer over top of cheesecake.

Cut cheesecake into individual wedges or place on a buffet and serve. Store, covered in plastic wrap, in the refrigerator for up to 1 week.

Irish Cream Chocolate Chip Cheesecake

MAKES 12 SERVINGS

Baileys laced throughout this creamy cheesecake is sheer heaven. This cake is probably the most popular dessert in the book. I prefer Oreo cookies (with the filling removed) for the cookie crumbs in this recipe.

See Tip below and "General Notes on Cheesecake," page 339.

---

2 CUPS CHOCOLATE COOKIE CRUMBS

½ CUP UNSALTED BUTTER, MELTED

¾ CUP SUGAR

3 (8-OUNCE) PACKAGES CREAM CHEESE, SOFTENED

3 EGGS

¼ CUP HEAVY CREAM

½ CUP BAILEYS ORIGINAL IRISH CREAM

¾ CUP SEMISWEET CHOCOLATE CHIPS

Mix the cookie crumbs, butter, and ¼ cup of the sugar. Pat mixture on bottom and up sides of buttered 10-inch springform pan. Freeze, covered, 30 minutes.

Preheat oven to 350F (175C). Set the springform pan containing crust on a baking sheet.

Beat the cream cheese and remaining ½ cup sugar in a large bowl until fluffy. Add the eggs, one at a time, beating until incorporated. Beat in the cream and Baileys until thoroughly blended. Fold in half of the chocolate chips. Pour batter into prepared pan over crust and scatter remaining chocolate chips over top. Gently press chips into batter with a spatula.

Place baking sheet with pan on middle rack of oven. Bake for 1 hour or until cheesecake puffs up and a knife inserted off-center comes out clean. Cheesecake center will continue to cook and become firm once cake is removed from oven; cake will sink slightly as it cools. Place baking sheet with pan on a wire rack. Cool cake to room temperature.

Run a knife around edge of cake to loosen from pan. Release latch and remove pan collar. Place cheesecake on a large plate and chill, uncovered, for at least 2 hours or overnight. Cut into wedges and serve cold. Store, covered in plastic wrap, in the refrigerator for up to 1 week.

TIP: When making a cheesecake with chocolate chips, candy, or fruit, that ingredient may sink to the bottom during the baking process. If you prefer the ingredient to be distributed throughout add half of the ingredient, bake for 15 minutes, and then scatter the remainder of the ingredient on top. Using this technique, the ingredient should be distributed throughout the cheesecake.

Designer Spirits as Gifts

A generic brand of schnapps, brandy, or inexpensive spirits can be spiced up by the addition of dried fruit, herbs, or whole spices. Add slivered dried peaches to a bottle of peach schnapps or mint leaves to peppermint schnapps. Bits of orange peel can brighten up a bottle of Triple Sec, and lemon twists can add zest to vodka or tequila.

For a real designer look, peel a lemon or orange so rind is one whole piece. Using scissors, cut little shapes from peel, such as fish, stars, or circles. Put shapes into bottles of spirits with compatible flavors.

This idea works well with whole spices, fruit rinds, berries, and edible herb sprigs. Grated spices, chocolate, and small seeds cloud the liquid, making it look dirty. Do not add anything that is nonedible, like flowers or tiny plastic stars.

Decorate the manufacturer's bottle by adhering dried flowers, whole spices, or small trinkets to the front of the bottle. Tie a bow around the neck and affix a gift tag to the ribbon.

Fancy Lemon Curd White Chocolate Cheesecake

MAKES 12 SERVINGS

Lemon curd topping adds a lively lift to this buttery, decadent dessert. In the past, I've used prepared lemon curd purchased at the grocery store to fill tartlets. The commercial curd pales in comparison to fresh curd.

See "General Notes on Cheesecake," page 339.

1 CUP (2 STICKS) UNSALTED BUTTER

2 CUPS VANILLA WAFER COOKIE CRUMBS

1 TABLESPOON FRESHLY GRATED LEMON ZEST

2 TABLESPOONS SUGAR

10 OUNCES GOOD-QUALITY WHITE CHOCOLATE, CHOPPED

3 (8-OUNCE) PACKAGES CREAM CHEESE, SOFTENED

3 EGGS

¼ CUP GRAND MARNIER

2 TABLESPOONS POWDERED SUGAR, TO DECORATE

HEAVY CREAM, WHIPPED AND SWEETENED, TO SERVE

LEMON CURD

6 EGG YOLKS

1 CUP GRANULATED SUGAR

½ CUP FRESH LEMON JUICE

½ CUP UNSALTED BUTTER, SOFTENED, CUT INTO TABLESPOONS

Melt ½ cup of the butter in a small saucepan over low heat or in a microwave. Allow the remaining ½ cup butter to soften at room temperature. Mix the cookie crumbs, lemon zest, sugar, and the melted butter. Pat mixture on bottom and up sides of buttered 10-inch springform pan. Freeze, covered, 30 minutes.

Preheat oven to 350F (175C). Set the springform pan containing crust on a baking sheet.

Melt the chocolate in top of a double boiler or in a small saucepan over a larger pot of simmering water. Remove from heat and cool 5 minutes. Beat the chocolate and cream cheese in a large bowl until smooth. Add the eggs, one at a time, beating until incorporated. Beat the ½ cup softened butter and Grand Marnier into mixture until thoroughly blended. Pour batter into prepared pan over crust.

Place baking sheet with pan on middle rack of oven. Bake 1 hour or until cheesecake puffs up and a knife inserted off-center comes out clean. Cheesecake center will continue to cook and become firm once removed from oven; cake will sink slightly as it cools. Place baking sheet with pan on a wire rack. Cool cake to room temperature.

Meanwhile, make the Lemon Curd: Whisk together the egg yolks, granulated sugar, and lemon juice in a medium saucepan. Cook over medium heat, stirring constantly so mixture does not boil, until mixture thickens, 8 to 10 minutes. When thickened, remove from heat and immediately stir in butter, 1 tablespoon at a time, until mixture is smooth. Cool completely. Cover and chill until ready to use.

Spread Lemon Curd in an even layer over top of cooled cheesecake. Place the cheesecake on a large plate and chill, uncovered, for 2 hours. When Lemon Curd has set, run a knife around edge of cake to loosen from pan. Release latch and remove pan collar.

Place a paper doily on top of lemon curd. Sift powdered sugar evenly over doily. Remove doily to reveal powdered sugar design. Cut individual wedges from cheesecake and serve cold with a dollop of whipped cream. Store, covered in plastic wrap, in the refrigerator for up to 1 week.

Toasted Almond Caramel Cheesecake

MAKES 12 SERVINGS

This light cheesecake recipe is without a doubt my favorite! Praline seem to be the latest trend in cheesecakes. A praline, in case you haven't been privy to all those wonderful Louisiana chefs who've become media stars, is a confection made of caramelized pecans. This dessert contains Amaretto, Kahlua, and cream, which happen to be the ingredients of the Toasted Almond cocktail.

See "General Notes on Cheesecake," page 339.

1 ½ CUPS GRAHAM CRACKER CRUMBS	½ CUP SOUR CREAM
½ CUP GROUND ALMONDS	1 CUP HEAVY CREAM
¼ CUP PLUS 2 TABLESPOONS UNSALTED BUTTER, MELTED	KAHLUA CARAMEL TOPPING
¾ CUP SUGAR	1 CUP SUGAR
2 (8-OUNCE) PACKAGES CREAM CHEESE, SOFTENED	¼ CUP WATER
2 EGGS	1 CUP HEAVY CREAM
⅓ CUP AMARETTO	3 TABLESPOONS KAHLUA
	¾ CUP SLIVERED ALMONDS

Mix the graham cracker crumbs, almonds, the ¼ cup butter, and ¼ cup of the sugar. Pat mixture on bottom and up sides of buttered 10-inch springform pan. Freeze, covered, 30 minutes.

Preheat oven to 350F (175C). Set the springform pan containing crust on a baking sheet.

Beat the cream cheese and remaining ½ cup sugar in a large bowl until fluffy. Add the eggs, one at a time, beating until incorporated. Beat Amaretto, creams, and remaining 2 tablespoons butter until thoroughly blended. Add Amaretto mixture to cream cheese mixture and beat until combined. Pour batter into prepared pan over crust.

Place baking sheet with pan on middle rack of oven. Bake 1 hour and 10 to 15 minutes or until cheesecake puffs up and a knife inserted off-center comes out clean. Cheesecake center will continue to cook and become firm once cake is removed from oven;

cake will sink slightly as it cools. Place baking sheet with pan on a wire rack. Cool cake to room temperature. Run a knife around edge of cake to loosen from pan. Release latch and remove pan collar.

Meanwhile, make the Kahlua Caramel Topping: Combine the sugar and water in a medium saucepan over medium-low heat and cook, stirring occasionally, until sugar dissolves. Increase heat to medium and bring to a boil without stirring until mixture turns deep amber, 12 to 15 minutes. Remove from heat and stir in the cream and Kahlua. Return to medium heat and cook, stirring constantly, until smooth, 3 minutes. Remove from heat and cool for 5 minutes.

Preheat oven to 450F (230C). Place almonds in a shallow baking dish. Bake 5 minutes or until lightly toasted.

Place the cheesecake on a sheet of waxed paper. Pour the caramel over top of cooled cheesecake, allowing it to drizzle down sides. Scatter the almonds over the top. Remove waxed paper and place cheesecake on a large dish. Chill, uncovered, for 2 hours.

Cut individual wedges from cheesecake and serve cold. Store covered in plastic wrap in the refrigerator for up to 1 week.

The Better It Looks, The Better It Tastes!

Modes of fashion travel from clothes to interior decorating to food, not necessarily in that order. A great presentation idea in the world of haute couture will ignite a new trend in haute cuisine. Remember all the geometric shapes printed on shirts and accenting sunglasses in the early 80s? Before long, restaurateurs were cutting potatoes into triangles and placing them beneath perfect medallions of beef. A reaction to the clean angles spawned the birth of the "dirty plate." Plates of food were served with their rims dusted with ground spices, minced herbs, or an artful sauce splash. A design trend in the late 90s juxtaposed two tones of the same color—for instance, a vibrant lime slice floating on green artichoke soup, creating a subtle but eye-catching effect.

Illusion is a very powerful tool within edible and nonedible cultural realms.

Behind the scenes at one of Los Angeles' best restaurants, I was aghast to learn that the secret ingredient in its most famous dish was a cheap can of soup doctored up by the chef. I quickly lowered my turned-up nose as I realized that everyone cuts corners in the interest of time. Shortcuts in the kitchen are smart, and we are lucky that the food wizards of today are sharing their tips and helping us all cook like pros.

Beautiful and interesting food presentation is important because the better it looks, the better it tastes.

ALTERNATIVE DISHWARE

In this "non-plate" presentation, food is offered in ceramic skillets and on makeshift griddles. This dishware can be a step-saver when food is cooked and served in the same vessel. A lovely example is in Japanese restaurants, where the food is placed in teak compartment boxes and sushi boats. The dessert world is always at the creative forefront, opting for wine and martini glasses or edible cups in place of the classic bowl.

ARCHITECTURAL FOOD

This is similar to Tower Food, except that items on the plate may resemble a building or natural structure. For example, a mixture of potatoes and egg can be baked into a flat slab with herbs running through it. When the slab is placed upright, supported by mashed potatoes, it may look like the face of a mountain. Few restaurants present their food in this beautiful manner, because it is too time-consuming to build the plates.

CONFETTI GARNISH

Minced vegetables of various colors are sprinkled on top of food or on the plate's rim. A combination of red, yellow, and green bell peppers seems to be the most popular.

DIRTY PLATE

Ground spices or sauce splashes accent the rim of a plate. Powdered sugar can be used on dark plates, and anything colorful is dynamic on a light plate. Turmeric or curry on a black plate looks like gold. The spice must be compatible with the food.

EDIBLE ACCENTS

Puff pastry can be cut into leaves or flowers with cookie cutters and placed on top of a pie. Or a puff pastry square can cover the top of a soup crock and be dressed with pastry shapes. Vegetables cut into shapes are healthy edible accents.

EDIBLE CONTAINERS AND HOLDERS

These can range from hollowed melons used as fruit bowls to rosemary sprigs used as appetizer skewers for chicken chunks. Most edible items that are both large enough and sturdy enough in raw or baked form can be containers for food. (See Easy Hors d'Oeuvre Cups with Gourmet Fillings, pages 109-124).

FAMILY STYLE

This Chinese restaurant style of dining is growing in popularity. Items on a menu are offered in large portions, serving 3 persons or more. The diners order a few dishes and share the meal. Lately, I've seen this presentation in Italian restaurants and restaurants featuring Basque cuisine.

Food and Condiments in Molds

Savory custards such as vegetable timbales and sweet dessert custards are prime examples of this technique as they are usually baked in a decorative mold. Butter, creamy cheeses and spreads, or even ice cream may be presented in molds. Place the softened food in a mold; as the food firms up in the refrigerator, it will take the mold's shape. Experiment with molds used for terrines, steamed puddings, cookies, and cakes.

Geometric Food and Garni

Colorful shapes are strategically placed around a plate. Three red pepper triangles are elegant on a plate rim. Sliced carrot circles or fruit peel dots add a fun decorative edge to side dishes.

Herbal Garnishes

This style is an extension of the classic parsley sprig. Parsley looks nice, and serves as a natural breath freshener. Whole sprigs and herbs are laid across the top of an entree or inserted into the food as a finishing touch. Sage leaves can float atop soup or dill sprigs can dress up a salmon fillet. Coarsely chopped or chiffonade herbs (the leaves are cut in thin strips) are beautiful as well. Herbal garnishes must be compatible with the flavors of the food because their purpose, other than aesthetic, is to highlight its aromatic qualities.

Landscaped Plates

Most restaurants with any aesthetic sense landscape food on the plate. There are chefs who draw their designs on paper, and the food must be replicated night after night according to that blueprint. Many presentation trends originate as a restaurant's specific plating technique and can become a signature for the chef.

ROBINSON CRUSOE PLATE

This is my least favorite style. The plate is emphasized because the food portion is minuscule. A scanty piece of tuna or a tiny crab cake is stranded in the middle of a huge plate like a castaway on a deserted island. This trend, popular in nouvelle cuisine, is practically extinct except in overpriced restaurants.

SAUCE POOLS

A pool of sauce is poured on the plate and the entrée or dessert is placed in its center. An easy way to make a round pool is to put the sauce in a gravy boat or vessel with a spout and pour about 2 tablespoons in the center of the plate. Tilt the plate at a slight angle and turn the plate until the sauce forms a pool of the desired size. Always serve extra sauce on the side.

SAUCE SWIRL ART

Sauce is poured into a needlenose bottle and artfully swirled onto the plate. The swirled lines can weave in and out like a spiralograph, using one or two different sauces. Or a cream sauce pool can have swirls of a different colored sauce, such as a sweet crème anglaise with raspberry sauce accents or a port wine sauce throughout a creamy savory base.

SPIRE GARNISH

This fried food art is the Warhol approach to toppings. Fresh pasta or pastry may be tied in a bow or shaped in an artistic squiggle and then fried to keep its shape. The shape is placed in the food and juts up like a spire. Tempura batter can be streamed into hot oil and fried until it hardens into an interesting shape. Fried wonton noodles and starchy vegetable sticks such as sweet potatoes, also work well with this technique. On the sweet side, caramel shards and Pirouette or tuile cookies are often used as dessert spires.

Tower food

Food is piled high in the center of the plate, and you must deconstruct it to eat it. For example, mini corncobs are placed vertically on a plate to support a layer of bound asparagus spears that hold a filet of salmon. Mashed potatoes or a whipped vegetable may adhere the layers together. Height is the goal here with a slight emphasis on design. Tower food is impressive to the eye and appetite-inducing with the demolition work that is involved.

Word art

Clean letter stencils are placed on the rim of a plate or on the food and the letters are filled in with ground spice or an edible item in dust form. I've seen flour letters on bread (the flour is applied prior to baking, and the bread cooks up with a message on top). Or the plate rim of a spicy fish dish can have "fish" spelled out in stenciled ground cayenne pepper.

Proportion Chart for Foods

This guide gives serving amounts of common party fare. The amounts are ample for guests with average appetites.

FOOD ITEM	HORS D'OEUVRE PORTION (AMOUNT PER GUEST)	DINNER ENTREE WITH 2 SIDE DISHES (AMOUNT PER GUEST)	BUFFET ENTREE PLUS 1 MORE ENTREE WITH 2 SIDE DISHES (AMOUNT PER GUEST)
Beef, Lamb, Pork (boneless)	2 ounces	6 to 8 ounces	4 ounces
Beef, Lamb, Pork (1 bone)		12 ounces	6 ounces

FOOD ITEM	HORS D'OEUVRE PORTION (AMOUNT PER GUEST)	DINNER ENTREE WITH 2 SIDE DISHES (AMOUNT PER GUEST)	BUFFET ENTREE PLUS 1 MORE ENTREE WITH 2 SIDE DISHES (AMOUNT PER GUEST)
Beef, Lamb, Pork (with ribs)		1 to 1½ pounds	12 ounces
Bread/Dinner Rolls		1½ pieces	1 piece
Cakes/Desserts		1 slice	½ slice
Chicken, Turkey, Poultry (boneless)	2 ounces	6 to 8 ounces	4 ounces
Chicken, Turkey, Poultry Fryer Pieces, (with bone)		12 ounces	6 ounces
Chicken, Turkey, Poultry (whole)		2 to 2½ pounds	1¼ pounds
Cookies		2 or 3 pieces	1 or 2 pieces
Dessert Sauce		¼ cup	2 tablespoons
Fish filet	2 ounces	6 to 8 ounces	4 ounces
Ice Cream		½ cup	⅓ cup
Pasta	1 pound/8 persons	1 pound/4 persons	1 pound/6 persons
Rice, Cooked		½ cup	⅓ cup
Salad/Lettuce		¼ head	¼ head
Salad Dressing		⅓ cup per lettuce head	
Vegetables and Side Dishes		½ cup	⅓ cup

HORS D'OEUVRE PROPORTIONS	HORS D'OEUVRES ONLY (AMOUNT PER GUEST)	HORS D'OEUVRES WITH APPETIZER BUFFET AMOUNT PER GUEST	HORS D'OEUVRES BEFORE DINNER AMOUNT PER GUEST
Total Number Prepared per Person	7 to 10	5 to 7	3 to 4

Proportion Chart for Beverages

*I*t is almost impossible to gauge specific beverage amounts needed for an event without knowing the guests' preferences. Some crowds are heavy scotch drinkers and others stay with wine or beer. You know your guests and probably have an idea of what they drink. As a caterer, I ask hosts about their beverage consumption experience with the invited crowd. Based upon their answer, I provide the average serving amounts for the popular drinks. I also bring backups of certain beverages based on the demographics of the crowd.

My backup beverage system is based on age and a West Coast crowd. For a younger group, 21 to 30 years old, I offer more beer and tequila. For guests who are 30 to 50 years old, I anticipate more wine and vodka. For the 50-plus age group, I concentrate on the spirits and always have a good bottle of scotch on hand. My

Nebraska relatives prefer beer, my Southern friends are big on bourbon, and my Californian family loves wine. These, of course, are very broad generalizations, but they may help you narrow your options and spend your money wisely.

BEVERAGE	SERVING AMOUNT PER PERSON IN (AVERAGE BOTTLE)	WINE AND BEER BAR ONLY WITH SODA, JUICE (AMOUNT PER 25 GUESTS)	FULL BAR WITH SODA, JUICE (AMOUNT PER 25 GUESTS)
Beer	1 serving (12 ounces)	24 bottles (1 case)	18 bottles (3 6-packs)
Champagne	5 glasses/(750 ml)		

Unless the event is for a special occasion, Champagne is rarely offered at the bar. When it is served, allow at least 1 glass per person.

BEVERAGE	SERVING AMOUNT PER PERSON IN (AVERAGE BOTTLE)	WINE AND BEER BAR ONLY WITH SODA, JUICE (AMOUNT PER 25 GUESTS)	FULL BAR WITH SODA, JUICE (AMOUNT PER 25 GUESTS)
Liquor	25 servings (750 ml)		1 (750-ml.) bottle each vodka, gin, tequila, bourbon, scotch

When serving a full bar, offer at least 1 bottle of each spirit, even if you think only 1 or 2 mixed drinks will be consumed. If you are featuring a specialty drink, such as margaritas or martinis, have 2 or more bottles of the spirit and a proportionate amount of mixers used in the drink.

BEVERAGE	SERVING AMOUNT PER PERSON IN (AVERAGE BOTTLE)	WINE AND BEER BAR ONLY WITH SODA, JUICE (AMOUNT PER 25 GUESTS)	FULL BAR WITH SODA, JUICE (AMOUNT PER 25 GUESTS)
Wine	5 glasses/(750 ml.)	6 to 8 bottles (white)	5 bottles (white)
		4 bottles (red)	3 bottles (red)

For sit-down dinners allow at least 3 glasses of wine per person.

BEVERAGE	SERVING AMOUNT PER PERSON	WINE AND BEER BAR ONLY	FULL BAR
Juice	6 glasses (1 quart)	1 quart (orange)	1 quart (orange)
		1 quart (cranberry)	1 quart (cranberry)
Soda/Tonic	6 glasses (1 liter)	4 liters club soda	3 liters club soda
		2 liters Coke	2 liters Coke
		2 liters Diet Coke	2 liters Diet Coke

BEVERAGE	SERVING AMOUNT PER PERSON IN (AVERAGE BOTTLE)	WINE AND BEER ONLY WITH SODA, JUICE (AMOUNT PER 25 GUESTS)	FULL BAR WITH SODA, JUICE (AMOUNT PER 25 GUESTS)
		1 liter 7-UP	1 liter 7-UP
		1 liter ginger ale	1 liter ginger ale
		1 liter tonic	1 liter tonic
Optional for full bar only			
Bloody Mary mix			1 liter
Sweet and sour mix			1 liter
Grenadine			12 ounce bottle
Garnishes			2 large lemon peels cut into twists
			5 limes cut into wedges
			1 small jar each: green olives, cocktail onions, maraschino cherries

ICE, CUBES (5-HOUR EVENT)	IN DRINKS ONLY AMOUNT PER PERSON	FOR CHILLING WINE OR BEER
Moderate Weather	1 pound	10 pounds per case
Hot Weather	1½ pounds	15 pounds per case

The Well-Stocked Cooking Bar

This glossary is an alphabetical listing according to brand name of the beverages used in the recipes. In some cases, the generic name of the beverage is so popular, as with Amaretto or any schnapps flavor, that the beverage is listed under the generic name followed by a preferred brand name. If you have on hand a favorite brand of beverage that you wish to substitute for the one specified in a recipe, read your brand's label and look for flavor characteristics similar to those described in the glossary below. Along with a description of the beverage, you'll find the average price range for a medium-size bottle, approximately 750 milliliters, as indicated by the following price guidelines.

$ $20 and below

$$ above $20

Absolut Vodka $

Very light-bodied Swedish vodka with a slight hint of licorice.

Absolut Citron Vodka $

Lemon-flavored Swedish vodka with a zesty tang that holds up beautifully during the cooking process.

Absolut Kurant Vodka $

Black currant–flavored Swedish vodka with the intense flavor of black currants. Use in recipes that contain dried fruits.

Aftershock Cinnamon Liqueur $

This hot cinnamon liqueur has edible crystals floating throughout.

Alizé de France Passion Fruit Liqueur $

Passion fruit gives this liqueur its tart flavor, but you'll also detect a hint of cognac. The blend is a nice one for spirited fruit sauces and vinaigrettes.

Amaretto di Saronno $

Although there are many brands of Amaretto on the market, Amaretto di Saronno is the absolute best. This pungent, sweet almond liqueur is already a baking favorite and can be substituted for almond extract.

Anisette $

Anise and licorice are basically the same flavor. There are countless anise-flavored liqueurs in many price ranges on the market and its wonderful rich flavor is great for baking. Anisette is found under the Hiram Walker label at a very affordable price.

Applejack $

Laird's, a wonderful brand of apple-flavored brandy, can be found for a very reasonable price. Applejack has more of a sweet rather than tart apple taste.

Apricot Brandy $

An apricot-flavored brandy most commonly distributed under the DeKuyper, Gaetano, or Hiram Walker brands.

B & B $$

A combination of Bénédictine liqueur and brandy, this longtime favorite cordial has the flavor of sweet herbs and spices.

Bacardi Añejo Rum $
Another Bacardi family gem flavored with molasses, vanilla, and butter.

Bacardi Black Rum $
A bit heavier than the others, this extremely dark rum is on the sweet side and has a faint taste of coffee.

Bacardi Gold Reserve Rum $
This golden Puerto Rican rum is laced with vanilla, caramel, and orange to name a few.

Bacardi Limon Rum $
One of the first rums to venture into the alternative flavor world, this lemony rum is on the sweet side.

Bacardi 151 Light Rum $
A straightforward, affordable Puerto Rican rum that is good for cooking and especially good for flaming due to its high alcohol content.

Baileys Original Irish Cream $
A holiday favorite and the first on my list for after-dinner drinks. Baileys is a fantastic liqueur for baking. Not only does its unique caramel and toffee flavor continue to shine in contrast to poor imitations, but the texture will lend a creamy richness when added to your baking. Try substituting an equal amount of Baileys in recipes that call for sweetened condensed milk.

Bärenjäger Honey Liqueur $
This liqueur is exactly what you'd expect—a sweet, honey-flavored elixir.

Black Haus Blackberry Schnapps $
This schnapps has the aroma of liquid blackberries laced with a touch of peppermint and a pleasant fruit taste that is not too syrupy sweet.

Blue Curaçao $
Tinted a novel blue, this liqueur has a hint of orange and usually can be found under the DeKuyper, Gaetano, or Hiram Walker brand.

Bushmills Blended Irish Whiskey, Old $
Bushmills has many fine whiskeys to its name, but this version is the most affordable. A wonderful blend whose most pronounced taste is that of malt.

Calvados Boulard, Pays d'Auge $$

This wonderful brand of French apple brandy is both sweet and spicy, like a perfectly mulled apple cider. Pricewise, the Pays d'Auge brand runs the gamut from $20 to $150 a bottle.

Captain Morgan Original Spiced Rum $

The "Original" label of this rum, as opposed to the "Private Stock" label, contains many classic baking spices such as cinnamon, vanilla, and nutmeg, which will highlight similar ingredients in your recipes.

Chambord Liqueur Royale de France, Royale $$

Excellent for baking and for pouring directly over vanilla ice cream. A luscious mélange of berries blended into a velvety liqueur.

Cherry Brandy $

A cherry-flavored brandy also known as kirschwasser and kirsch. DeKuyper, Gaetano, and Hiram Walker all have versions.

Cherry Heering $

The wonderful aroma of very ripe black cherries of this liqueur is richly intense with a bit of tartness to it.

Chivas Regal 12-Year-Old Blended Scotch Whisky $$

One of the most popular and complex blended scotch whiskies. This favorite spirit is very smooth and with many complicated flavors, ranging from sweet to smoky.

Christian Brothers Brandy $

A very sweet but strong brandy that won't lose its potency during the cooking process.

Christian Brothers Frost White Brandy $$

Smooth and crystal clear, this brandy is on the dry side, with some of the characteristics of a fine distilled white spirit.

Christian Brothers Spiced Brandy $

Perfect for a mulled cider or holiday glogg, this spiced brandy has traces of cinnamon and sweet apples.

Cinnamon Schnapps $

Schnapps with a cinnamon flavor highlights the spice and gives it a bit more zing. Look for DeKuyper, Gaetano, and Hiram Walker brands.

Cointreau The exclusively orange-flavored liqueur is the perfect complement to anything with a hint of citrus or chocolate dessert.

Coruba Jamaica Rum $
This excellent potent rum has a great caramel color and an unbelievable taste of spiked sugarcane fields.

Crème de Banane $
A spirit flavored with sweet, ripe bananas found under the DeKuyper, Gaetano, or Hiram Walker brand names in every area.

Crème de Cacao (White and Dark) $
The use of these spirits is a very cost effective way to add the cocktail dimension to your baking. Both are very light and have a trace of chocolate flavoring. The main difference is in their color, as the two names suggest, with the dark tasting more like cocoa and the white tasting more like white chocolate. Look for DeKuyper, Gaetano, or Hiram Walker brands.

Crème de Cassis $
A black currant-flavored spirit, lighter in consistency than a liqueur and easily found under the DeKuyper, Gaetano, or Hiram Walker brand names.

Crème de Menthe (White and Green) $
Many of the schnapps and fruit brandy manufacturers like Hiram Walker and DeKuyper also make crème de menthe. White crème de menthe is clear and has more of a crisp, peppermint bite. Green crème de menthe is green, with a smoother mint flavor and a liqueur consistency. Both are usually very affordable under the DeKuyper, Gaetano, or Hiram Walker brand.

Crème de Noyeaux $
An almond-flavored liqueur very similar to almond extract that can be found under the DeKuyper, Gaetano, or Hiram Walker brand names in most areas.

Cuervo 1800 Tequila, Jose $$
An amazing high-end tequila that goes down like liquid silk and comes in a beautiful perfume-type bottle.

Cuervo, Especial Gold Tequila, Jose $
Made from the core of the agave plant, it is wonderfully sweet and smooth. Go for the gold tequila in cooking.

Cuervo Mistico Tequila, Jose $
Infused with a blend of citrus, this smooth designer tequila is an excellent new ingredient for both margaritas and cooking.

DeKuyper Brand $
One of the major producers of inexpensive yet tasty fruit brandies, schnapps, and liqueurs that are great for cooking on a budget. Available in almost every area.

Espresso Liqueur, Borghetti Caffé Sport $
This smoky, syrupy liqueur is very rich and bakes into a superb roasted coffee bean essence, like a satisfying shot of espresso in the late afternoon.

Finlandia Vodka $
This vodka from Finland has delicate traces of herbs and grains. Finlandia also has a cranberry-flavored vodka which is quite good.

Framboise $
A luscious, ruby, raspberry liqueur with a silky finish that will bring an outstanding taste and moist texture to all your baking. Try adding framboise to your jams and preserves for a touch of something special. Bonny Doon vineyards has an excellent framboise.

Frangelico $$
Another fine liqueur that is becoming a premiere ingredient in gourmet kitchens. Its flavor is the most fabulous extraction of the hazelnut you will ever taste.

Fruit Brandies, Liqueurs, and Schnapps $
See DeKuyper, Gaetano, and Hiram Walker.

Gaetano Specialties $
They offer almost every flavor of brandy, liqueur, cordial, schnapps, and spirit imaginable at very affordable prices. Although all of their items are not available in every area, I always see the Gaetano Amaretto and Coffee Liqueur, which are a great budget buy. If you do find some of their more exotic items like Butterscotch and Blueberry Schnapps or Crème de Strawberry, definitely pick them up as they are delicious flavorings for cookies and other desserts.

Galliano $$
This beautiful golden liqueur is flavored with herbs to give the slight taste of root beer, especially when mixed with cola.

Glenfiddich Special Old Reserve Speyside Single Malt $ $
For the true scotch lover, this straightforward spirit is top shelf.

Godet Belgian White Chocolate Liqueur $ $
A lovely and elegant liqueur as perfect for baking as it is for sipping. This creamy vanilla and chocolate liqueur tastes as good as it sounds and will blend with just about any baked good imaginable.

Godiva Chocolate Liqueur $ $
The Godiva name lives up to its exquisite reputation with this blend of chocolate and sweetness in a bottle. Your dessert experiments will have excellent results when the ingredients have the Godiva name.

Goldschlager Cinnamon Schnapps Liqueur $
This glitzy, intensely flavored cinnamon liqueur has gold flecks floating throughout that are edible! A fun and extremely potent (53 percent alcohol) liqueur to cook with.

Grand Marnier Cordon Rouge $ $
Another outstanding French liqueur for baking and cooking, Grand Mariner has a distinct sweet orange flavor that has made it a classic for years.

Guinness Stout $
This Irish stout has a creamy, molasses taste that works in hearty recipes.

Harvey's Bristol Cream Sherry $
An affordable, solid sherry that can be found in almost everyone's collection. Its sweetness with a slight nutty edge is perfect for baking.

Hennessey VSOP "Privilege" Cognac $ $
A bit more fruity and certainly more affordable than others under the Hennessey label, this top of the line cognac has flavor overtones of smoked apples and pears.

Hiram Walker Brand $
Another major producer of very affordable, good-quality fruit brandies, schnapps, and liqueurs that are great for cooking without breaking your wallet. Available in almost every area.

Irish Mist $ $
Much sweeter than its Irish whiskey distant cousins, this liqueur has an overall taste of honey and herb.

Jack Daniels Old Time No. 7 Tennessee Whiskey $

The much loved JD has the sweetness of a bourbon with a whiskey punch.

Jägermeister $

A swift kick of herbs that is best consumed in one quick shot.

Jameson Blended Irish Whiskey $

One of the sweeter Irish whiskeys, this blend has elements of oak and apple.

Jim Beam 4-Year-Old Kentucky Straight Bourbon $

A crisp, clean Kentucky bourbon that is great for cooking with its subtle vanilla and cocoa flavors in a sweet spirit.

Kahlua Licor de Café $

Better known simply as Kahlua, few can touch this excellent coffee- and chocolate-flavored Mexican liqueur, though many have tried. It is my absolute favorite for baking, especially in rich, decadent chocolate desserts. Any cheap substitution for this is a big no!

Kirschwasser $

Another name for cherry brandy.

Macallan 12-Year-old Speyside Single Malt $$

This whiskey has a sherry flavor at its core that makes it sweeter than many other scotches.

Malibu Rum $

More like a liqueur in consistency, this rum has a terrific coconut flavor.

Myer's Platinum White Rum $

A high-quality and affordable Jamaican white rum with a slight sweetness balanced by a fruity essence.

Myer's Dark Rum $

This rum relies more on spices such as anise and pepper for flavoring than many dark rums with a sweeter base.

Midori Melon Liqueur $

A green melon liqueur with a syruplike consistency but a very light texture. This refreshing Japanese import has an excellent aroma and as unique a flavor as bubblegum.

Peach Schnapps $

This is a terrific combination of mint mellowed by sweet peaches. Look for DeKuyper, Gaetano, or Hiram Walker brand.

Peare de Brillet Liqueur $

This liqueur tastes like the perfect pear—not too ripe, not too sweet and a bit lighter than the average liqueur.

Peppermint Schnapps $

This spirit is like drinking a candy cane. Look for DeKuyper, Gaetano, or Hiram Walker brand.

Port Wine $

Most reasonably priced Ports are fine for cooking. However, watch the sugar content in the recipe as this wine is so sweet, it may obscure any other flavors. I like to counterbalance the use of Port with the bitterness of nuts or the acidity of a fruit.

Pucker Sour Apple Schnapps $

More of a liqueur than a schnapps, this trendy spirit tastes like a green apple Jolly Rancher candy.

Raynal VSOP Napoleon Brandy $

There are many brand names of Napoleon brandy on the market in many price ranges. The Raynal brand balances a blend of citrus, nuts, and fruits, among other flavors.

Remy Martin VSOP Cognac Fine Champagne $$

One of the most respected cognac makers, Remy Martin has such an elegant bouquet and a smooth texture that it should be used in simple recipes to allow the true flavor of the cognac to come through. This version has deep undertones of musk and herbs.

Rumple Minze Peppermint Schnapps $

A great blend of peppermint and herbs, this brand of schnapps is particularly smooth.

Sambuca Liquore Classico, Romana $

A fabulous black licorice-flavored liqueur that is so pure you'll think you're eating candy. There are many licorice-flavored liqueurs on the market; this is one of the best.

Sambuca, Romana Black Liquore di $

Richer and more intense in flavor than classic Sambuca. One can taste the herbs as well as the licorice in this deep black liqueur.

Schnapps $
See DeKuyper, Gaetano, or Hiram Walker brands.

Seagram's 7 Crown American Blended Whiskey $
This favorite whiskey is like a spirited liquid candy: It definitely has that whiskey nip when sipped, but it mellows into a light caramel flavor when cooked.

Southern Comfort $
A little touch of orange and a little touch of sweet has made this liqueur a big favorite. It's great for cooking and baking when you want to add the hint of a spirited citrus.

Stolichnaya® Vodka $
A high-quality Russian vodka with a real kick and a faint licorice and herb blend.

Stolichnaya® Gold Vodka $$
My husband's personal favorite, this excellent Russian vodka is as clear as a bell on the palate with a surprising silky white chocolate aftertaste.

Stoli® Kafya Vodka $
The essence of coffee flavors this Russian vodka. Add this for a hint of coffee without turning the dessert into a cup of espresso.

Stolichnaya® Limonnaya Vodka $
A wonderful burst of lemon, this flavored vodka is more than just a novelty and is great for sipping as well as cooking. I'd recommend trying this flavor as an accent in lemon desserts or vinaigrettes.

Stolichnaya® Ohranj Vodka $
Another flavored vodka that is right on target. The strong, sweet taste of orange makes it a real winner for cooking. Light and refreshing, this vodka will add another dimension to fruit- or citrus-based recipes.

Stoli® Persik Vodka $
Rich in flavor with the ripest peaches you can imagine, this vodka smells as great as it tastes.

Stoli® Razberi Vodka $

This raspberry-laced vodka is just as spectacular as its relatives and perfect if you want a light raspberry flavor without the heaviness of a raspberry liqueur.

Stoli® Strasberi Vodka $

The bouquet of this strawberry vodka is just as good as its taste and even better in a baked good.

Stoli® Vanil Vodka $

What could be more suitable for baking than a vanilla-flavored vodka. Try using it along with vanilla extract to highlight its flavor. On its own, it acts as a terrific flavor binder in baked goods.

Stoli® Zinamon Vodka $

This combination of cinnamon and vodka is wonderful. As with the Stoli Vanil, this cinnamon-flavored vodka will enhance the spices in your baking without interfering with all the other flavors. Stoli Zinamon would also be great in sauces spiced with curry, cumin, or dried fruit.

Tanqueray Special Dry English Gin $$

Pure and smooth with a slight citrus edge, Tanqueray's quality is key, because you can trust this gin to mellow into a wonderful juniper berry essence when cooked.

Tia Maria $

Much lighter than most coffee liqueurs, Tia Maria has captured the sweeter nuances of the coffee bean.

Triple Sec $

With Triple Sec you'll get that saturated orange taste of the high-end liqueurs without paying the high price, but little else in the way of that special handcrafted flavor. Triple Sec is usually available from major distributors like DeKuyper, Gaetano, or Hiram Walker.

Tuaca $

The terrific butterscotch with elements of caramel, toffee, and nuts makes this a great addition to sweet baked goods.

Villa Massa, Liqoure di Limoni $

A zesty liqueur made from the ripest lemons imaginable. It is extremely sweet and great for enhancing the natural lemon flavors in your recipes.

Wild Turkey Straight Kentucky Bourbon $

It doesn't get much straighter than this! The true sweet bite of bourbon with musky overtones and the slight taste of nut and oak.

Wild Turkey Rare Breed Straight Kentucky Bourbon $$

Right out of the barrel this 101-proof bourbon is matured to perfection and is as smooth as silk on the palate.

Index